Wish You Were Still Here
The Scottish Seaside Holiday

ERIC SIMPSON

AMBERLEY

This book is dedicated to the memory of my late beloved wife and helpmate, Kathleen Hazel Simpson, who encouraged my researches and who loved our trips doon the watter on the paddle steamer Waverley.

First published 2013

Amberley Publishing
The Hill, Stroud
Gloucestershire, GL5 4EP

www.amberley-books.com

British Library Cataloguing in Publication Data.
A catalogue record for this book is available from the British Library.

ISBN 978 1 4456 1529 5
E-Book 978 1 4456 1552 3

Typeset in 10pt on 12pt Adobe Caslon Pro.
Typesetting and Origination by Amberley Publishing.
Printed in the UK.

Contents

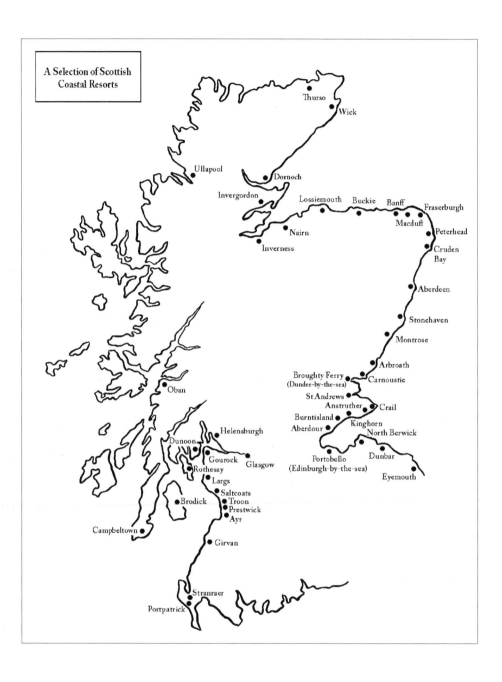

A Selection of Scottish
Coastal Resorts

Thurso
Wick

Ullapool
Dornoch

Invergordon
Lossiemouth Buckie Banff Fraserburgh
Macduff
Peterhead
Nairn
Cruden
Inverness Bay

Aberdeen

Stonehaven

Montrose

Arbroath
Broughty Ferry Carnoustie
(Dundee-by-the-sea)
St Andrews
Anstruther Crail
Burntisland
Oban Aberdour Kinghorn
North Berwick
Helensburgh Portobello Dunbar
Dunoon (Edinburgh-by-the-sea)
Gourock Eyemouth
Rothesay Glasgow
Largs
Saltcoats
Brodick Troon
Prestwick
Ayr
Campbeltown

Girvan

Stranraer
Portpatrick

Introduction

In brief, this book can be described as an illustrated social history of the once vibrant seaside holiday sector of the tourist industry. As one of our key forms of leisure and mass entertainment, tourism was one of the major growth industries of the nineteenth century and this growth continued into the twentieth century, but in greatly altered forms and patterns. Starting in the golden age of the Victorian and Edwardian resorts, the author explores the ways and means whereby the Scottish people were enabled to enjoy the benefits of seaside and other holidays. This includes how they travelled, the things they did and where they stayed. The book, therefore, is not just about the holidaymakers but embraces too the many people in the resorts who made their livelihood in the tourist industry. A wide choice of pictures and other illustrations, even some naughty postcards, are used to explain the nature of the traditional seaside holiday and how holiday resorts and holiday-going changed and developed during the course of the twentieth century and in the early years of the twenty-first. Sporting activities, and for spectators no less than participants, were and still are very important, especially golf. So too was swimming and one of the extraordinary features of the early twentieth century was the craze for building open-air seawater swimming pools in a country that is not renowned for great warmth. As the author shows, many Scottish towns, both large and small, were quite prepared to run into debt to construct the very many open-air swimming ponds that once dotted the coastline. In the wee quiet places where there was little in the way of ready-made entertainment, holidaymakers had to find their own ways of spending their time. In such resorts bathing, tennis, golf and other sports were, therefore, favoured activities.

Holidays and places of resort took many different forms. Whereas many tourists, summer visitors as they used to be called, headed for the big, brash coastal towns with their Pierrot shows and other forms of popular entertainment, others preferred remoter locations. While the villages and small towns that laid some claim to being a resort were widely spread from Galloway to the far north, there were concentrations in Ayrshire, Lothian, Fife and Angus. With their sandy beaches and links golf courses, these strings of resorts had their own special appeal. The author gives the smaller resorts their due weight, but naturally most attention is given to the most popular resorts – such as Aberdeen, Broughty Ferry, Dunoon, Portobello, and Rothesay. Large or small, near or far, all were brought to new life and vigour when the Glasgow Fair and other visitors arrived in some force.

The story unfortunately is the classic economic story of growth to maturity and then decay and decline. The later decades of the twentieth century saw the Scottish seaside resorts face fresh challenges and the onset of a period of decline. Why this happened and how the resorts have faced up to these challenges is part of a story, which is very much a continuing one. Nevertheless, today the Scottish tourism sector as a whole sustains nearly a quarter of a million jobs – more than the combined totals for fishing, farming, forestry and electronics, and the traditional seaside

BATHING POOL & BAY, TROON. 182

Troon's stylish 1930s swimming pool was built at a time when the building of local authority open-air pools was fashionable. Behind it there was an Italian Rock Garden, and then the prom with its shelters and seats. Built at a cost of over £20,000, this very ornate pond was for those days a very substantial investment.

resorts, some now being reinvented, retain a not insignificant share in the economic benefits thus engendered. At the very least, these once popular summer playgrounds retain a sentimental hold on the Scottish public and the story of their twentieth-century rise and partial fall is both an important part of our social history and an engrossing one in its own right.

THE AUTHOR

Eric Simpson, a former Head of History at Moray House College of Education in Edinburgh, has written and lectured on many different aspects of Scottish History and Heritage. His books include *Going on Holiday, Discovering Moray, Banff & Nairn, The Auld Grey Toun – Dunfermline in the time of Andrew Carnegie 1835-1919, Dalgety Bay – Heritage and Hidden History* and he also has three titles on the Amberley list. When not exploring seaside places, he heads for the hills, and he has climbed all 282 Munros (Scottish 3,000-foot-plus mountains). A native of Buckie, his learning was enhanced by the facilities and teaching provided at the town's public library, the local High School and Aberdeen University. He has resided at Dalgety Bay in Fife since 1966. For the last three years he has been historical adviser for the BBC Scotland TV series Grand Tours of Scotland.

CHAPTER 1

Off to the Coast: From Victorian Heyday Till the End of the First World War

The 23rd of May 1871 was a landmark day in the history of Portobello, then one of Scotland's leading seaside resorts. An enthusiastic crowd had assembled for the opening of the town's latest – and greatest – attraction: a promenade pier, 1,250 feet long with, at the seaward end, a substantial pierhead topped by an imposing pavilion. The new pier, with its restaurant, bar, and bandstand, was built not for serious trade and commerce but solely for holiday treats and pleasures. As such, it was the first, and the last, of its kind to be built in Scotland. Present at the opening were the civic dignitaries of Edinburgh, Leith and Musselburgh and, of course, Portobello itself which was then, like Leith also, an independent burgh. It was a proud day too for the designer of the cast-iron pier, Thomas Bouch, a railway engineer who had himself contributed much of the capital for the Portobello Pier Company. In later years Bouch became notorious as the engineer who constructed the first ill-fated Tay Bridge. Although it had a chequered history, his promenade pier proved to be more durable than his Tay Bridge masterpiece.

The fact that the pier was to be open on Sundays was a considerable draw in those days of strict Sabbath worship. The pier company had to overcome local opposition to Sunday opening. When the necessary enabling act was still before Parliament, Provost Wood of Portobello had hurried to London to try to secure for the town council a voice in the regulation of the opening times and manner of using the pier on Sundays. Rejecting his protests, the chairman of the parliamentary committee scrutinising the pier company's proposals remarked: 'You are a very peculiar people in Portobello to desire such a holy atmosphere.' Even after the work had been completed, the Sabbatarians kept up the pressure. The pier company, they complained, was 'trading' on the Sabbath and others would thus be encouraged 'to follow their occupations for gain on what should be a day of rest'. The resort, they further lamented, had lost the custom of families who had been accustomed to holiday at Portobello. Respectable visitors, the Sabbatarians claimed, were going elsewhere 'in consequence of the scenes of rioting and drunkenness which unfortunately abound on the Sunday, and which render it unsafe for well-dressed females to appear on the streets without being exposed to insult'. The pier, nevertheless, was a very popular feature. The special holiday granted to mark the centenary of the birth of Sir Walter Scott brought a record number of visitors. Despite many counter attractions held to mark the event, no fewer than 2,500 people, the local Leith newspaper enthused, paid the one penny admittance charge to the pier that August day of 1871.

The success of Portobello Pier and indeed of the resort in general depended on the large number of visitors who were now arriving by train. Mass tourism was the product of the railway age, except obviously for those resorts like Dunoon and Rothesay on the Firth of Clyde which owed their initial growth and development to the steamboat. Well-to-do summer visitors, accustomed to spending a month or six weeks in a resort, all travelled by train. But the railway companies had learned to exploit another market by organising day excursions, which even working people

Portobello Pier in Edwardian days.

could afford. As far back as 1853 the 'Magnificent Spectacle' of the herring fleet departing for sea had brought huge crowds from Edinburgh to Dunbar. Portobello Pier, on the other hand, was no ephemeral attraction. Day-trippers flocked to Portobello not just from Edinburgh and round about but from much further afield. On Saturday 8 July 1871, 600 excursionists arrived by special train from Larkhall. Another 700 came from the iron towns of Newmains and Wishaw and 2,000 spilled out of trains from Galashiels. Nearly forty years after its completion, Portobello Pier was still drawing in the crowds. Due to the recurrent costs of storm damage, it was, however, not a paying proposition. In Edwardian days, it was kept in repair by the North British Railway, whose excursion steamers (run by its subsidiary the Leith-based Galloway Saloon Steam Packet Company) operated an extensive schedule of summer sailings. For many holidaymakers a trip to the Isle of May or a sail across the Forth to Fife was the highlight of a visit to Edinburgh-by-the-Sea.

In the early years of the twentieth century, Portobello, now since 1896 part of the City of Edinburgh, gained a great new visitor attraction, its Marine Gardens. The mere name Marine Gardens fails to convey the size and scope of this major facility which, as the inaugural press advertisements proclaimed, constituted 'a new era in the History of Amusements in Scotland'. The buildings which comprised this privately-owned leisure complex had first been erected in Edinburgh's Saughton Park for the 1908 Scottish National Exhibition. When the exhibition closed, the buildings were dismantled and transferred in the following year to Portobello and re-erected on a neglected seafront site, which had aptly been described as 'a howling wilderness'. Its proprietors claimed for it: 'the largest rink in Scotland [for roller-skating], the finest bands procurable, the most refined concert programmes, the most lavish display of electricity, and the newest amusement devices.' The amusement devices included a mountain slide, a scenic railway, joy wheel, hall of mirth and a zoo – Bostock's Jungle and American Animal Arena. There was dancing in the ballroom; music, operettas, and films in the concert hall; pierrot shows in the open-air theatre; and invitation bands in the Band Court. On gala occasions there were balloon ascents, parachute demonstrations and high diving (into a small tank from a 70-foot-high tower). The most curious of the exhibits was the Somali village with genuine tribesmen and women – a feature which nowadays would be condemned as grossly patronising and politically incorrect. Nevertheless, for pleasure seekers, the

Edwardian-era Portobello beach scene packed with day-trippers clothed in their Sunday best. Note the bathing machines or coaches, as they were termed in some resorts.

Marine Gardens provided an unrivalled amenity. In the Edwardian glory days of 'Good Old Porty', they boosted the resort's image and popularity, and, as with the pier in its early days, attracted hordes of trippers by train and by passenger steamer direct to the pier, and not to be forgotten, great crowds borne by tramcar from the city itself.

The early 1900s was a boom time for the Scottish resorts. On festive occasions, particularly at the start of the summer holidays, crowds of people spilled out of the cities and industrial towns and villages – masses who were only too eager to get away from their normal abodes and places of employment. Although for most people it was still unpaid, a complete week's holiday was becoming the general rule for tradesmen and industrial workers. Even as far north as Elgin, we find, according to the *Banffshire Journal* of 2 July 1900: 'As an experiment, all tradesmen have suspended work for a week on the method adopted by the people of Glasgow at the Fair.' It should be remembered, though, that in many forms of employment, the important fishing and agricultural industries for example, there were no such concessions. On the other hand, industrial workers were often given an extra-long break, not as a special treat, but as a means whereby employers saved money when trade was poor. When at the time of their Trades or Fair Week holidays industrial towns virtually closed down, the demand for transport services was enormous. A Hawick veteran, the late William Landles, recalled the days when folk from the Borders went en masse to Portobello and other resorts for their annual holiday. Provided they were in regular employment, many working people were able to save enough to enable them to go off for the entire week. In the early twentieth century, four special trains left Hawick at the start of the Trades Week. Three went south: to Whitley Bay, Silloth (on the Solway Firth) and Spittal (by Berwick); and one steamed north to Portobello, which had its own station then. For youngsters the train journey itself was a great adventure – the sounds and smells taunting their senses. In those days of the annual mass exodus from factory towns, holidaymakers might rightly enjoy a change of scene and air, but one thing didn't change: they would still encounter many of the same people they met every day in their home towns. For working-class families from factory towns, holiday going was a collective experience and had a reassuring familiarity. As William Landles recalled, 'You travelled together and returned together. Just walking along the prom meant meeting your workmates, friends and neighbours and always

Part of the Marine Gardens complex, which included a zoo and real-life Somali villagers. A section of the scenic railway can be seen on the right.

posing the same questions: "Hae ye got guid lodgings? Is yer landlady a guid cook?'" The Landles family (mother, father and five bairns) favoured Portobello and, having found a good landlady, returned to the same digs year after year. While Mrs Arthur, their landlady, cooked for them, Mrs Landles provided the food. Travelling up on a Saturday, Mrs Landles took sufficient supplies with her to cater for the weekend until she could do some food shopping on the Monday.

As a youngster William Landles loved the beach at Portobello and recalled with great nostalgia the pier, the white-garbed pierrots, and the hucksters' stalls lining the prom. Going to swimming galas at the indoor baths and gasping at the high diving displays was one of the highlights. There was unwanted excitement on one occasion when his father took the bairns out in a rowing boat. When the weather broke, Mr Landles, Senior, watched by a crowd of anxious spectators, had to row back to the beach in a storm of thunder and lightning. Coming from an inland town, the family enjoyed going to Leith harbour to view the great ships and all the stir and bustle of the docks. For the thrill of climbing the Scott Monument or seeing the castle, they took the tram up to Edinburgh. Large families by necessity patronised the cheaper restaurants. One eating-house, as William Landles recalled, had a notice on the window: 'tatties and gravy for the bairns two pence [old money]'.

Day excursions, laid on by the different railway companies, were also highly popular with working-class folk and their families. In his book *Among the Fife Miners*, Kellogg Durland painted a graphic picture of excursion fever in the mining districts of West Fife. Durland, an American sociologist who in 1901 spent some months living and working in the mining community of Kelty, accompanied his collier friends on two day-long excursions – one to Aberdeen and another to Inverness. Since the railway fares were low, whole families could afford these trips, jaunts they called them. Durland had been warned that these jaunts were 'fearful crushes', the trains always very late, and the trips marred by excessive drinking. But drunkenness, he found, was 'conspicuous by its absence'. With regard to the Inverness trip at any rate, the local *Inverness Courier* had no critical comments to make – just remarking that 'the weather was bright and sunny, and the visitors apparently enjoyed themselves'. The excursionists (over 1,000 according to the *Courier*, much less than Durland's estimated 3,000) were crammed into three special trains. Although it was already full and did not stop, the first train into Kelty station, loaded with people from other West Fife towns and villages, received a tremendous welcome. Let Durland tell the tale:

It was a glorious July morning, and the spirits of the crowd ran high. As the first train approached a great shout went up that was echoed back with a right royal will. It was the first holiday in several months, and the pent-up feelings were given full freedom. The tumultuous enthusiasm was contagious, and I found myself shouting too. The singing and the shouting lasted all day, all the way to the Highlands and back.

Day excursionists, once they had reached their destination, made an obvious and not always welcome impact especially when large parties were decanted into small towns. When in 1910 the North British Railway Company laid on two special excursion trains to North Berwick, the peace and quiet of the 'Biarritz of the North' was rudely shattered. Some 800 visitors passed from the station in 'a state of high excitement, not a few singing the latest music hall renditions.' Generally, this exclusive resort, as we are informed rather ironically by the North British Railway Official Guide, was not popular with trippers nor did the locals then set out to cater for them. But this guide *The Beauties of Scotland* (1914 edition) was not aimed at day-trippers but at potential middle-class customers. North Berwick was a town where amenity was so important that the gas works was flitted in 1904 into the country mainly to preserve its character as a holiday resort. But no matter how poor the facilities and how miserable the weather, day-trippers were prepared to enjoy themselves in a variety of ways.

Although Northern Ireland, the Isle of Man and other parts of Scotland and England, too, were coming into favour at Glasgow Fair time, the big crowds still opted for a 'doon the watter' or 'Coast' holiday. West of Scotland folk in those days did not speak of going to the seaside. They went 'to the Coast' or alternatively went 'coasting'. While the railways were playing an ever-increasing role in the holiday traffic, there were, in the summer of 1900, no fewer than forty-six vessels working on the Clyde, with a total passenger capacity of 52,000. Rival railway companies had, however, pushed lines westward down by the Clyde and thus took business away from the all-the-way paddle steamers, which left from the Broomielaw in the heart of Glasgow. Many travellers now preferred to take the train to, say, Wemyss Bay or Gourock and then embark on what would be a much shorter sea voyage. At the start of the Glasgow Fair, all the railway stations were packed with a surging mass and enormous queues. The well-to-do setting off on a long-stay holiday had arrived by cab and had servants and porters to help them. Their main luggage would have been dispatched in advance. The rest had taken the tram or had walked, mothers often pushing a pram laden with luggage. Ironically, comic postcards best convey, albeit with a degree of exaggeration, the trials of a journey to the coast when tired and fractious weans (children) roared and cried while distraught parents made their displeasure only too evident. Although the weather was atrocious, the start of the July 1914 Glasgow Fair holiday as described in the *Glasgow Herald* was fairly typical:

Notwithstanding the unpropitious weather, large numbers of excursionists left by rail and steamer. Fair Saturday is the occasion of the one-day tripper, and this year was no exception to the rule. At all the railway stations heavy traffic was experienced. From early morning right on to the afternoon train after train was despatched, all the ordinary ones being run in two or more portions. The main rush was to the Clyde coast, but other holiday haunts claimed a large share, notably the towns on the Fife seaboard. The trains for the Highlands and also for London and the popular resorts in England and Ireland carried full complements.

On the other hand, a steamboat journey doon the watter was, weather permitting, very much part of the holiday experience. Better weather on Fair Monday in July 1914 meant that more day-trippers ventured doon the watter than on the Saturday. It was estimated that the fleet of eleven steamers sailing from the Broomielaw carried over 13,000 passengers, about 3,000 more than on the Saturday. The purification of the river, which resulted from new sewage schemes, ensured that, by that time, a sail on the Clyde was a more pleasant experience than hitherto. That summer of 1914 excursionists saw shipyard after shipyard – all with ships on their stocks, many of them great warships that, within a short period of time, would be armed and manned to help resist the might of the German High Seas fleet. But the July trippers had pleasure on their minds. Maw and the weans would have listened to the band, while Paw slipped down below allegedly to 'see the engines' but in reality to savour the liquid delights of the saloon bar. Until the outbreak of war in August 1914, German bands had been particularly popular, the players often university students earning some holiday cash. Sometimes too there were thrills for passengers, and spectators on land too, when rival steamers raced for a particular pier. Although competition between rival captains was one of the great spectator sports of the Clyde, it could be a hazard to both vessels and passengers. Smoke pollution from coal-burning steamers was another menace and was a source of constant complaint. Attempts made to prosecute offenders met with limited success. When in July 1900 Captain Stewart of the *Benmore* was fined at Rothesay Burgh Court for permitting black smoke to issue from his steamer, he asserted in his defence that steamer captains had enough to do in the busy season 'keeping a lookout for small boats and so on without watching how their engineers and stokers did their work.'

As for long-staying visitors, it was the custom, each summer, for middle-class families to book accommodation at their favoured resorts – rooms or whole houses – for an extended period of four to eight weeks. The father of the family, however, took a shorter break – a week or two at the most. He, however, travelled to the family's resort from his place of business in, say, Glasgow each weekend. Faster travel, by steamboat and train, even meant that from some resorts daily commuting was possible. Since no respectable person would travel on the Sabbath, even if suitable trains or boats had been available, the exceptionally busy Monday morning train or boat became one of the recognised social phenomena of the time. A favourite postcard showed a crowded Brodick pier on a Monday morning with, as well as the morning commuters, lots of women and children. The womenfolk were present to wave farewell to Papa and the other departing males, and no doubt

Doon the watter steamers departing from the Broomielaw, Glasgow.

to display their finery and sense of fashion. Neil Munro painted a verbal and idealised portrait of the typical holiday girl on the pier 'so fresh, so tanned, so rosy with the wholesome air of the sea.' She, his Edwardian 'Summer Girl', clad in muslin and chiffon, a Tam o' Shanter on her head and walking-stick in her hand, stood on the jetty waving 'studiously graceful adieux after her friends bound for the city'.

August was the month when visitors from south of the Border arrived in numbers. A census of visitors in the town of Stonehaven, taken on 8 August 1898, reveals that out of a total of 1,433, no fewer than 390 had arrived from England and thirty from abroad, the rest coming from Scotland with Aberdeen (234), Glasgow (197), and Edinburgh (191) well to the fore. The classification employed is revealing. Adults were listed as being Ladies, Gentlemen, and Maids. Since the census had presumably been taken on a weekday when many of the males were at work, there were nearly twice as many Ladies as Gentlemen. The Maids, domestic servants brought to the resort by their employers, numbered 165, part of their work being to look after the 298 children under the age of fourteen.

In time, holidaymakers from the West of Scotland began to make even more of a mark and for Stonehaven July became the highpoint of the holiday season, with the time of the Glasgow Fair the busiest week of the year and, as it coincided with the Aberdeen holiday, the town was bursting at the seams. There was no doubt too that the Glasgow visitors knew how to enjoy themselves. Stonehaven's August visitors, it was said, were much more staid. As this extract from a contemporary Doric (Scots) poem illustrates, the guid folk of Stonehaven welcomed the annual influx.

> A few days hence and then 'twill be
> The annual Glesca fair
> An' weel ye ken that it will be
> An unco grand affair.
> An' men an' weemen, auld an' young,
> Their herties filled wi' glee,
> Will a' be steamin' northward
> To Stonehaven by the sea.

Although very few had the benefit of holidays-with-pay, a rise in the general standard of living permitted some working-class families, by scrimping and saving, to have enough cash to pay for holiday fares and cheap, albeit crowded, lodgings for a few days or longer. Some were lucky enough to find accommodation with friends or relatives. And for those who could not find or afford suitable lodgings, there was the option that was often taken in resorts of sleeping out of doors. In Rothesay a favourite place for makeshift howffs was the town's Skeoch Wood, ironically known as 'Hotel-de-Skeoch'.

When the masses arrived, the ultra-rich moved out. Centrally located mansions in Dunoon and Rothesay, once the residences of wealthy Glaswegians, were sold and converted into hotels, boarding houses or convalescent homes. Resorts like Rothesay, Dunoon and Millport continued to prosper thanks to their popularity with canny, well-doing working folk and a greatly expanded middle class. The Edinburgh bourgeoisie, too, had long since abandoned Portobello and spent their vacations in North Berwick or Dunbar or in the golfing resorts of Fife. Glasgow professionals and businessmen were also smitten with the golf craze, Ayrshire in their case being their favoured playground. The socially exclusive 'Arran set' also took to golf in a big way. That island, despite the

Rothesay's famous 'pointing porters' touting for custom. The porters were licenced by the burgh and each had his own identifiable number. As steamers approached the pier, they pointed towards passengers with luggage to try to book their services.

generally poor standard of accommodation, had retained social cachet, due in large part to the feudal restrictions that had for long been imposed by the dukes of Hamilton. For the comfort-seeking 'better class of visitor', and for English tourists passing through, there were upmarket hotels like the Marine in North Berwick and the hydropathics, two of the latter in Bute – the Kyles of Bute Hydro at Port Bannatyne and the Glenburn in Rothesay. The latter, with its 125 bedrooms, was a self-contained all-the-year-round holiday centre. As well as the usual reading room and billiard room, the Glenburn could boast a recreation hall with stage and scenery for theatricals. Within the grounds there were tennis courts, croquet lawn and putting green, and, close at hand, an 18-hole golf course. In its heyday the Glenburn was a very profitable concern. In 1897, as John Burnett has shown, it made £2,360 profit on a turnover of £11,843.

The big city shops ensured that their well-to-do customers were suitably attired for the holidays. Prior to the holiday season, they placed advertisements in newspapers like the *Glasgow Herald*. Upmarket Glasgow firms like R. W. Forsyth of Renfield Street and Gordon Street advised customers preparing for the Fair Holidays that they stocked such necessary items as ladies' dress baskets, hat cases, bonnet boxes, and carriage cases, also Coast hampers and luncheon baskets. Another shop had made 'a great purchase' in anticipation of the 1900 Fair Holiday. Since their customers were heading not for the Riviera but doon the watter, their holiday sales list was a prudent one. Topping the list were ladies' waterproofs, rubber capes and mantles. Nominated 'as the best travelling companion' in another less than optimistic July-dated advertisement was an item that was highly appropriate for a Scottish summer holiday, namely the 'Drooko' umbrella.

There were worse perils to come, though. On 4 August 1914, Great Britain declared war on Germany. Six days later, an entertainer in the Bachelor Boys pierrot company playing at St Andrews posted a card to a friend in Crieff. He joked that he could write because he had 'a few minutes to spare before the Germans capture us'. Quite a few holidaymakers took the threat of German attacks more seriously, with the result that they cancelled their holiday arrangements. Initial reports from the resorts, as printed in the *Glasgow Herald* of 12 August, revealed considerable variations in the immediate impact. While Stonehaven was doing all right, at Brodick, on the other hand, everything was much quieter than usual and Rothesay was seriously affected by cancellations. It was not only those who let houses that felt the pinch. In September 1915 a pierrot, a member of a troupe playing at Aberdour, appeared before the Small Debts Court at Dunfermline. The accused had failed to pay for his board and lodging. The entertainer explained that the war had meant that the number of visitors had gone down sharply and that the troupe's takings had consequently suffered. The court was unsympathetic and ordered him to pay off his debt and pay the expenses of the case. Despite appearing before the court 'in gay summer garb', this was one pierrot who, thanks to the war, finished the season in a far from merry state.

Spy mania was rife. Not that that was anything new. Before the war, after the Admiralty had started to construct a torpedo range on Loch Long, many foreigners, principally 'heavily-moustached Germans from the Fatherland' had come to Arrochar to climb the Cobbler. For suspicious locals, it had been the view of the Loch Long torpedo range rather than the scenery that had been the attraction. The musicians of the German bands came under similar suspicion. The bands had, of course, disappeared but so had most of the excursion steamers. Since shallow-draught paddle steamers made ideal minesweepers, the navy requisitioned many excursion boats, including the entire Galloway fleet. Hotels and many other buildings were likewise adapted for military use. The army, for instance, took over the Marine Gardens at Portobello. One of the soldiers billeted there in 1916 sent a postcard with a prewar view of the ballroom being used as a roller-skating rink. His message read: 'This will give you some idea of the place we sleep in. There are beds 8 deep in the floor. Am on bombing [practising with hand grenades] this week. Love Billy'.

To protect the shipping and towns of the Upper Clyde from hostile attack, a boom was built across the Firth from Cloch Point to Dunoon. This resulted in a dramatic reduction in the traffic to the island resorts, particularly Rothesay and Arran. The pier income at Rothesay was reduced to such a degree that in 1917 pier charges were introduced – one old penny for each passenger. With the remaining excursion steamers restricted to the upper waters of the Firth of Clyde, Dunoon gained at Rothesay's expense, as did the quiet village of Lochgoilhead which enjoyed a spell of unusual popularity. More threateningly perhaps Blackpool also profited from the restrictions on the Clyde passenger traffic. As John K. Walton, the Lancashire town's historian, tells us, Blackpool had a prosperous war. For some resorts, the presence for the duration of the war of considerable numbers of naval and military personnel compensated for the loss of their normal quota of visitors. With the new naval base of Rosyth close by, accommodation at Aberdour, for instance, was at a

One of the Pierrot troupes who performed in Edwardian Aberdour.

premium. Aberdour House was occupied by the dashing Admiral Beatty, who commanded the battle-cruiser squadron at the battle of Jutland and latterly the entire British Grand Fleet. The presence of many service personnel and their families ensured too that the hotel and boarding-house keepers of Dunoon were kept busy. War or no war, the Sabbath was still sacrosanct. When Army bands started playing in Dunoon's Castle Gardens on Sunday afternoons, the town council put a stop to it. Troops could slaughter each other on Sundays, but light music was quite another matter. Concern was expressed about the decline in moral tone, since the presence in Dunoon of so many servicemen attracted prostitutes to the town – 'undesirables' being the euphemistic term employed. Although the removal of so many coastal steamers badly affected some towns, the Fife and Ayrshire resorts, easily accessed by rail, took up the slack. Travel congestion and the removal by the railway companies of cheap fare concessions meant that, as Dr A. J. Durie has pointed out, holidaymakers were reluctant to travel great distances. Full employment and the comparatively high earnings gained by women in the munitions and related industries meant a large number of working people had money to spare for holidays and excursion trips. By 1918 the volume of Glasgow Fair traffic was at least as great as in pre-war years. Not surprisingly, with many young men in reserved occupations having money to burn, there were complaints about heavy drinking.

The wear and tear resulting from military occupation had a deleterious effect on many requisitioned buildings, including Portobello's Marine Gardens which never recovered their former glory. Only the ballroom survived and ironically it too was a casualty of wartime neglect and abuse, but this was during the Second World War. A bus depot now occupies the site. Sadly, Portobello Pier, opened to such acclaim away back in 1871, did not survive the war. Storm damage had rendered it unsafe, so early in 1918 it was demolished. For the Galloway Saloon Steamer Company, which in the palmy days of the 1890s had owned six steamers, the outlook was bleak. With the other Forth piers and landing stages used by the company in a poor state of repair and all their steamers gone, the company went into voluntary liquidation. While excursion steamers did eventually return to the Forth, it was with a much more limited programme. For East of Scotland sea-borne excursionists, it was the end of an era. As for Portobello, every few years proposals and plans for a new promenade pier were brought forward but they all came to naught.

The *Wemyss Castle*, a Galloway steamer, at Elie in the company's Edwardian heyday.

CHAPTER 2

On the Beach:
The Lure of the Seaside

Elie has a most pleasant, dry and healthy situation. The shore is sandy, and shelving gradually, is remarkably well adapted for sea-bathing; and is, of late, much resorted to for that purpose.

The Statistical Account of Scotland, Parish of Elie, 1794–5

It was in the eighteenth century that sea bathing became fashionable when some influential medical practitioners began to recommend bathing in the sea, inhaling the fresh sea air and even drinking seawater for a variety of ailments, both real and imaginary. The sea, too, whether lapping gently on the sands or crashing onto rocks or harbour walls was a source of perennial fascination and poetic reflection. For people from inland places, the sea was elemental and strange, its surging power a source of wonderment and romance. Ships outward bound and carrying full sail were seen, too, as a link to romantic faraway places. For all sorts of reasons then, it became the done thing for well-to-do people to resort to 'salt water quarters' for the summer season. Lodgings were found at accessible fishing villages and seaports, preferably those with, as at Elie, good sandy beaches. In consequence, some of these places came to be regarded as holiday resorts or, in the parlance of the time, seaside watering places.

For Elie and similar watering places, the description 'much resorted to' was a relative one. In the eighteenth century and in the early 1800s, few people could afford the time or the cost of a seaside holiday. But, as we have seen, by the late nineteenth century more and more people had the means and the time for, if not an extended holiday, then for at least the occasional day excursion. As bathing for health became less important, the family holiday aspect took over. At resorts like Ayr, Saltcoats and Broughty Ferry with ample stretches of sand, it was still the beach and its immediate hinterland that was the main attraction. You went to the beach not only to bathe or paddle or, in the case of the weans, to make sandcastles and play all sorts of games. You also went there to be entertained. It was on the shore, or adjacent natural links or manmade promenade, that Punch and Judy booths, pierrot platforms, bandstands, and other shows were to be found. For many people on the margins of society, the beach at holiday times was a retail opportunity. Gypsies brought their donkeys there and other showmen set up swing-boats and roundabouts or hired out deck chairs. And there were always plenty of ice-cream carts and sweetie stalls and beach photographers on the prowl. In time, the various local government authorities set out to inspect and regulate these amenities with, for example, vets checking the condition of donkeys and ponies. Councils also profited by charging for the licences, which they imposed on stallholders, showmen and other providers.

At the more organised resorts, town and county councils provided extra facilities like bench seats and shelters and, as cars and motor-buses became more numerous, car parks and access roads.

A heavily clothed, and not too happy-looking, child, on a donkey at Portobello beach.

A paddling pool for the kiddies and maybe too a yachting pond were also regarded as desirable adjuncts. Montrose provided useful information in the form of a tide table. The town council also provided the bathing coaches. In the early 1900s, the Montrose bathing coaches were divided into First Class (cost four old pennies) and Second Class (two pennies). Juveniles when sharing paid half price. The time allowed for each dooker (bather) was 30 minutes. A horse to haul the coaches was hired for the sum of 18 shillings a week, the owner feeding it and accepting all risks. Some years later we find the council buying a horse for the beach and selling it at the end of the summer season. Councils naturally expected some return for their expenditure. At the end of each season, the Sea Bathing Committee of Montrose Burgh Council drew up an annual report. In 1900 the total number of bathers using the coaches was 3,931, the greatest number on any one day being 178 and the daily average thirty-six. With fifty-eight days of the season being wet, the profit for that summer amounted to a mere £2 and 9 shillings. The convener of the committee caustically added: 'Bathers apparently object to fresh water externally especially in the form of rainfall but plenty of evidence is afforded from the number attending that fair weather is essential for financial purposes.' Some councils hired out costumes, towels, and deckchairs. At Prestwick, where, like Montrose, a horse and a man were hired to operate the bathing machines, six old pennies was the charge in 1921 for the hire of a machine, and two pennies each for the use of a bathing costume and a towel. Other councils gave franchises for such services. In 1933, though, North Berwick Town Council turned away applicants who sought permission to hire out deck chairs. No one, the council insisted, should charge for a seat in their town.

Rows of bathing coaches were a feature of some beaches. Kate Grimman, recalling her childhood days, described the coaches in 1920s Carnoustie:

The coaches had big iron wheels and double doors; as the doors were quite high up, we had to mount a few small steps to get in. On a hook beside the door hung a pail, which was provided for the purpose of rinsing feet … On the floor inside was a draining board; there were benches and hooks, and a rather fascinating little port-hole high up on the back wall … We had barely unrolled our towels when the best moment was upon us. There was a clanking noise, then the coach vibrated and lurched into motion. Jean pulled open the upper part of the door, so that we could admire the powerful, gleaming flanks of Barney, the big carthorse … as he performed his duty of pulling us down to the water's edge. As we rode, I leapt up on to the bench to peer out of the little port-hole at this unusual view of the retreating beach.

For Kate and her sister Jean hiring a bathing coach was a rare treat. Bairns more often tried to get a free ride by sitting on the coach's rear steps. For the bathers inside, it could be quite a bumpy ride. At Aberdeen beach, the woman in charge of the Edwardian-era machines yelled out this warning: 'Haud on yersel!' Bathing machines, as they were also called, had first come into use in the eighteenth century to protect modest bathers from prying eyes. By the late 1920s, though, they were regarded as out of date and were gradually phased out. Some were retained and just used as stationary changing huts.

In the early 1900s bathing places were generally segregated with separate areas set aside for males on the one hand and for women and children on the other. 'Mixed bathing', as it was called, was regarded as the kind of practice dodgy Continentals got up to and was prohibited, sometimes by local byelaws and otherwise by unwritten rule. An 1896 guide for Crail asserted that one of Crail's 'recreative laws', which, it hoped, would be 'honourably observed' was that the main bathing beach at Roume Bay was available for men only up to 8 a.m. Once any hardy early morning male dookers had departed, women and children were left with the beach to themselves. Change was on the way, however. A decade later at nearby Elie, although Ruby Bay was reserved for women and young children, mixed bathing was permitted at all times of the day elsewhere. Nevertheless, at Rothesay men and women retained their own bathing stations, each fitted with dressing rooms and well screened from 'public observation'. The weans had their own 'Children's Corner', the one place, in the town itself, with a modicum of sand.

No matter what the rules said, there were always some rebels who defied the conventions, as we see from a letter to the *Glasgow Herald*. A visitor to Ayr, in the summer of 1900, scandalised to see twenty naked men on the beach, wrote to the press calling for action. If nothing were done, this correspondent asserted, then the town council should just remove the bathing machines from the beach and burn them. Generally, it was day-trippers whose conduct raised eyebrows. Young working-class men and women out on the spree could be rather too high spirited for the more staid middle-class long-stay visitors. It was maybe not Club 18–30, but even in Edwardian days sexual

Postcard view of Montrose beach in the early 1900s. Notice the rescue boat and also the advertisement on one of the bathing coaches for which the council charged ten shillings per annum. A few of the women are using a bathing raft as a seat on the sands. Deckchairs are conspicuous by their absence.

restraints were loosened at the seaside. In 1910, according to a Fife newspaper, respectable visitors to Aberdour were outraged by the 'shameless effrontery' of couples lying 'locked in each other's arms … in a shameless defiance of the conventionalities that are protective of virtue.' Drunkenness and gambling were other causes of offence. On some town beaches, in the days when most forms of gambling were highly illegal, groups of men would gather on the shore to bet on cards or pitch-and-toss. At the first hint of a police raid, these gambling 'schools' scattered very quickly. One Kirkcaldy veteran recalled how he when a boy profited from these raids. 'After this happened, we would go and search in the sand where they had been playing, and I have to admit we often found shillings and sixpences, great riches for us!'

In the early twentieth century in more out-of-the way places like Newburgh in Aberdeenshire, there were few day-trippers and a more carefree atmosphere prevailed. When the Bishop family arrived there from Aberdeen for their annual six weeks' summer vacation, the first thing the children did was to kick off their gymmies (sandshoes) and for much of the time run about bare-foot. The young Edith Bishop revelled in 'the happy sense of freedom to run without stockings held up by tapes to stays!' The children dressed and undressed among the sand dunes. Sometimes, as Edith Bishop recalled, they did not even need towels as rolling down a sand hill was just as effective and more fun. To heat themselves up after bathing in the cold North Sea, the Bishop bairns ran races and played tracking games on the dunes and the moor behind. For visiting children and locals alike, the shore was a matchless adventure playground. They could dig caves in dunes, build sandcastles, dam burns, send stones skimming across the waves, gather shells and seaweed and explore rock pools. At Newburgh, the Bishop girls and their friends, armed with cleeks (iron hooks), hammers and with old gymmies (sandshoes) on their feet, hauled crabs out of their hiding places. The hammers were used to break down rocks to secure easier access. Once caught, their pincers were tied and the crabs strung on a piece of twine. 'Once we had seventy crabs! Many wash-house boilers were cooking that evening!' Not all parents were so lenient. Amy Stewart Fraser, recalling family holidays at Stonehaven in 1904, watched as girls happily paddled with their frocks tucked into their knickers:

> My mother would not have dreamed of letting us make such an exhibition of ourselves, so we walked demurely on the Esplanade with our parents, in our kilted skirts, our blouses with sailor collars, and our round straw hats, watching other children paddling and building sandcastles. We were not envious; we realized that such ploys were not for us.

Sandy beaches were ideal locations for sandcastle-building competitions, which were popular events and sometimes sponsored by newspapers. In 1905 the 'sand modelling' competition at North Berwick attracted no fewer than 185 contestants. On popular beaches expert sand 'sculptors' put on special displays. Their technique involved piling up quantities of sand first thing in the morning, damping it down and then proceeding to sculpt figures of considerable complexity. For visitors, there was fascination too in watching other people still hard at work. On some shores there might be salmon fishers launching their boats or drying and repairing their nets and elsewhere maybe fisher folk baiting their lines for the next trip out to sea. For holidaymakers the way of life and work of the fisher folk was a source of perennial fascination. Some fishermen, though, had found that hiring out rowing boats and taking summer visitors for trips round the bay was less laborious and easier money than their traditional mode of life. Steep, shingle beaches, as at Dunoon, were not ideal for bathing or for children's play. But they were very suitable for boating which could be

MODEL YACHTING AT LARGO.

The rock pools at Largo were a perfect playground for children. The girl on the left is wearing oil-proofed paddlers or waders. These were manufactured just along the coast by John Martin & Co., of Cellardyke, a firm that also supplied oilskins and tarpaulins for seafarers.

enjoyed at all stages of the tide. In Dunoon in the 1930s there over 200 boats for hire – all of them licensed by the town council.

In the freer and easier 1920s, mixed bathing came to be accepted. Fashions changed too. Women's skirts were shorter and so too were bathing costumes. The bright young things of the Jazz Age refused to wear the old one-piece loose-fitting garments, which reached to the knee and buttoned close to the neck. In the early 1930s, less absorbent, synthetic materials came into favour. Swimsuits were still one-piece but more revealing than before. There were still some restrictions, as we see from a 'referendum' conducted in 1930 by Wolsey Ltd., the Leicester garment manufacturer, to ascertain which styles were to be permitted that summer. Although most of the Scottish resorts polled had no regulations, Broughty Ferry and Edinburgh had rules prohibiting garments made of transparent material during mixed bathing. What defined 'transparent' was unfortunately not explained. At any rate, old-style stockinette garments could be clingingly revealing when wet. The questionnaire also asked about colours. At Aberdeen, it transpired, two-colour costumes, were all the rage.

Unfortunately, there was the occasional drowning tragedy. In the years 1869 to 1889, twenty-one people were drowned at Aberdeen beach, fifteen drowned while bathing and six off small boats near the beach. Many resorts, therefore, took responsibility for beach safety by appointing lifeguards – 'beach rescue men'. Aberdeen, Broughty Ferry, Montrose and St Andrews were some of the places that had standby rescue boats. In 1900 Montrose Burgh Council appointed Alexander McDonald as 'Rescue' at the Bathing Station at a weekly salary of 25 shillings, plus the Sunday takings from the hire of bathing coaches. At the end of the season, he was commended for 'his most exemplary conduct and attention to his duty', which included keeping order in the Bathing Station area. That year he had rescued from danger three persons, thus ensuring that the bathing season ended free from fatalities. As for the three people rescued, the danger was 'entirely due to their own foolhardiness and that in spite of timely warnings.' The poles shown in the Montrose beach postcard were another safety device. In 1910 the Montrose Town Improvement Association paid for poles with ropes attached to enclose the part of the beach in front of the Bathing Station 'for the safeguarding of bathers.' Bathers were advised to keep within the lines. Voluntary lifesavers often helped out too, as in 1930s North Berwick where the members of the Lifeguard Corps were available to help the council's beach-ranger. Aberdeen had another safety measure – a Children's

At the Beach, Broughty Ferry

In this postcard, based on an 1896 photograph, we see some of the Broughty Ferry fishing community shelling the mussels needed to bait their hooks. This was the kind of picturesque but carefully posed scene that artists and photographers loved to record.

Shelter for Lost Children. Security-conscious parents pointed it out to their bairns as the place to head for if they got separated in the beach crowds.

There were other unseen dangers. Too often insufficient attention was given to the location of sewage outlets with their evident risks to public health. Public toilets were an obvious necessity, but once more the provision was inadequate. In July 1947, for instance, complaints were made about the nuisance caused by sewage discharge at one corner of Aberdour's popular Silver Sands beach. Correspondents wrote in scathing terms to the local press complaining not only about this issue but also about the filth engendered by the presence on Sundays of 2,000-odd people and the consequences of having no public conveniences 'within reasonable range'. Five years later the situation did not seem to have improved any, as the County Clerk of Fife County Council had to draw attention to the problems created by the enormous crowds visiting the Silver Sands area. In addition to the 'exceedingly difficult' policing problems, which arose, there were 'the attendant questions of sanitation and disposal of litter'.

For those seeking thrills and spills there was, on some resort beaches, motorbike and car racing. St Andrews was just one of the resorts which sanctioned such events. From 1909 till the 1950s, motorcycle speed championship races attracted large crowds to the town's West Sands. Since beaches, Carnoustie's for example, where there was a firm stretch of sand could also be turned into landing strips, travelling aerial circuses entertained the crowds with acrobatic displays and also gave, what was then a considerable novelty, the chance of a flight. In 1932 low-flying aeroplanes were a source of annoyance for the more stuffy North Berwick residents. One of the companies operating pleasure flights had to apologise for the nuisance caused by its pilots flying over the town 'during the hours of divine service on Sundays'.

With the various churches seeking to take the gospel 'to where the people were', the beach too became the place for seaside missions. The Church of Scotland specialised in running beach missions for children. From two centres in 1934 – at Millport and North Berwick – the Kirk was, by the late 1980s, running thirty-two centres, led by lay volunteers and trainee clergymen as well as ministers. From the parents' point of view, it meant that they could go off and do their own thing, only too glad to have their children taken off their hands for a spell. And many children were only too happy to participate. The Children's Own Club at North Berwick, as described in 1939, was

Competitors rounding a bend at St Andrews' West Sands around 1950. At their peak, motorbike and car races attracted over 2,000 spectators. These events required the sanction of St Andrews Town Council.

fairly typical. 'The day begins with the bright singing of old and new choruses and then goes on to games and scavenger hunts on the beach.' In 1938 Aberdeen Presbytery ran a children's 'happy hour' every forenoon. The activities included a nativity scene and pageant presented by local children and a play entitled 'Stanley Finds Livingstone'. On another occasion one of the boys of the mission was dressed as a Roman soldier to illustrate an address entitled 'The Whole Armour of God'. With evening talks at the Links on subjects like 'Christian Athlete', the adults were not neglected. Not all evangelists were welcome, though. In Edwardian St Andrews there were complaints to the local press about Jacob Primmer, an ultra-Protestant preacher, 'bawling' on the Embankment and 'hot gospellers' from Oxford with a portable organ holding services for children at night when they should have been in bed. There were overzealous evangelists at Lossiemouth too. In the summer of 1950, holidaymakers at the Moray resort complained of being pestered even in their beach huts. When, accordingly, the local Youth for Christ team sought permission to hold religious meetings on the beach, they were turned down. Since two other groups had been given the go-ahead, the result, the town council feared, would be to create 'religious pandemonium on the beach'. The beach and adjacent areas of public resort, like the Castle Hill in Dunoon, could also be used for political demonstrations. In the early 1900s, the Women's Freedom League (WFL) headed for the summer resorts to campaign for votes for women. A 1908 report in the socialist newspaper *Forward* reads: 'Yes, I think Dunoon is converted, and everywhere doon the watter. Those who come to scoff buy badges and postcards … in which we do a roaring trade.' (*Forward*'s editor was Tom Johnston who in 1945 became the first Chairman of the Scottish Tourist Board.)

For visitors to the seaside, leisurely strolling or promenading on the beach was an essential part of the daily ritual. You could enjoy the view, chat with other holidaymakers and, at the same time, feel that you were contributing to your well-being by inhaling the fresh sea air. After all, doctors had for many years been commending the virtues of sea air for its tonic-like qualities. Invalids and convalescents had, according to accepted medical opinion, to take account of the effect of the local climate on their particular condition. According to Dr Neville Wood's *Health Resorts of the British Isles* (1912), Oban, like other West Highland resorts, was suitable for convalescents and others, including the 'overwrought and the neurasthenic' who required 'pure air, a sedative climate, and the quiet enjoyment of beautiful scenery.' The east coast resorts, on the other hand, were generally

THE PROMENADE, LARGS.　　　210202

Strolling on the prom at Largs in 1930. Women with young children would have been glad to find a seat where they could put their feet up.

regarded as dry and bracing. Nairn was strongly recommended for the quality of its air, in winter no less than summer. St Andrews was regarded as extremely bracing – very windy in other words. In the autumn and early winter months, it was much in favour 'with those, who coming from the relaxing, damp west coast require a dry, bracing climate to recuperate in after debilitating illnesses.' It was the same with Kinghorn which was why, in the 1930s, the Dowie family from Edinburgh spent their holidays there. A holiday house on the promontory overlooking Pettycur, the family doctor advised, would give them a plentiful supply of sea air.

To get full benefit from the ozone, to use the favoured term of the time, convalescents and other visitors wanted a safe place on which to promenade. At the same time, developing seaside resorts needed to protect the houses and hotels that were going up from the onslaughts of the sea. The Victorians, accordingly, went in for coastal protection in a big way. From building sea walls on their sea-fronts, they went on to provide 'added value' in the form of access roads and paved terraces – esplanades or promenades as they were called. For the more sedate visitors, a promenade provided a place for a pleasurable saunter – much better than scrambling over sand dunes or sinking into wet sand or, even worse, into mud. Rothesay's foreshore was one place that definitely needed tidying up. A local chronicler described this work, combined with the building of an esplanade, as the greatest improvement in the town carried out in the nineteenth century. Largs, too, benefited from the sweeping away of derelict boats and sheds that littered the foreshore.

For an ambitious resort a prom became an essential amenity and, as at Burntisland, something for guidebook writers to boast of. That burgh's beach esplanade, built between 1899 and 1905, was commended for 'its broad level pavement and comfortable seats'. At Thurso various 'public-spirited citizens' raised funds for the construction of an esplanade in 1882 and then for an extension in 1919. The Townswomen's Guild was largely responsible for the shelter built in 1933 and the Town Improvement Committee donated a block of bathing boxes in 1949. Dunoon's esplanade, more than two miles long by 1939, transformed 'a narrow and dangerous roadway … into a broad and handsome promenade where a delightful seaside constitutional can be enjoyed.' Once it was lit (first by oil, then gas and ultimately electricity) promenading, and often too dancing on the prom, might continue well into the night. If there was no band, a gramophone filled the gap. Even on the prom, though, there were social distinctions. One regular visitor to Portobello observed that: 'The would-be elite gravitated to the eastern end towards Joppa'. The hoi polloi, on the other hand, headed westward where the funfair was located.

Where there were links by the shore, promenading and all sorts of activities, including golf, cricket and horseracing, could be accommodated. It was on links land that the game of golf developed and evolved over the centuries. An Aberdeen historian reckoned their 'fine breezy common' to be one of the greatest public benefits possessed by the city. For this ambitious city, however, a proper esplanade was still a necessity. Even industrial towns, Greenock and Kirkcaldy for instance, built proms. A plaque on the latter's prom tells us that this Sea Wall and Esplanade was built by the Corporation of Kirkcaldy in the years 1922–23 'during the above years of great trade depression in order to relieve unemployment.' For the socially inclined the promenade was above all the place where you went to meet people – to see and to be seen. Since, as we have observed, entire towns emptied at the same time, you would meet friends from your neighbourhood or from your work. But, in addition, you had the chance of making new friends or resuming an acquaintanceship started on a previous holiday. For young men and women, too, the beach or the prom was the place to find a 'click'. The chance of a holiday romance, or at least a mild flirtation, was for many young people the main attraction of the seaside holiday.

In England a large number of resorts built a different kind of promenade – one that extended over the sea – by building a pier designed for that purpose. The Portobello Pier was the only one of this type to be built in Scotland, since proposals to build promenade piers at Aberdeen, Ayr and Nairn came to naught. There were plenty of other piers in Scotland, but they tended to be more functional. The steamer piers at Rothesay and Dunoon were, however, substantial structures and were natural gathering places for visitors and natives alike. Watching the steamers come and go was very much part of the doon the watter holiday. Today we can still experience something of the stir and excitement of former days when the paddle steamer *Waverley* sails up to the piers at the Firth of Clyde holiday resorts. Elsewhere, however, we need the local museum or heritage centre to tell the story of a very different past, of the time when Scottish proms and beaches were just as crowded and lively as their sun-kissed counterparts in today's highly favoured hot-climate resorts.

CHAPTER 3

Holiday Destinations: From Early Beginnings to the 1930s Depression Years

There is no such thing as a Planned Holiday Resort. There are only a great and increasing number of places which have 'cashed in' on a growing demand for a seaside holiday. The but-and-ben has swollen into a villa. The villa has bulged into a boarding house, the hamlet has put on housing-of-a-kind weight and Seaside Resort is truly a name which covers a multitude of sins and architects' blushes.

Councillor the Revd John P. Crosgrove, Convener of Housing, Rothesay, writing on 'The Psychology of the Seaside Resort' in *Transactions of the Royal Sanitary Association of Scotland*, 1950.

This statement by the reverend councillor was not strictly correct, as some UK resorts, Lundin Links in Fife for example, were planned. Projected originally by the Standard Insurance Company, the arrival of the East Fife Railway in 1857, it was hoped, would stimulate growth. Despite its eligibility as a golfing and sea-bathing resort and its situation on Largo Bay, which apparently rivalled 'the beautiful Bay of Naples in point of scenery', progress was slow until the completion of the Forth Railway Bridge in 1890 opened up a much wider market. By then an enterprising laird John (later Sir John) Gilmour was transforming Lundin Links. Thanks to his efforts, the North British Railway Company was obliged to have all its trains stop at the local station. He helped to promote Lundin Links as a golfing resort and laid out ground for feuing. He had an 'excellent' road built to the station, drained the links and, very important for a health resort, introduced a gravitational water supply. Robert Black, Clerk to Largo Parish Council, paid fulsome testimony to the laird's qualities. Through his 'enterprise and liberality, much of late [1897] has been done to further improve and popularise the place.' With 2,090 inhabitants in 2001, Lundin Links continues to thrive, albeit with a high percentage of retirees. Helensburgh, too, was a model village but one that was planned as an industrial settlement not as the resort and commuter town it eventually became. It was steamboat travel pioneered on the Clyde by Henry Bell, the proprietor of the local Baths Hotel, and then the arrival of the railway that transformed its prospects.

Although parts of some other resorts were planned, most developments were of a piecemeal nature. Proximity to a great urban mass of population was the key to the rise of resorts like Helensburgh, Portobello and Broughty Ferry. They developed initially because, firstly, they were deemed by popular opinion to be suitable 'salt water quarters' for valetudinarians and other holidaymakers and, secondly and what was equally important, they were easy to get to. Just as the tentacles of increasingly wealthy Glasgow were extended to Helensburgh, Gourock and other doon-the-watter resorts, so summertime Portobello was transformed into Edinburgh-by-the-Sea,

BATHING POOL & BEACH, LOOKING EAST, HELENSBURGH. A.2399.

On the summer day in 1935 when this photograph was taken, Helensburgh beach was packed and likewise the outdoor pool. The Granary Restaurant was a prominent feature on the seafront. As its name suggests, it was a former grain store. The North British Railway had wanted to build a railway along the seafront as a link to the pier, but the citizens blocked this environmental affront.

and Broughty Ferry became the favoured resort for the populace of Dundee. Aberdonians, although their city was a substantial resort in its own right, saw nearby coastal communities, most notably Stonehaven, as alternative destinations for dooking and other holiday pleasures. Since Saltcoats was the first of the resort stations on the line from Glasgow to Ayrshire, it was for the poor of the city the cheapest to reach. It has been said that the locals knew when the Glasgow Fair arrived 'as the streets filled with poor souls, many suffering from rickets.' As means of transport were improved especially with the extension of steamboat and railway services, the better-off holidaymakers began to range much further in their search for an ideal holiday location, preferably one that avoided over close contact with the hoi polloi of the cities.

The Rosneath peninsula on the Firth of Clyde, to the west of Helensburgh, was one area, where in the heyday of Victorian enthusiasm for seaside watering-places, a number of small ribbon-development settlements were built. The population of this comparatively isolated peninsula trebled once convenient steamer communication had been established. These mostly affluent newcomers had been lured to new settlements like Cove and Kilcreggan by the splendid views and sheltered waters, ideal for boating and sailing. The ruling elite ensured also that that there would be none of the kind of developments that might draw in the 'wrong type of visitor'. Coulport on Loch Long, on what had been till then the undeveloped side of the Rosneath peninsula, was one of the later developments. In 1880 a steamer pier was built and ground set aside for feuing for what the speculators hoped would be a grand new watering place. For a while, the pier attracted some steamer excursions and, indeed, was favoured for a time as a place for evening and special excursions. This initial flurry of development was, as we shall see, not to last.

Roseneath Pier.

In the early 1900s, the village of Rosneath was a place of convalescence for invalid and wounded soldiers (five of them in this image) who had been sent home from the Boer War (1899–1902). This was a temporary provision, but quite a number of permanent convalescent homes were established in the Firth of Clyde resorts. This steamer pier was built in 1893 and was one of eight such piers on the Gareloch, built in the days when the Gareloch was a prestigious holiday destination – a rich man's paradise. Today's nuclear submarine base at Faslane somewhat detracts from its charms.

From these examples, it is obvious that there are many and diverse places – ranging from village-size to city-size – that, at one time or another, could claim to be considered a seaside resort. For some places, Dunoon and Rothesay most obviously, the holiday trade was their lifeblood. For others, the city of Aberdeen for instance, tourism was, and still is, very important but it was only one among a number of significant industries. There were quite a number of other places from Buckie in the north-east to Campbeltown in Kintyre which were not primarily seen as resorts, but which tried to develop tourism as a very useful ancillary source of income. Some resorts like Nairn and North Berwick on the east coast and Innellan, near Dunoon, on the west side of the country, were rather select; others like Rothesay and Portobello were much more popular, catering for the masses rather than the few. With such a degree of diversity, it is difficult to be precise as to the definition of a resort. I would not, for example, classify Edinburgh and Dundee as seaside resorts, despite each having a lengthy coastline and despite having swallowed up their neighbouring resorts, Portobello (1896), on the one hand, and Broughty Ferry (1913) on the other. Since both Portobello and Broughty Ferry had become well established as resorts before their loss of independence, they continued to be regarded by natives and visitors alike as resorts in their own right. It is therefore convenient to categorise them as separate entities.

It was visitor demand that made Portobello and Broughty Ferry what they used to term places of resort. But visitors needed the means of getting to their destination, places to stay, and, in course of time, a range of things to do, especially when the weather was bad. To meet the needs of these visitors, individual entrepreneurs, many of them outsiders, were prepared to make the necessary capital investments in transport, accommodation and leisure facilities. Then, as tourism grew increasingly important for local economies, municipal authorities started to become involved and, as we shall see, make investments in, for example, leisure amenities. The seaside became established as not just a place to go to for bathing but also, for the masses in particular, as a venue for a wide range of sports and entertainments. In consequence, in some places, Portobello, for example, there was a substantial degree of private investment in entertainment facilities, which drew large crowds. Conversely, for more discerning and/or snobbish visitors, there could be just too many attractions, and for them the word popular was not a recommendation. For the average middle-class family, easily accessible places, like Portobello and Broughty Ferry, came to be regarded as just too trippery. Portobello, for example, was, according to the 1875 edition of Murray's *Handbook for Scotland*, a 'pleasant seaside town'. But in the 1894 version it was downgraded to being 'a seaside town and second-rate watering place'. In October 1906, concerned citizens attended a protest meeting in Portobello Town Hall. The rowdism and vulgarity on the prom and beach during the past summer, it was claimed, was keeping the locals from visiting the prom during the summer months. Although describing Portobello as 'a favourite suburban residence and bathing place', Black's *Shilling Guide to Scotland* (1898 and 1906 editions) added insult to injury by casting doubt on the purity of the seawater.

North Berwick, on the other hand, was assessed very differently: 'the favourite watering-place for the Edinburgh upper classes', according to Murray. Dunbar, too, had its middle-class devotees; Nairn in the north-east was another burgh with an upmarket clientele, very many coming from England. This self-styled 'Brighton of the North' had become established in Victorian days as a fashionable health resort and like North Berwick and Carnoustie (yet another 'Brighton of the North') their excellent golf links ensured their continued prosperity. (Incidentally, the term 'Blackpool of the North' was only used in a derogatory way.) The increasing popularity of golf was an important factor in the changing fortunes of towns with good golfing ground – Prestwick and Troon being two other prime examples. Golfing resorts like these became middle-class redoubts. Troon, for instance, was described in a *c.* 1945 Official Guide as a thriving resort 'free from the 'tripper' element'.

Nairn golf course, with local laddies serving as caddies, in an image which, though not posted till 1914, can be dated to 1894. For wealthy southerners, the fact that there were no large industrial towns anywhere near Nairn was a major attraction. That ensured that there were no unwelcome day-tripping hordes.

For many small communities the opportunities afforded by the ever-expanding tourist industry offered a hope of salvation in the face of declining industries. In many small towns and villages, the holiday trade brought new wealth into impoverished or decaying, but nevertheless picturesque, wee places, like Dornoch in the north and Portpatrick in the south-west. Murray in 1894 had reckoned the first to be insignificant and inaccessible and the second 'a poor little place'. In the early 1900s their popularity with golfers, improved hotel accommodation and access by rail brought them new life and vigour. It was in 1902 that Dornoch got its branch line. Stagnant fishing towns and villages, newly accessible by rail, were tidied up and had their facilities enhanced to secure a share in this great urban seasonal migration. For the old-world burgh of Crail in the East Neuk of Fife, as in so many other towns and villages, it was the coming of the railway in 1883 that wrought a veritable revolution. Fife journalist, Henry Farnie, had stated *c*. 1860 that this ancient royal burgh was 'little known for summer quarters. It lies for one thing completely off the beaten track; and the inhabitants living like so many snails in their shells, do not care to put themselves about for enticing visitors'. As in a number of other towns, a forceful Provost, James Peattie in this case, pushed through essential improvements – most importantly a new water supply and drainage system. With the natives now 'enticing' visitors, this ancient burgh was now able to boast of its tennis 'greens', which were well patronised by the ladies, and from 1892 a bowling green. Three years later golfing legend Old Tom Morris was employed to lay out a new golf course at Balcomie Links to replace an inadequate 9-hole one. Picturesque corbie-stepped gables, cobbled thoroughfares, auld kirks and tolbooths did not in themselves attract summer residents. In these respects Culross in the west of Fife could easily match Crail in the east. But, while a few artists and antiquarians found their way to this historic burgh, families found it less appealing. This was because, with virtually no sand, the Culross foreshore was unattractive. There was no links suitable for golf either and, unlike the East Neuk fishing ports, there was no harbour to bring life and colour to an otherwise quaint auld toun.

A proportion of the money brought into such communities was reinvested in better housing and facilities like village halls, bowling greens and tennis courts, which served locals and visitors alike. In the small communities, in particular, the regular summer visitors often helped with fund raising for local good causes. They put on concerts and contributed to charity bazaars and such like and helped

The Stotfield Hotel at Lossiemouth, photographed in 1926, was one of two large hotels built hard by the first tee of Moray Golf Club's championship course. As with the neighbouring Marine Hotel, it was built to meet the convenience of golfers. Jessie who posted this card in August 1931 had enjoyed fine weather and was 'quite sunburnt'.

to keep some of the local kirks economically viable. In Lossiemouth, for example, St Gerardine's, a Church of Scotland kirk, received invaluable support from well-to-do summer residents during the fishing depression of the interwar years.

Communities, whether highland or lowland, adapted in other ways too. As stated above, except where landowners exercised a measure of feudal control and planning as at Helensburgh, development, by and large, had been haphazard and unregulated. Rapid expansion had, though, created problems that required communal solution. Among the doon-the-watter resorts, towns like Campbeltown and Rothesay were already royal burghs, but Helensburgh, Gourock, Millport, Dunoon, Saltcoats, Largs, and even tiny Cove and Kilcreggan had become 'police burghs' before the end of the nineteenth century. The new elected town councils thus gained the responsibility for overseeing various major public services and duly embarked on schemes for better water supplies, drainage and public lighting. For such towns, their image had to be protected. In 1937, two East Fife burghs, Pittenweem and Crail, decided not to publish the latest report from their Medical Officer of Health. Provost Milne of Crail was quoted in the *East Fife Observer* as saying that there were statements in their report 'which might excite people'. He went on to say that 'it would be wrong to publish anything that might be harmful to Crail as a holiday town.' Shades of Ibsen's play *An Enemy of the People*!

While, in providing such public utilities, the coast towns were doing no more than their counterparts elsewhere, they had the additional incentive of safeguarding their image as health resorts and desirable places of permanent residence. Nevertheless, there was by no means universal approval for the policy of spending ratepayers' money on holiday attractions. Cost to the ratepayers was always an issue. In the 1930s the ratepayers of Fraserburgh rejected a town council proposal for the construction of an outdoor seawater bathing pool. A similar project in Leven, as we shall see in chapter 6, met a similar fate. Although one would have thought that a public park was an essential amenity for an aspiring place of resort, away back in 1880 the ratepayers of Dunoon had rejected such a proposal on the grounds of cost. It was not till 1903 that Dunoon acquired its park. Commuters and people who had retired to a holiday town for a quiet life had generally little interest in promoting tourist activities. John Strawhorn, the historian of Prestwick, noted that, during the 1920s, party politics played little part in local elections. The principal division of opinion, he observed, was 'between those who wished to develop the holiday trade and those residents who felt disturbed by the growing number of visitors'.

Nevertheless, seaside towns spent a great deal of money on tourist attractions, including, as we have seen, esplanades and shelters, facilities for bathing and other forms of entertainment. There was investment, too, in concert halls and pavilions, like those at Dunoon and Gourock. Opened in 1905, the Dunoon Pavilion was, it was claimed, the first place of entertainment to be built by a municipality in Scotland. Dunoon, a burgh since 1862, and Millport, since 1864, recognised the need to purchase and thus control their steamer piers, so important were they for their economies. Millport followed the example set by other towns by passing in 1900 byelaws to regulate, for example, the hiring of ponies and donkeys, boats and other vessels and also the bathing places where, of course, males and females were segregated. With regard to ponies and donkeys, the town council insisted that all animals had to be kept in good condition and that no one over the age of fifteen be permitted to ride on the donkeys. Some council regulations were sensible; others less so, as when, in the 1930s, St Monans Town Council stipulated that the lessee of their beach refreshment hut was not to sell refreshments on Sundays. Early on, the value of advertising was recognised. In 1904, for example, Prestwick Town Council delegated to a house-letting committee the task of

Glasgow Street and Esplanade, Millport   RELIABLE SERIES 534

By ensuring that the town was clean and tidy and that its facilities were well regulated, Millport Burgh Council provided a safe environment for the like of these Edwardian girls clustered round the fountain.

issuing lists of houses available for summer letting and, in addition, advertising the town as a resort. Two years earlier bathing machines had been introduced. Further features were added, following the formation of an Attractions Committee. Among other tasks, it saw to the improvement of the beach seats, the licencing of rowing boats, the granting of franchises for the sale of ice-cream, the erection in 1910 of a new concert pavilion (£800 having to be borrowed for this), and, one year later, the construction of a putting green. Other pre-1914 improvements included the building of a sea wall and esplanade and, at least as important, an underground urinal.

Leven Burgh Council in Fife was another that pursued a proactive tourism policy in the interwar years. As part of a policy which older historians called 'municipal socialism' and some more recent ones 'municipal capitalism', the council made significant investment in visitor-orientated amenities. In this important golfing resort, the town council feued the golf course from the Durie estate and then leased it to the three local clubs who had formed a joint committee to manage it. But the council also recognised the need to provide other amenities. In 1921 the council borrowed £1,000 to erect a ladies' shelter which, despite its name, included gents' as well as ladies' lavatories. At the same time it went ahead with the construction of a putting green at the beach. More ambitiously, the council sought to acquire Leven Beach. With the proprietor, R. M. Christie of Durie, agreeing to feu the ground to the burgh, the council borrowed another £1,000 for this purpose. But the council's territorial ambitions were by no means complete. In 1924, the councillors unanimously decided to acquire Spinkie Den, a local beauty spot, compulsorily if necessary. There were already some privately operated recreational facilities in the den, a pierrot stance and an open-air fresh-water swimming pond both built with the consent of the laird, the self-same R. M. Christie. After protracted negotiations, Mr Christie did agree to hand over the den, the annual feudal payment to him being £105. Fortunately, a local farmer John Letham, came forward and gave the council £1,000, which sum, he said, suitably invested would go some way towards meeting the feu-duty. For his generosity, a grateful council changed the den's name to Letham Glen. In that same year, 1925, the burgh erected ornamental gates at the entrance to the glen. Five years later Mr Letham donated another £500 to pay the cost of the gates and railings. The council proceeded to make a number of improvements to the glen, including the construction of a putting green.

Councillors and business leaders in the resorts were conscious of the need to promote their community not only as a tourist destination, but also as a suitable place for industrial development.

Castle-Building at Leven

The Ladies' Shelter at Leven beach from a 1920s postcard.

In 1907, for example, Montrose Town Council agreed to spend from £20 to £30 in 'advertising the town in various Journals during the coming season' and also pay £3 and three shillings for a page advert in Leng's *Golfer's Manual*. Along the coast Broughty Ferry Council had their own publicity campaign, buying posters and advertising in West of Scotland newspapers. Many towns had a promotional body which also helped with publicity costs. These organisations were as often as not co-operative ventures between councils, voluntary bodies and individual business people. For instance, Campbeltown Town Council formed in 1906 an Advertising and Development Committee with power to co-opt non-members. Receiving only a small annual grant from the council, it had to raise money to fund its activities which included publishing a guidebook in 1907 (with interesting contents but typically dreary cover) and opening a tourist information office. Generally early guidebooks were just that – a guide for visitors telling them what there was to do in a specific town or area and where to go with an emphasis on local history.

In 1910, Broughty Ferry Merchants' Association organised a gala to draw in and entertain visitors during the peak holiday period. This became an annual event. Montrose Town Improvement Association also played a significant part in developing the town both as a health resort and as an industrial centre. In the smaller resorts, voluntary groups played a proportionally greater role in preserving and developing local amenities. Brodick in Arran, for example, had an Improvement Trust, formed in 1892, whose principal task was to preserve the amenity of the village particularly the foreshore. Portpatrick had, we are told in the *Third Statistical Account: Kirkcudbright and Wigtown* (1965), a Village Improvements Committee that for almost sixty years had helped to make the village 'more attractive and comfortable for the inhabitants and summer visitors'. Yet another committee, post-1945 vintage, produced a brochure on behalf of the proprietors of the Portpatrick boarding houses.

Most guidebooks, usually undated and generally anonymous, were produced for the councils by commercial concerns and published by them, with copious local advertisements. If the publisher had the permission of the council, the resultant booklet would bear the label of an 'Official Guide'. In the post-Second World War years Aberdeen's Publicity Department, however, issued its own guides. Councils also took out adverts in the railway companies' own publications. In 1937, for example, Cullen Town Council had a full-page advert in that year's *LNER Holiday Handbook*.

Cullen (population in 1931 – 1,688) was confidently described as yet another 'Brighton of the North'. The burgh was, the advert declared, 'the prettiest and healthiest summer resort on the shores of the Moray Firth'. Guidebooks emanating from the smaller towns tended to focus on their strengths as family resorts, like the interwar Invergordon guide which stressed the long, clear summer nights and the absence of vulgar holiday crowds and 'the strident noises of popular watering-places'. Girvan was 'a family town … free from the steamers and bustle of other Clyde towns'. Likewise, the Campbeltown Advertising Committee boasted, in a leaflet issued in June 1939, that their town succeeded as a resort due to 'its beautiful environment and wealth of natural charms, rather than to any pose or ostentation, so common a feature of the gaudy and artificial type of resort designed solely for pleasure'. Some attempts to find a suitable advertising slogan savoured of desperation rather than inspiration – witness, Girvan 'the Atlantic Resort' and, even more idiosyncratic, Campbeltown 'the Peninsular Resort'. Occasionally you can find disparaging comments about rival resorts. It was presumably a local patriot who, in an early 1920s *Official Guide to Elgin and Lossiemouth*, wrote that, while nearby Nairn had splendid golfing and bathing facilities, there was otherwise 'little to attract the attention'. The editor, though, saw nothing incongruous in carrying a full-page advert for a gravestone manufacturer and another advert for a draper whose 'Requisites for the Beach' included Speyside wool blankets. Maybe, though, when a snell (sharp) north wind was blowing thick blankets might have been quite appropriate.

Resorts also often benefited from bequests and other gifts bestowed on them by grateful current or former residents. The Traill brothers, one of Melbourne in Australia and the other of West Bromwich, granted over £2,000 for the construction of a pavilion at Montrose. This edifice, which was ceremoniously opened in August 1913 and which continues in use, was intended to be 'a resting place and shelter for the citizens and others visiting the beach'. William Mowat, a large-scale tanner, provided the cash for a promenade at Stonehaven. This prom, built in 1895 using duckboards, did not last long, however. This prom may be likened to a poor man's version of the boardwalks found in Continental resorts like Deauville. It is important to remember, too, the contribution made by business people of all kinds. Dundonian entertainer, Henry Melville (or Harry Marvello to give him his stage name), was certainly one. He had come to Portobello in 1905 with a concert party and did so well that two years later he bought the Tower Hotel on the seafront. He then formed a company, which built the 1,000-seat Tower Pavilion in the garden that fronted the hotel and did good business with the variety shows and other entertainments he provided there. Nor should we forget the essential role played by the small-scale entrepreneurs, the small men and women who sold ice cream and lemonade and hired out boats and donkeys, and thus helped to make a day by the sea such a pleasurable experience. What constituted a tourist attraction varied enormously. William Bissett of Leven supplied his hometown with two of its tourist sights. From the 1920s, he and later his son James ornamented the family home and garden structures with shells gathered from the seashore. Over the years, the Buckie House and Shell Bus, as they were known, featured in many of the postcards sent by visitors to the town. After James Bissett died in 1979, attempts to sell this attraction as a going concern met with no success, and the site was cleared.

Scottish seaside towns had nothing to rival the huge 'people's pleasure palaces' of Blackpool and the other large English resorts. But, in relation to their size and relative importance, a number of burghs invested considerable sums in their recreational facilities. Aberdeen is a prime example of how a vigorous city council and individual entrepreneurs promoted the holiday industry. The Aberdeen Swimming Baths Company built indoor baths at the Links which, with 109,000 bathers in 1888, proved very popular. In the early 1890s, the city council, however, sent investigators to a large variety of seaside resorts both in England and in France. Following their report, the council bought and further improved the company's baths. Completed in 1898 the Corporation Baths was one of the largest of its kind in the country. Other private ventures included a funfair with a ramshackle-looking 'American Switchback' (1889), a skating rink and small zoo. There was also a boating pond which a visitor in from the country for the day couthily described, in a postcard, as 'a place like a mill dam wi a curn (few) boaties in't nae muckle bigger than tubs'.

Real pioneers, the council examined the possibility of introducing 'a motor-car' service to the beach. It was suggested that councillors visit some of the other places 'where such cars are to be seen'. In the event, the Corporation constructed an electric tram line which, when opened in 1901, provided easy access to the Bathing Station and to the handsome esplanade which was built and extended over the years. At this time open-air concert performances were very much in vogue. In 1902 two London-based performers took to the stage at Aberdeen beach, paying the council £25 for the privilege. Catering for the family market, this pierrot ensemble provided 'fun without vulgarity'. Three years later, the council erected a modest pavilion. According to a local guidebook this timber building with a corrugated iron roof was a 'commodious and lightsome structure'. David Thomson, a very able comedian, was the impresario in charge. While the 'minstrels popularised the beach', Aberdeen Town Council, according to a 1908 guide, made a good thing from 'the substantial rent exacted' from its Beach Pavilion. These minstrels gave three performances a day weather permitting. Talent competitions were a popular feature with a young Harry Gordon one of the winners. In later years, Harry Gordon became one of the stars of David Thomson's concert party and, after Thomson's death, became joint-lessee of the pavilion. Clean, wholesome but very couthy entertainment was guaranteed: 'You may always be sure of a clean, healthy show and the best we can provide.' Recalling those early days of the 'finest family entertainment I have ever come across', Edith Bishop enthused over, among other first-class artistes, 'the fabulous Scott Skinner playing lively dance music on his fiddle and dancing at the same time'.

In the 1920s, with Harry Gordon's Entertainers enjoying unprecedented popularity, the town council invested in a new building. With a seating capacity of only 750, the new Beach Pavilion, which was opened in 1928, was the perfect theatre for the kind of friendly and intimate performances that were Harry Gordon's trademark. An Aberdonian himself, his sketches in the north-east Doric

Maggie, who had relatives in the audience when this postcard photograph was taken, wrote that the weather on that day, the May Holiday, was glorious but since then 'it has been so windy and cold that the poor pierrots have had to perform to empty chairs.' The place was Aberdeen beach and the year around 1912.

dialect, as a local wifie or as one of the characters in his fictional village of Inversnecky appealed very much to locals but were also made comprehensible to outsiders. This canny impresario, however, ensured that a glamorous chorus line gave his shows sex appeal. As the star of the show and as producer and director, Harry was the mainspring. Not content with that, he also designed sets and programmes and wrote some of the songs and sketches. By the 1930s Harry was also the sole lessee. He was able to entice many of the stars of the interwar and immediate postwar years to come north to do a turn at the city's Beach Pavilion. One local cynic, with perhaps the city's exposed location very much to mind, alleged that Harry Gordon was possibly the only real attraction that the Aberdeen beach ever had.

But from 1929 the city had another major attraction – its new Beach Ballroom. It was opened with some pomp and ceremony with some 1,000 'gay masqueraders' dancing on what was claimed to be the 'silkiest and most alluring dance floor in the country'. The corporation built this prestigious building at a time when ballroom dancing had attained an extraordinary degree of popularity. It was also an era of confidence and economic stability. Unfortunately, this confidence was not sustained. It was shattered by the economic depression that followed the Wall Street Crash of October 1929. However, an English entrepreneur, John Henry Iles had taken over the ballroom on a five-year lease, agreeing to pay 50 per cent of the net annual profit to the council. Iles (1871–1951) was a remarkable character who played a major role in the popularisation of brass bands. On a visit to North America in 1906 he was greatly impressed by the kind of amusement parks that he saw there. On his return, he introduced roller coasters, 'scenic railways' they were called then, to Blackpool and London's White City. Initially, his business acumen impressed Aberdeen Town Council who also leased a piece of ground to him where he built an amusement park whose most

The scenic railway, until it was burned down in 1940, was the dominant feature in the Aberdeen Pleasure Park. But with the Codona family also having a funfair at the beach, there were, as we can see from this 1930s postcard, many and varied forms of entertainment.

notable feature was a 100-foot-high scenic railway. Iles's involvement in Aberdeen was only a small part of his empire. He had major interests in amusement parks in Barcelona, Berlin, Brussels, Cairo, Copenhagen, Paris and Pittsburgh and also in Margate, which was near his home in Kent. His relationship with Aberdeen Council was not, however, a happy one. Iles, on his part, was unhappy about the restrictions placed on the running of the ballroom, which made profitability difficult to attain. Councillors, on their part, were soon expressing their doubts about the way the ballroom was being run, and were querying, too, his financial viability. Consequently, when the lease expired in 1934, it was not renewed. The council took over the running of the ballroom, putting a manager in charge. The council's doubts about Iles's financial stability were confirmed when, in 1938, he was declared bankrupt.

A 1930s guidebook writer had, prior to visiting the city, wondered why Aberdeen had become such a favoured spot with holidaymakers from Glasgow, Dundee and other industrial towns. When he saw the golden sands and all the beach area amenities, he concluded that Aberdeen had 'everything that makes for gaiety and hilarity'. It was the nearest approach to Blackpool that he had seen. Making the city's amenities pay, particularly the Beach Ballroom, in the years of the Great Depression was no easy task. The ballroom lease, it was claimed, had too many restrictive clauses. Alcohol was banned, but that was the case with most dance halls. The council had also decreed that, as well as there being no dancing on the Sabbath, the dancing entertainment had to be 'free from vulgarity'. In the postwar years of grey austerity, the management did their best, plugging the ballroom as combining 'the alfresco atmosphere of the beach with the gaiety and glamour of a London west-end spot'.

In the 1930s 'gaiety and hilarity' were badly needed. The Wall Street Crash had sent the financial markets into freefall and the world economy into chaos. The 1929 Great Crash plunged the world into a trade depression of unprecedented severity. Scotland, with many of its important industries already in decline, suffered very badly. With business after business failing, unemployment soared. In 1932 the number of unemployed in Scotland was around 400,000 or 27.7 per cent of the insured workforce. By the following year there was a slight improvement but it was still at 25.5 per cent. This may be compared with the percentage figure for the South East of England at 9.4 per cent. Some places were worse off than others. In 1934 Motherwell, 37.4 per cent of the insured workers were unemployed, the heavy industries being the worst affected. Although it may be assumed that the long-term unemployed had to stay at home, the effects of the Great Depression on holiday going seems to have been variable. In late August 1930, the Glasgow *Evening Times* gave a favourable report on the 'Coast holiday harvest' for the previous three months. There might have been fewer Glasgow Fair visitors, but the ever-increasing number of English visitors coming to the Clyde provided compensation. The Coast landladies, the *Times* declared, gave a good deal of the credit to the 'Come to Scotland' movement (The 'Come to Scotland Association', a voluntary body, had been formed in the 1920s to promote Scottish tourism). A number of Clyde Coast resorts devised their own variant on this slogan by running a 'Come-to-the-Clyde' advertising campaign. Though limited in scope, the campaign that year, 1930, seems to have paid dividends for the participating towns – Rothesay, Dunoon, Gourock and Helensburgh. It was not easy to raise funds for such projects, though. Rothesay was in the best position as the profits made from its entertainments financed its advertising. On the other hand, Dunoon had a voluntary assessment and the other Clyde towns just relied on voluntary contributions. Largs, which had previously contributed to the Clyde Advertising Scheme, had withdrawn from it in 1929. Their local organisation, the Largs Advertising Association, had dropped out because the scheme was oriented towards 'the steam-

SEAMILL BEACH AND ARRAN HILLS

Thanks to the motor car, the middle-classes had a wider choice of holiday destinations. At some beaches, as we see from this 1935 postcard of Ayrshire's Seamill Beach, you could even drive right on to the sands. The car on the left foreground is a 1925 Morris Cowley and next to it is a new 1935 Morris.

boat excursions point of view.' Largs now, the association maintained, relied more on the motoring public, whether travelling by private-car or charabanc. From their point of view, steamer traffic was much less important.

As the Depression continued to bite, the *Rothesay Express*, looking back on the events of the year 1931, declared that, due to the slump, there had been fewer visitors that year. In the following December, it could report that visitors were still coming to the town and that was partly due to the fact that fewer people were going abroad, but the newspaper noted, too, that holidaymakers had less money to spend. This ties in with evidence that withdrawals from the Glasgow Savings Bank for the Fair Holidays were well down compared with pre-Depression levels. It was the same story across in Fife where in November 1931 the Leven Town Band faced a financial crisis. The band's only source of income were the collections at its summer recitals at the town's Letham Glen. But 'due to trade conditions' the sums raised had been getting smaller each year with disastrous effects on the band's finances.

Notwithstanding the Depression and extremely high levels of unemployment, large numbers of people were still intent on either going away from home for a holiday or at least taking advantage of local day excursions. In July 1933, in Cardenden in the heart of the depressed Central Fife coalfield there were, according to the local press, heavy bookings for the cities and coast resorts. The exodus by train and bus was 'slightly heavier' than during the previous few years, although that summer's very good weather would have boosted the holiday trade. In Dunfermline the rail bookings both for period and day trips were 'well up to standard'. In Glasgow, at the start of the Fair Holiday that same year, an estimated 250,000 left the city by all means of transport – by train, bus, steamer, car and bicycle. Of the then existing two major railway companies, one, the LNER, dispatched 120 special trains from the city. From the LNER's Queen Street station alone, 46 specials departed on Fair Saturday, many of them bound for the Fife coast resorts. Perhaps it was that the worse things were, the greater the need to escape. There were also, as Alastair J. Durie has noted, age-group differences. In some areas, he found that, although there were fewer family parties setting off, young people without encumbrances were going off in numbers.

With an estimated 15,000 holidaymakers arriving at Aberdeen, no wonder it was said that Fair time meant that 'Aberdeen belongs to Glasgow'. Among the around 2,000 arriving at Stonehaven,

A busy day at Aberdeen's alternative beach at Bay of Nigg. There was no roller coaster here but there were swings and ice-cream vans and stalls.

however, there were many Aberdonians, since the Glasgow and Aberdeen Trades Holidays coincided. On Saturday 22 July 1933, at the end of a week of splendid holiday weather, the staff at Aberdeen Joint Station, according to the *Press and Journal*, supervised a 'gigantic quick-change act'. Along with the hordes departing to the West of Scotland, and a few hundred going back to Fife, came a fresh influx of holidaymakers from Dundee and Edinburgh and, of course, Aberdonians returning from southern resorts. On that Saturday, in addition to the ordinary trains, there were eight specials from Dundee and six from Edinburgh, though some of these travellers were going further north. 'At times,' we are told, 'everyone in Aberdeen seemed to be carrying luggage'. As well as Aberdeen, the smaller east-coast fishing towns, Buckie, Fraserburgh, Anstruther and Eyemouth for example, where the once profitable herring fishing had collapsed, tried to cash in on this new potential bonanza. In these towns, as we have seen, great efforts were made to encourage the development of tourism.

Many families stayed at home, some by choice but most probably by necessity. The stay-at-homes, though, could take advantage of the numerous day excursions laid on by local transport services. They could also enjoy simple, traditional pleasures. In 1933 in Aberdeen for example, while incoming Glaswegians up for the Fair flocked to the sea beach with its funfair and other attractions, many locals, the *Press and Journal* stated, opted for a simple stay-at-home holiday. Heavily laden with pots, pans and kettles, 'Mr and Mrs Aberdeen and family' headed for a less fashionable beach at Bay of Nigg where, heedless of the sewer outlet, they could light a fire and enjoy an old-style picnic. There was a fresh-water tap where they could fill their kettles and on this pebbly beach plenty of dry flotsam and sticks for their fires.

By 1936, there were signs that things were picking up. The August Rush at Rothesay, it was said, was greater than any for the past ten years. So great were the piles of arriving luggage that it

ABERDEEN FROM THE AIR

As we can see from this 1930s aerial view of Aberdeen beach, we have at top left tennis courts and a bandstand and top right the Beach Ballroom. On the centre left we see the children's pony track and beyond that, three tramcars. The building with the big lum is the bathing station and next to it the Shelter. On the sands there is a row of bathing coaches and some wee sheds for selling ice cream and other goodies.

was late at night before it was all cleared. Nevertheless, the once so prosperous Glenburn Hydro Hotel, which was up for sale, stood empty and it was another three years before it reopened. Small, peripheral Clydeside settlements, like Blairmore on one side of Loch Long and Coulport on the other had also suffered. These middle-class outposts were developments too far. Created, as George Blake, that astute observer of the Firth's social mores, later commented 'in the mighty flood of Victorian prosperity [they were] left stranded and slightly pathetic in the ebb'. On the east side of the country, on the other hand, there were indications that recovery was on its way. According to the *East Fife Observer* of 12 August 1937, the August influx to the east-coast towns was larger than it had been for many years. This upturn, the paper continued, was 'generally attributed to the increase in the number of persons employed throughout the country since the beginning of the year.' The fact that, by the late 1930s there was a dramatic increase in the number of workers who were being paid for their annual holiday, also helped to boost recovery, particularly at the lower ends of the holiday market. Professional and white-collar workers had long enjoyed the advantage of paid annual leave. But now, largely through the medium of collective agreements, manual workers were making gains in this field. By March 1938, according to Ministry of Labour estimates, 42 per cent of workpeople in the United Kingdom enjoyed the benefit of paid holidays. The Holidays with Pay Act in 1938 established the principle that employees should have at least one week's holiday with pay, with initial implementation, however, to be still on a voluntary basis. Full implementation of this Act had to wait till more peaceful times.

There were other more serious matters facing the people of Britain in that year. Hitler's aggression in Czechoslovakia in 1938 and threats to Poland in the following year brought war ever closer. But the *Press and Journal* headline of Monday, 17 July 1939, 'Aberdeen Casts Care Aside', shows that

Evacuees newly arrived at Buckie railway station. The police sergeant, as he was then, was the author's father.

holiday fever was as intense as ever. According to this newspaper report, on the previous Saturday, the start of the Glasgow Fair, a trainload of visitors arrived at the main railway station every eight minutes from early morning till late at night. Railway officials subsequently reported that Aberdeen had more holidaymakers than the previous year. In addition, many visitors arrived by special bus. The conjoining of the Aberdeen and Glasgow trades holidays meant that the railways and bus companies had to cope too with the hordes of Aberdonians who were also holiday bound. On that same Saturday the main bus company, W. Alexander & Sons, had forty extra buses in service to accommodate those departing from the Granite City. Although on 18 July the government plans for evacuation in case of war were front-page news, the pleasure seekers were not deterred. On the following Saturday, as the Glasgow folk departed, twelve special trains arrived bearing a fresh contingent of holidaymakers, this time from Edinburgh and Dundee. By the end of August the threatened war edged closer, as at least one holidaymaker noted. In a card posted from Aberdeen on 29 August, he described Aberdeen as a lovely place but added, 'It is an anxious time owing to the recent crisis.'

When by the beginning of September 1939 war with Germany became inevitable, even more arrivals were recorded with more special trains than ever before. This time they brought not holidaymakers but evacuees from the danger zones – children of primary school age and mothers with under-five-year-olds. In Britain as a whole, a million and a half were evacuated to small country towns and other rural centres. Holiday towns received large numbers, in Campbeltown's case 445. In north-east Scotland, by 3 September 1939 when war was declared, 12,000 mothers and children had arrived. They came from Edinburgh, Glasgow, Dundee, Rosyth and Clydebank. Cullen in Banffshire, for example, received nearly 100 evacuees from Portobello and neighbouring Buckie around 200. Among the latter were two Portobello bairns who were accepted into their home by the writer's parents.

CHAPTER 4

The Rothesay Experience:
Sabbatarian and Feudal Restraints

The town and bay [Rothesay] all summer long make up a brilliant scene. There are steamers constantly coming in from the outer world with crowds of gay and happy folk, then going off, with dusky plumes of smoke and dazzling tracks of foam, across the blue waters that wind into the far recesses of the hills. There are yachts that come sweeping with white wings silently round cape and inlet. And there are the little boats that dance everywhere merrily on the sparkling sea.

George Eyre-Todd *Doon the Watter – Caledonian Excursions Official Guide,* 1906

Although Dunoon's inhabitants would have disagreed, the most popular, and certainly the largest, of the Coast resorts was Rothesay on the Isle of Bute. Rothesay, a historic royal burgh, had sprung to prominence in the early nineteenth century as a watering place for the well-to-do merchant and professional classes. From its early days, the town had been, its townsfolk claimed, the Madeira of Scotland. As a health resort, it was a refuge for patients suffering from consumption (tuberculosis) and other bronchial complaints. Catherine Sinclair, writing in 1840, quoted the heartfelt cry of a sick young friend suffering from the snell winds of Auld Reekie (Edinburgh): 'Oh, what would I not give for one breath of Rothesay air!' In addition to its relatively mild climate, the town could boast of a most scenic backdrop. The view across Rothesay Bay towards Cowal and remote, hill-girt Loch Striven inspired many a writer. George Eyre-Todd (see above) was only one of many authors who waxed lyrical on its charms.

By the late nineteenth century, popular tourism had arrived, and consequently at the July peak time, during the Glasgow Fair, Rothesay, like the other Coast towns was, as Neil Munro observed, no place 'for the contemplative pilgrim, the sensitive poetic soul'. Wealthy Sassenachs, going down the Clyde on MacBrayne's prestigious steamer, the *Columba*, en route to their Highlands and Islands shooting lodges, were dismissive. Describing the town as Glasgow-by-the Sea, they compared it to the Cockney masses' favourite destination – Margate. For working-class Glaswegians, on the other hand, the town, with its late Victorian tenement blocks, seemed to be a homely-like place and a place that they could identify with. Yet Rothesay, like Margate, was by no means devoid of middle-class visitors. There was a large choice of impressive houses and apartments to let in the burgh and in the smaller Bute resorts like Port Bannatyne and Kilchattan Bay. The Glenburn Hydropathic, with a wide variety of spa-type treatments, and the Kyles of Bute Hydro at Port Bannatyne catered for valetudinarians and other moderately well-to-do visitors. According to *The Buteman Guide to Rothesay*, the burgh was a safe place of residence. Being an island was one safeguard, as it kept tramps away. More significant was 'the absence of a rough and lawless class of inhabitants', there being neither workable minerals nor any other trades employing a rough population.' What the

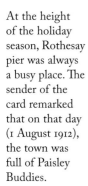

At the height of the holiday season, Rothesay pier was always a busy place. The sender of the card remarked that on that day (1 August 1912), the town was full of Paisley Buddies.

guide does not mention is that extra police were required at Glasgow Fair time when there was a great deal of drink-induced disorder. In 1907 Rothesay Town Council borrowed a sergeant and six stalwart, and presumably Doric speaking, bobbies from Aberdeen to help cope with the problem.

The constant coming and going of steamers was one of the great attractions of Rothesay, thus ensuring a very wide choice of possible excursions. However, even then Rothesay's preeminence was being challenged. By the outbreak of the First World War in 1914, it was beginning to be apparent that its best days were over. Even in the early 1900s many were tempted away to rival resorts in the east and other parts of Britain. The *Glasgow Herald*, at the start of the 1914 Fair, stated that some people, as a result of recent experiences, were abandoning the Clyde, heading instead for English and Irish resorts or opting for 'the quieter charms of the Highlands'. A few years earlier local business people had clubbed together to form a Rothesay Advertising Association, which set out to attract visitors from south of the Border as well as from the Glasgow conurbation. It advertised the town in the press of the industrial towns of the North and Midlands of England. The result was an immediate boost to the number of August visitors, thus extending the season. The association also published guidebooks and set up an Information Bureau to help not only visitors but prospective residents as well.

Developing seaside towns attracted investment from outwith the area, and Rothesay was no exception. When the burgh was still on the up-and-up, a group of Edinburgh entrepreneurs set up, in 1879, a company to build a tramway system. The horse-drawn cars of the Rothesay Tramway Company linked the town centre to its northern suburbs and continued from there to Port Bannatyne. The trams were a great success, quickly becoming one of Rothesay's distinctive features. In 1883, the year after the system opened, over a quarter of a million passengers were carried in the three summer months from June to August. The system was electrified in 1902 and three years later extended to Ettrick Bay on the west side of the island, making a total length of just under five miles. Most of the trams, it was optimistically decided, were open-sided cars though these were employed only in summertime. Later, for summer use two roofless 'toast-rack' trams were introduced. Designed to carry eighty passengers, the 'toast-racks' sometimes carried as many as one hundred. The trams, on one August day in 1907, carried some 2,000 trippers who had arrived at Port Bannatyne by excursion steamers and were then transported to Ettrick Bay by this 'scenic electric railway'. During the summer months, Ettrick Bay's sandy beach was a prime attraction as a children's playground but to enhance its appeal the tramway company organised children's sand-castle competitions. A shelter-cum-pavilion was built and a programme of entertainments instituted. There were pierrot shows, sports, concerts, lectures and dances. In 1907 the area round the pavilion was landscaped and the building itself extended, raising its capacity to 1,000. The tramway company also offered 'evening cruises' by tram to Ettrick Bay, but unfortunately for the company it was soon to suffer from restrictions imposed by the Bute Estate.

In an early 1920s guidebook no fewer than twelve places of worship were listed in the town. Not surprisingly, Sabbatarian views were strongly held. In Victorian days, the introduction of Sunday steamers had met with a lot of opposition (see chapter 7). Although by the 1920s that battle had been lost, clergymen still fulminated against the Sunday boats. In Rothesay the Sabbatarians sermonised also on the issue of Sunday trams. The religious susceptibilities of the councillors ensured that no trams ran on Sundays. When in 1902 the possibility of running a Sunday service to Port Bannatyne was raised, the Wee Frees (the breakaway Free Church of Scotland) were up in arms. If that dreadful circumstance came to pass, then the next stage, they asserted, would be the opening of an ice-cream shop in the village. Such an establishment would be 'a source of much mischief to the conduct and morals of the juvenile population.' Although in 1921 the tramway company did gain, after a plebiscite, a large majority of householders in favour of Sunday running, the town council remained firmly agin any change. The absence of public Sunday transport to Ettrick Bay meant that, as the tramway company sourly observed, the holiday bairns would just have to potter about 'in a little bit of dirty sand' at Rothesay's Children's Corner. In 1925 the council was persuaded to hold its own plebiscite and this time accepted the need for change and commenced that year a limited service of Sunday cars.

Year after year during the 1920s and 1930s Sabbatarian issues and controversies hit the local headlines. In 1929 the Glasgow Independent Labour Party applied to the town council for the use of the Meadows for their annual excursion and also sought permission for their band to play, as it was to be a Sunday. Concerned to maintain the social tone of their burgh, some council members wanted to restrict the ILP band to sacred music and to prohibit dancing and singing. The town council did grant the application but left it to the Parks Committee to set the conditions. By reinforcing outsiders' perceptions of Scotland as a narrow-minded Calvinist stronghold, such Sabbatarian restrictions and protests, however, had a long-term deterrent effect on the Scottish tourist economy. In April 1929 the *Rothesay Express* drew attention to an article in a Sunday newspaper, which mentioned a possible boycott of the Coast towns. Their Sabbatarianism, many

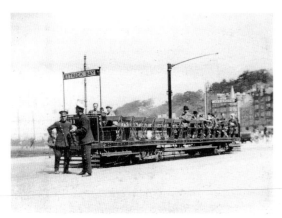

A 'toast-rack' tram with a few passengers ready to leave for Ettrick Bay.

held, was driving visitors away. The *Express*, though, cast doubts on this assertion. If Rothesay, however, did go over to a 'continental Sunday', the class of people 'we would gain by adopting it form a class we can very well do without. There is no need to pander to degeneracy.' Rothesay, the *Express* continued, already had Sunday steamers, driving, swimming and so on; and Sunday golf, tennis, and boating will 'probably come in a short time.' In the following spring Sunday boat hiring was permitted but not with speedboats. Two months later Gourock followed suit. The bubble had been burst. By the mid-1930s there were Sunday concerts at Ettrick Bay and then in 1936 Rothesay Town Council sanctioned Sunday concerts at the town's Winter Gardens, but reserved the right to vet the programmes and insisted that one-third of the profits should go to local charities. The conditions would seem to have been too restrictive, as the company stopped the concerts after three weeks stating that they did not pay. The fact that 'quite a few' shops were now open on Sundays was another indication that attitudes were beginning to change. Sunday golf was quite another matter, though, and it was still forbidden.

There were other restraints though at Rothesay which inhibited the full-scale development of the kind of facilities that might have helped the town to compete with the more popular English resorts. The Bute family, the dominant landowners, often opposed developments that, in their eyes, would have spoiled the beauty and natural simplicity of the island. Though the 3rd Marquis of Bute (1847–1900) was popular enough in Rothesay to be elected as Provost in the 1890s (he had made gifts to the town and had opened woodlands to the public), he had initially been hostile to proposals for a tramway system. 'Bute was no place for tramways,' he had asserted. In 1915 an interdict obtained on behalf of the 4th Marquis of Bute (1900–1947) meant that the tramway company had to stop its Ettrick Bay concerts. The estate feared the introduction of Blackpool-type entertainments and it even objected to the bathing tents and boxes that the company had provided. Nevertheless, with no decent beach on the east side of the island, the visitors flocked to Ettrick Bay. In the 1920s there could be as many as 100,000 visitors in one week at Ettrick Bay, but there were bitter complaints as to the lack of entertainments. The *Rothesay Express* was forthright in its support for the Rothesay Tramway Company when, in 1929, it sought a Parliamentary Order, as part of a wider Bill, to secure extra powers: 'We think that the Marquis' position is unreasonable and against the desires of the community and visitors.' Oddly enough, the *Express* continued, he has licensed fortune-tellers and

Another Edwardian view, this time of one of Rothesay's boat hiring stances.

'other people of a very different class of attraction in this very place.' According to another critic, the only entertainments at Ettrick Bay were donkey rides and palmistry. Despite the Bute Estate's opposition, in 1930 the Rothesay Tramway Company secured the Parliamentary Commissioners approval for the holding of concerts at Ettrick Bay. The removal of the old restrictions brought, as we have already noted, new life and vigour to Bute's holiday mecca.

Their ownership of most of the island gave the Bute family what many on the island considered to be too dominant a role, a role that inhibited job-creating developments. It was the same in the Cumbraes where many people in Millport were also aggrieved by estate restrictions. In 1932 plans to extend the foreshore at Millport were vetoed, the claim being that it would 'make Millport too much like Blackpool'. It was said, with regard to the Isle of Great Cumbrae, that nothing was built at the north end of the island in case it spoiled the view from the Marquis' seat of Mount Stuart on the east side of Bute. The *Rothesay Express* was highly critical of estate policy, which ensured that for many years there had been virtually no building construction in the two islands:

> The only obstacle to the development of both Cumbrae and Bute as holiday and health centres is the difficulty in obtaining land for building and development purposes. If the restrictions were lifted in this direction there is no limit to the possibilities of these islands.

Only the shortage of houses, the editor asserted, writing in those heady days just a few months before the Wall Street Crash, limited the number of visitors. Another critic of Bute's feudal system bitingly remarked that 'sometimes it was as difficult to build a henhouse, let alone a residence.' Restrictive though this policy may have been, looking at it in hindsight, there were perhaps long-term benefits to an island where today's emphasis is on green tourism. Feuing restrictions meant that there were no 'shackland' clusters in Bute and the idea of a large Butlin-type holiday camp on Bute would have been laughable.

Rights of way were another bone of contention. One of the bus companies had been running trips to Scalpsie Bay, where there was another good bathing beach just 5½ miles from Rothesay on the south-west side of the island. In 1934 the estate tried to stop access by stationing 'a private constable' at the gate. The *Rothesay Express* thundered its disapproval of the way whereby the estate was inhibiting development and the spread of tourist traffic: 'the trade of the island will languish'. Opposition by the 4th Marquis delayed the construction of the much-needed road that would provide a link to a ferry at Rhubodach on the Kyles of Bute. The islanders, therefore, had to wait a long time for a suitable road and car ferry. Ironically, the chairman of the company operating the first car ferry was the Marquis of Bute, who had apparently changed estate policy.

As for Rothesay itself, an active town council provided an 18-hole golf course, tennis courts and in 1921 a putting green. For the golf course, charges per round went up during the busy months of July and August. Ladies, it may be noted, paid less than males for both golf and tennis. In the 1920s and 1930s the burgh entertainment facilities were extended. Outstanding among the new buildings was the Art Nouveau-ornamented Winter Gardens Pavilion of 1924. Built on the esplanade, this prefabricated cast-iron structure, a product of Glasgow's Saracen Foundry, replaced the town's Victorian bandstand. The first bandstand was erected in 1873 but it was dismantled in 1885 to make way for a larger one. It in its turn was replaced by the Winter Gardens. In the pavilion's heyday, the Rothesay Entertainers, performing twice nightly, drew large audiences. Many famous artistes kick-started their career at Rothesay, as, for example, when in June 1930 the *Rothesay Express* commented favourably on a bright opening to the season. According to the *Express*, a new artiste, the tenor, Robert Wilson, sang pleasingly a wide variety of songs and well deserved the ovation he received from the audience. This engagement marked the start of Robert Wilson's remarkable career as the 'Voice of Scotland'.

That same year the Palace Cinema was equipped for 'talkies', the first in the town, and then, in late July, the fairy lights on the Esplanade were switched on for the season. This new 'permanent illumination' was greatly admired. At the end of August extra illuminations, fireworks and a fancy dress parade brought thousands to 'Scotland's greatest carnival of light.' Out in the bay there were no fewer than thirteen steamers packed with sightseers. In 1929 a new attraction came in the form of speedboats, with the council agreeing to allot two stances for their use. Consideration was given also to the need to improve the bathing facilities on the West Bay. There were, as we have seen, two separate bathing stations – one for each sex. Each was surrounded with high walls, surmounted by spikes and barbed wire. English visitors were astonished by this antediluvian arrangement, the more especially since the sexes bathed together all along the shore. In 1929, however, the system was relaxed and the sexes could mix together at the West Bay station. Five years later the old bathing stations were incorporated into a new up-to-date lido, which, it was argued, had all the amenities of a pool without the disadvantages. As the accompanying photograph shows, the Lido was a highly popular facility. It lost a lot of custom, though, when the Victorian-era Aquarium was converted into indoor baths, which had the advantage of filtered and purified seawater pumped from the bay and was heated to 72 degrees Fahrenheit. The baths were dual purpose, serving both as swimming pool and as a health centre offering seaweed baths and other spa-type treatments. In the same year, 1938, a new cinema, the Ritz, was opened with a seating capacity of 834. Another palace of entertainment opened in 1938 was Rothesay's new pavilion. Its internal Art Deco features were described by the *Glasgow Herald* as 'ultra-modern'. The pavilion could seat over 1,500 and with its Canadian red birch dance floor, which was supported by coiled springs, proved to be a favourite place for dances. Like other resorts of that period, Rothesay had its beauty competitions and 'seaside girl parades' sponsored by newspapers like the *Daily Record*. Success in the Miss Rothesay competition ensured that the lucky lady would then go on to the Miss Scotland final.

The burgh, on the other hand, did not offer much for children. There was 'children's corner' with a poky amount of sand and Uncle Phil's Punch and Judy show. For a real beach experience, the only alternative was to take a tram or bus to the spacious sands at Ettrick Bay. Once the restrictions at Ettrick Bay were removed, the Rothesay Tramway Company splashed out money on its Ettrick Bay pavilion and, keeping very much up-to-date, also bought a radio gramophone. Now, with late trams and buses laid on, there could be evening concerts and dances, firework displays and illuminations, and even the putting green was floodlit. In 1931 Scottish Motor Traction (SMT) bought the tramway company. The new owners, although replacing the trams with buses in 1936, tried hard to promote Ettrick Bay and its amenities. Although it dispensed with trams, SMT did introduce a miniature railway for the young of all ages. Aeroplane flights and stunt flying displays were another attraction. Flights could be had from five shillings per person; 'looping' cost fifteen shillings and flights over Rothesay twice that.

For one weekend at the end of August, the town burst into life. The great attraction was the famous Rothesay Illuminations which in 1938 were blessed with exceptionally fine weather. Out in the bay, according to the *Glasgow Herald*, there were an estimated 15–20,000 spectators on steamers, yachts and motor-boats and another 30,000 viewed the display from the shore. In addition to the normal decorative lighting, padella lights (shallow pan-shaped oil lamps) rimmed the full circle of the bay, and coloured flares illuminated the woods above the town. The Winter Gardens and other

FYFE & FYFE Ltd. Present The Famous ROTHESAY ENTERTAINERS, Season 1936.

JOHN FYFE.   A. C. LOTHIAN.   BERT DOW.   JIMMY BURNS.   J. N. ALEXANDER.   BRYCE MACKAY,   TOM VERNE,
LEYLAND WHITE.   SANDY CONNOR,   CHARLIE KEMBLE,   JACK ANTHONY.   BILLY OSWALD,   PETER SINCLAIR,
HELEN GLEN CAMPBELL,   JEAN MACDOUGALL,   MARGARET REID,   JEANNETTE ADIE,   AGNES CAMPBELL,   BABS EADIE,   KATHERINE GIBSON

The smartly-attired line up of the Rothesay Entertainers in season 1936. Charlie Kemble and Jack Anthony were two of the best-loved comedians of the day. See also chapter 5.

Rothesay lido, photographed in 1934. See also chapter 6.

It was John Sword, founder of Western SMT, who brought this 15-inch gauge miniature railway to Ettrick Bay, as photographed in 1938. Parked nearby are two old tramcar bodies.

public buildings and many private houses were also lit up. And, of course, there was dancing and other entertainments which went on till the wee small hours.

The illuminations apart, the brevity of the summer season was a constant headache. Accordingly, the Advertising Association promoted, in late September 1936, a £4 All-In-Week. Hotels, boarding houses, catering establishments, etc. participated in this embryonic package holiday scheme. With only some thirty to forty persons taking up the offer, the 'experiment' was, it was judged, 'not up to the sanguine expectations of some'. One bonus was the reopening in the following spring of the Glenburn Hotel Hydro. The availability of the new pavilion gave the new owner the prospect of benefiting from conference work. Rothesay, however, did not benefit from a new phenomenon – the growth of package-type bus touring holidays. The *Rothesay Express* drew attention to a list of bus tours published by a Glasgow firm in 1936. In this 336-page book, there was no mention of Rothesay at all. That would be put right, the *Express* hopefully continued, once a road link to the Kyles of Bute ferry was built, but, as we have seen, there was going to be a long time to wait for it.

When in 1939 war broke out with Germany, the Clyde resorts were selected as safe destinations for housing evacuees. Accustomed though they were to dealing with masses of holidaymakers, Rothesay folk were shocked by the state of some of the Glasgow weans despatched there. Out of the 1,494 children sent to the town no fewer than 650 were, according to the Town Clerk, of 'a very undesirable class, very dirty and very unruly'. In the summer of 1940, although in that same year France had been defeated and the British army forced to evacuate from the Continent, Glaswegians, nevertheless, poured into Rothesay for the Fair. Effective publicity on the part of the Advertising Association and the fact that some of the rival resorts were now off limits helped Rothesay's holiday trade. The town was packed to capacity, with several hundred sleeping out on Fair Saturday – in the woods, on the seats along the shore, in sheds, in boats, and even on boxes on the pier. On the Sunday, when Henry Hall and his band played at the Pavilion, thousands had to be turned away. At the end of the year, looking back at the 1940 travel season, the *Buteman* considered that 'in all the circumstances it had been a profitable holiday season'. But Rothesay like the rest of the Clyde resorts had gone to war, and soon, in addition to the evacuees, naval and other service personnel arrived to fill otherwise empty holiday accommodation and for them at least there was no short season.

The Kyles of Bute Hydropathic in Port Bannatyne was a prestigious spa-cum-hotel. In the Second World War, it was requisitioned by the navy, who named it HMS *Varbel*. It accommodated naval personnel who trained for the very dangerous tasks of operating midget submarines and human torpedoes. Latterly, it was used as a convalescent home. Nothing remains of it now.

CHAPTER 5

Pierrots, Palais de Danse, Funfairs and Other Attractions

A herring man frae Paisley
Cam aw the way tae me
To see if I could keep his fush
Frae smellin, don't you see.
Says I, 'My man, I'll tell to you
Wi'oot the slightest chaff
The way tae keep your fish frae smellin's
Cut their noses aff.

Going to see the pierrots was one of the must-do features of the early twentieth-century seaside holiday. Most holidaymakers enjoyed their dancing and songs and revelled in the patter from the comics and 'light comedians'. Troupes of banjo-playing pierrots or concert parties, as the more sophisticated preferred to be called, were to be found at all sizeable resorts, and very many small ones too. The pierrots, derived from the Italian commedia dell'arte troupes, wore a clown-like garment with pom-poms down the front and a cone shaped hat on the head. Later the males tended to favour naval-style peaked caps and blazers. Providing simple, often homespun, entertainment for people in holiday mood, they played wherever crowds gathered, and that usually meant the beach or the prom. From a very distinguished source, Professor David Daiches, we have a sample of a comic song he heard while holidaying at Leven in the early 1920s. As we see from the extract above, which is from one of Ian Maclean's 'sub-Harry-Lauder' ditties, the humour was gentle and very simple.

In the early days open-air pitches were the rule, with companies performing on the prom or on a basic open-to-all-the-elements platform erected, as often as not, on the beach. If the weather was bad, however, the troupe had usually made prior arrangements to transfer the show to a nearby hall. Colin Clark, who, with his wife Grace, formed the comedy duo of Clark and Murray, related that, in the 1920s when playing at Dunbar, the Corn Exchange was the wet-weather venue. The members of the troupe, plus piano, were transferred from the park to the hall on the back of a horse-drawn coal lorry. On their way through the streets, they cried out to bystanders: 'Corn Exchange tonight!' just like they were selling coal. As long as there was a covered enclosure available, a rainy day, however, could be good for business. With a far-from-captive audience, the pierrots not only had to advertise the show but had also to master the art of cajoling cash from reluctant spectators – 'bottling' they called it in the trade. It was a skill at which some excelled more than others. A good line in patter helped. Troupe managers, when advertising for performers, stressed that candidates had to be good bottlers. Selling souvenir postcards of the troupe was another source of income. Fortunately, many of these went into postcard collections (a favourite

CASSELS' PIERROTS, MONTROSE, 1908.

In 1908, Mr J. A. Cassel paid Montrose Town Council £30 for the privilege of putting on al fresco entertainments at the beach. If the weather was inclement, the pierrots flitted to the Burgh Hall.

hobby of the Edwardians) and thus helped ensure their survival. Selling sheet music was another source of income. In 1932 one optimistic composer, a member of Jack Ashwood's Merrymakers, tried to get Leven Town Council to help with the cost of printing his song 'When You're Leevin' in Leven'. Although the council not surprisingly ignored his request, he did get his song published and duly sold it to the public for six old pennies a copy. Whether or not it was a hit with the local populace, we have no means of knowing.

Children's talent competitions were a favourite and cheap way of drawing in customers. In the late 1930s, a very wee but precocious Ronnie Corbett entered one in St Andrews and managed to win a prize of a cricket bat. Later in life, as a professional comedian, he achieved some of his early success in seaside shows. Many another star got his or her feet on the ladder after serving a hard apprenticeship with small beach shows. Bud Flanagan, later a music hall and cinema celebrity, played at East Wemyss in the summer of 1920. The great Harry Gordon of Aberdeen Beach Pavilion fame found the Fife seaside shows at Kinghorn and Burntisland to be an excellent training ground. Local allusions and jokes were always popular. Charlie Kemble at Rothesay was famous for his ability to pick on members of the audience and improvise ditties that related to local worthies and even members of the audience

Some residents and the more perjink visitors regarded pierrots as a nuisance, especially when singing near-the-knuckle songs. In the years prior to the First World War, there were objections to troupes playing at Aberdour West Beach, where there were two competing groups, each trying to outsing the other. In 1913 one seafront proprietor went to the Sheriff Court and secured an interdict against one of the concert parties – the Gay Bohemians. His objection rested on the nuisance caused by the assembly of large crowds of spectators who created a lot of noise and disturbance and

"SAMMY TAKES THE CAKE"
FRED COLLINS' BEACH PAVILION ENTERTAINERS.
BURNTISLAND — — — SEASON. 1915

In this 1915 postcard of Fred Collins's troupe, Nellie, writing to friends in Leith, described the Burntisland Pierrots as 'awfully good this year'. No wonder since Fred Collins's Entertainers included the young Harry Gordon and Jack Holden, later to be Harry's feed. Harry learned a lot of the business of being an impresario from Fred Collins, who later went on to found a major theatrical agency.

furthermore trespassed on his property. By flitting to the nearby Public Park, though, the pierrots managed to keep in business. In St Andrews some residents objected not only to itinerant preachers and other 'hot gospellers', but also to nearby seaside entertainers, the Ethiopian Serenaders in this instance. The ancient city, such critics claimed, was being transformed 'into a sort of 3rd-rate Portobello'. The better class of visitor, they feared, was being frightened away. The Burgh Police (Scotland) Act of 1892 had given town councils the power to ban or control places of entertainment, refreshment and bathing establishments within their bounds. In March 1907, Kinghorn Burgh Council resolved not to sanction the use of the Braes for concerts that summer because of the untidiness that was created and the unsavoury nature of some of the pierrots' songs which, as one councillor said, were 'not conducive to good morals.' For the 1908 season the council relented and gave a new company, the Gem Entertainers, a licence to perform at the Braes. According to the *Fife Free Press*, this troupe met with a good response:

> The Gem Entertainers opened their season at Kinghorn. There was a large and appreciative audience. Will Stewart delighted the company with several humorous and descriptive songs, including 'Sandy Boy'. Little Peggy, a young girl between six and seven years, gave a splendid exhibition of dancing; Gilbert Lees, a comedian, gave a rendering of 'How wid ye like tae be me'; Douglas and Clark, comedians, gave a rendering of 'Put me among the girls'; 'Scotland Yet' and 'Killarney' were sung in capital style by Miss Minnie Lemore who is the possessor of an excellent voice. The accompaniments were played by Mr Stewart Ferrier.

It was fairly common for companies, when denied performing rights within a town, to cock a snoot at authority by renting ground outwith the burgh bounds. In 1920, for example, Leven Town Council banned concert parties from the beach. But a troupe, the Bumble Concert Party, obtained a site outside the burgh boundary and managed to attract several hundred people to their first performance. Mrs Leo Bliss did the same when her company the Busy Bees lost the Carnoustie concession in 1924. She erected a canvas marquee on ground she rented and provided competition for the Rebels, the local company who played on the council's own pitch.

Another Nellie, Nellie Philips, had fond memories of the Kinghorn pierrots of her 1930s childhood. Not that they were the first priority for all visitors. She remembered that, when evening excursionists arrived by train or bus, many of the men opted for the pub. But the rest headed for the shore pavilion where Jack Allison's Concert Party provided some great entertainment. When it was the Glasgow Fair time, the compere assumed a Glasgow accent, and for the Edinburgh Trades a mock posh one. The Glasgow Fair audiences liked all-Scottish and Irish programmes. And there was always a quota of landlady jokes. Audience participation was important, with the comic and his feed ensuring that the children got involved with chants and singing. In this respect, the old pantomime-style 'Spot the ghost' routine was a perennial favourite. Nellie also recalled the time when a train came along and blew its whistle, just as the soprano was reaching her top notes in 'Oh, for the wings of a dove!' She and the other bairns killed themselves laughing. When she was just six, Nellie Philips was entered for one of the Kinghorn talent shows. Although she had to sit on a cushion to reach the piano, she won the first prize with a piece called 'On the Sea'. The last night of the season was a topsy-turvy night, with the cast swapping roles. After the finale, the ladies received bouquets and the men cigarettes. They all ended singing:

> Kinghorn! Kinghorn!
> It's the finest place I know.
> Kinghorn! Kinghorn!
> Bordered on the sea,
> It's a nice wee place to come to,
> And the seashore is divine.
> If you ever come to Kinghorn,
> Come up and see me sometime.

Despite the usually poor changing facilities, the pierrots often had to make quick-fire costume changes. At Kinghorn, children were able to crawl under the pavilion stage where they could look up through cracks in the floor. When the tap dancers changed their outfits, the bairns, Nellie Philips confessed, peered up through the cracks and tried to spot the colour of their pants. Florence Tudor, writing in the *Scots Magazine* (August 1981) described the primitive nature of the pierrots' pavilion at Millport. In the 1940s, when she played there, the 'theatre' was a large tented erection with a corrugated-iron roof. If it rained, the noise of the rain stotting on the roof meant that the performers could hardly be heard. The dressing room was so pokey that there was hardly room to turn, and there was no toilet. 'Of course, we were surrounded by fields so we just had to make do with them.' The inadequacies of many of the so-called pavilions, combined with the undoubted popularity of the pierrots' shows, induced, as we have seen, a number of municipal authorities to invest in purpose-built pavilions. Some, like Aberdeen's Beach Pavilion, were fairly substantial buildings and, as such, were available for other purposes. Others, as at St Andrews, were small, single-purpose structures. In 1927 that town council decided, despite vociferous opposition from some nearby residents, to invest in a new pavilion, complete with electric lighting and a fenced enclosure. Lessees were to be charged £100 rent for the season, which was just over 1/5 of the estimated cost, and provide their own piano and moveable furniture. Some performers were opposed to playing in enclosed premises. When, in 1930, North Berwick Town Council proposed to erect a new pavilion, Joe Anderson, whose troupe had been performing on the esplanade for some years, argued, unsuccessfully it may be said, in favour of continuing with the old-style, open-air type of show. Many performers preferred the al fresco show for its more intimate atmosphere where they felt more in touch with their audience.

Jack Allison's concert party on stage at the Kinghorn pavilion, with more spectators outside the enclosure than inside. Observe the ladder leading to the cramped changing room at the rear. When not in use, the chairs were taken into the pavilion and the swing doors shut and locked.

The minutes of Leven Town Council reveal the kind of sometimes tortured relationships that developed between municipal authorities and concert party impresarios. In December 1921 Ian McLean of Glasgow offered £40 for the stance at the east end of Leven Beach. The council accepted his bid but insisted that there would be no Sunday performances without its approval. The councillors also insisted that the pavilion he used be closed when not in use. Presumably they did not want to see the basic timber and canvas canopies that some showmen used. They stipulated too that it be removed immediately at the end of the season. When McLean's lease was renewed in 1922, the councillors stated that they were to consider the erection of a proper pavilion. The council was in no hurry, however. In 1924 it was decided that a sub-committee should visit some other places which had 'covered-in pavilions for pierrot performances and report back to the full council. Two years later, Ian McLean, anxious because he was going to face 'serious opposition' from a rival pierrot group that were to be playing in Letham Glen, wrote to the council stating that, if the burgh were to build a permanent building on the seafront, he would be prepared to up his rent to £100 per annum (the council too had concerns about this rival troupe. It was conceded, though, that, since this pierrot 'shelter' was outwith the burgh boundaries, it had no powers there.). In the event, the council did agree to build a seafront pavilion at a cost of around £1,250, but the total rental would be £160. With the construction costs, however, ever rising, the final price came to £2,141 and McLean's rent went up to £200. When the pavilion was opened in June 1927, the name was changed – from Pierrot Pavilion to Beach Concert Hall. This gave the council a multi-purpose hall, which was available for general community use. There were even occasional Sunday performances but not of the conventional pierrot type. In 1929, for instance, Ian McLean was given permission to give two orchestral concerts in the hall, provided that he gave a donation to the local hospital.

If Leven councillors were dilatory, they were speedy compared with their opposite numbers at Carnoustie. In 1914 Gilbert Payne, whose troupe had played at Carnoustie for many years, offered to build a concert hall, which he would lease for five years, and then the council could buy it if it was so desired. Certainly the outbreak of the Great War in that same year was no encouragement. Nevertheless, another twenty years passed before Carnoustie had its hall. Appropriately enough, the concert party playing in the new Beach Pavilion in that inaugural year was Gilbert Payne's Jolly Jesters.

The pavilions at the busier resorts tended to be more imposing, but none more so than the one built at Dunoon in 1905. Until 1932 it was run by the town council, then the concession to run shows was granted to Harry Kemp. In the busy postwar years, Chalmers Wood, a Glaswegian, paid no less than £2,000 for the summer rights to the pavilion and the adjacent Castle Gardens, which were used for open-air performances. Unfortunately, in April 1949, the pavilion was destroyed by fire. The town council moved quickly, purchasing two war-surplus hangars and linking them to provide temporary accommodation. It was another nine years, though, before the replacement theatre, the Queen's Hall, was ready. It is very much a 1950s building, its design and materials inspired by the 1951 Festival of Britain. At Saltcoats, George Kemp opened La Scala as a cinema in 1913. Like the Regal in Kinghorn and some other seaside venues, it was used both as a cinema and a variety hall, and sometimes combined both forms of entertainment. It was George's son Harry who, in 1922, started summer shows at La Scala where he had great success with his 'Scotch Broth' revue. In the interwar years quite a number of new pavilions were built. Largs Town Council built one known as Barrfields in 1929. It was erected on land gifted by local man Robert Barr who also donated £1,000 towards the cost of the building. The first lessee, who had paid £1,000 for what in that depression year was a doubtful privilege, failed to make it pay. In subsequent years, it was leased to a more experienced producer, Harry Kemp who, in addition to his shows at Saltcoats, was operating, as we have seen, at Dunoon and also Troon. Barrfields, with shows that ran from June to October, was a very popular venue. Gourock could boast of its stylish Cragburn Pavilion opened in 1936. That summer Tommy Morgan 'Scotland's Favourite Comedian' headed a cast of thirty-five 'in the largest and most ambitious Coast Show ever produced in Scotland'. This new pavilion, along with the Ashton esplanade, the open-air swimming pool and other amenities, was evidence, according to a contemporary Official Guide, of the Gourock councillors' wisdom and farsightedness. The

PHOTO HAMPTONS   HARRY KEMP'S "REGAL REVELS", SALTCOATS 1932   GLASGOW AND LARGS

As the number of performers indicates, Harry Kemp's 1932 'Regal Revels' at Saltcoats was a fairly sophisticated kind of show.

anonymous author praised the burgh's civic rulers: 'Generally they have shown a wise progressiveness and an inspired enterprise that have materially helped the town forward on its march of progress.'

There was inspired enterprise, too, from some of the Coast impresarios, most notably Ben Popplewell at Ayr. That seaside town had, in the late 1920s, two theatres providing summer season entertainments, both run by the Popplewell family. Ben Popplewell from Bradford had purchased and restored an old theatre and in 1925 opened it as the Gaiety. At the Gaiety he offered holidaymakers and locals twice-nightly vaudeville attractions. In the Ayr Beach Pavilion, which Ben Popplewell leased from the Town Council, his shows were on concert party lines with matinees 'during inclement weather'. This canny Yorkshireman, aided by other family members, made a financial success of a building that had cost the ratepayers around £8,000 but that locals had deemed to be a waste of money. In the early 1930s competition from the new talkie films hit the variety shows, so from then on the Pavilion was used mainly as a dance hall. Ben Popplewell responded by putting the Gaiety upmarket, engaging some of the best-known variety performers of the day and making the summer show, the Gaiety Whirl, into one of the best in the business. Like Harry Gordon at the Aberdeen Beach Pavilion, Ben Popplewell insisted on providing clean, family-style entertainment. In the 1930s and 1940s, Glasgow comedian, Dave Willis, was the lynchpin of the show. Audiences loved it when he came on stage as a wartime ARP Warden, singing: 'Wi' ma wee gas mask' or when he ran on stage reciting: 'Fuzzywuzzy wis a bear, Fuzzywuzzy had nae hair, Fuzzywuzzy wusnae fuzzy, wus' he'.

After the Second World War, tastes began to change. Competition from other forms of entertainment, television mainly, meant that pierrot-type shows had lost their appeal, and with the resorts declining in popularity, cash-strapped councils and private owners began to close, or convert to other purposes, their beach pavilions. St Andrews' pierrot pavilion was converted into a café-cum-ice-cream-stall which, after standing empty for some years, was recently demolished and a restaurant erected on its site. The Cosy Corner, once one of Dunoon's favourite entertainment centres, was torn down in 1960. Another once popular variety theatre, Leven's Jubilee, was demolished in 1973, and that town's Beach Pavilion survived but was used for other purposes. By 1973 there were only four summer shows left in Scotland. But the entertainment scene was not completely blank, as the larger hotels and holiday camps started to provide some cabaret-style entertainment for their guests. The great survivor is the Ayr Gaiety, which suffered, in 1955, a devastating fire and then in 1972, after being refurbished, was threatened with demolition. Fortunately, like the Rothesay Winter Gardens, the Gaiety was reprieved, its being listed as a historic building a significant factor in keeping the developers at bay. In 1973 the town council purchased the Gaiety for £72,000. Its troubles, though, were by no means over and it was closed for a number of years. With the support of South Ayrshire Council, the volunteers of the Ayr Gaiety Partnership are in the process of restoring it as a multi-purpose theatre. Although there is more work to be done, it reopened in December 2012 for a Christmas pantomime. As Ken Dodd, just one of the many great stars who have performed there, put it: 'A wonderful theatre, this, as famous in the business as the Palladium, London.'

In the smaller resorts the facilities were rather more limited. The more prosperous visitors often organised concerts and dances, with the profits going to local good causes. In Kinghorn, for instance, a 'Visitors' Concert' was promoted in July 1901 'by a number of gentlemen at present holidaying in the district', with the proceeds going to the hall fund. Where there were no theatres or cinemas, the village hall served as a substitute with the Saturday night dance or weekly cinema show the highlight of the week. At Montrose the Burgh Hall was converted, in the 1920s, into a municipal cinema and advertised as: 'Our Own Cinema'. In the early 1900s, films were a great novelty and attracted great crowds to ready-made or adapted cinemas. They provided a cheap form of wet-weather entertainment. In 1913, on Glasgow Fair Monday, an estimated 12,000 people went to one or other of Rothesay's picture-houses. The first half of the twentieth century was, of course, the great age of cinema going, and no resort with any pretensions could afford to be without at least one picture-house. Largs at one time had three and Rothesay four. By 1938 Ayr had no fewer than six, and there were another two at neighbouring Prestwick. One reason for Aberdeen's popularity with visitors was the great choice of cinemas – no fewer than nineteen in 1939. Of Campbeltown's former two cinemas, one, the Picture House, happily survives.

In the middle years of the twentieth century, ballroom dancing was also at its height of popularity, and every sizeable resort offered a choice of dance halls. Asked by the author (in July 1998) about the provision of dance halls in Arbroath, Anita Walker, who was standing on the esplanade at the time, enthusiastically replied: 'Dance halls, now you're telling me! We're very close to one of my places – the Seaforth Hotel for the ballroom, which was the place to dance at the weekend. But there was the Marine Ballroom, which had dancing on almost every night. There'd be dances in the Red Triangle Hut, which was the YMCA hut and then, of course, we had the midnight dancing at the side of the pool. There'd be somebody doing a Strip the Willow or an Eightsome Reel and trying not to fall in the pool. But it was good fun.' Like the theatres, many of the concert pavilions, Dunoon's and Rothesay's for example, were multi-purpose and were highly popular for dancing. The ballroom at Portobello's Marine Gardens was also multi-functional. In its early days, as we have seen, this huge dance hall was also used as a roller skating rink. As a ballroom, it attracted large crowds from all over Scotland. For the 'modern dance' craze of the 1920s and 1930s a good floor was essential. In the early

BALLROOM, MARINE PARK, PORTOBELLO   751/55

The Marine Ballroom in Portobello was a very popular dance hall but was once also used as a roller-skating rink. When the First World War started in 1914, the ballroom was requisitioned for military use. It suffered the same fate again in the Second World War, and the damage caused ensured that this once highly popular venue was finished as a ballroom.

1920s, Rothesay's 'high-class' palais de danse, situated in Battery Place, guaranteed a 'perfect floor and the latest music'. But every wee place had its palais de danse or village hall where, as in the big resort ballrooms, it was, for young folk especially, the ideal place to meet the opposite sex, to eye up the 'talent' and get a 'click'. To keep the Lord's Day sacred, all dancing finished at midnight, although, in the exceptional conditions of wartime, some dances were held on Sundays. In Aberdeen, in 1947, there was what was described as 'a short-lived experiment' with Sunday dancing which was popular with the public, but, with the kirks hostile, the city magistrates put an end to the experiment.

Where the multitude went, so did the showmen. If the crowds went to the seaside, so did the show people. They set up their stalls and merry-go-rounds on beaches, proms or on some nearby vacant piece of ground, paying a rent, of course, for any ground they occupied. In the smaller towns and villages, the showmen were usually itinerant, spending only a short time on any particular pitch. In the more popular resorts like Portobello and Aberdeen, there were permanent amusement parks. In its Edwardian heyday, one of the Marine Gardens' prime attractions was its extensive funfair, which included a three-tier scenic railway. In later years in Portobello, it was the Codona family's Fun City that drew the crowds. It had all the usual fairground attractions – a figure of eight railway, helter-skelter, merry-go-rounds, chair-a-planes, fortune-tellers, and hoop-la and roll-a-penny stalls. Intriguingly, the helter-skelter matched the shape of nearby pottery kilns. At Girvan, the showground at the harbour drew the visitor, according to the Official Guide to 'this gay centre'. Funfairs also attracted a lot of criticism. Many locals and the more sedate visitors loathed the noisy crowds, the bright lights, and loudspeakers blaring out the popular tunes of the day. St Andrews Town Council, for one, made it quite clear that, the traditional Lammas Fair excepted, there would be no noisy mini-Golden Mile in their town.

Some kinds of sound were more acceptable. In the 1890s, it has been estimated, there were around 40,000 brass and silver bands in the UK as a whole, and music played by military and civilian bands attracted sizeable audiences. In Edwardian Rothesay, the town council employed 'a first class professional band' which played every afternoon and evening to large crowds. In resort after resort, a bandstand was seen as a considerable social asset. Rothesay's first bandstand was gifted in 1873. It was later replaced by an even larger model, which in its turn was supplanted by the Winter Gardens. Helensburgh got its bandstand in 1902 and St Andrews followed suit three years later. At the latter, however, the council stipulated that there would be no Sunday concerts. Whereas in most Scottish resorts, during the first half of the twentieth century, councillors regarded variety shows and amusements on the Sabbath day as anathema, they cast a kindlier eye on musical entertainment. In the interwar years Leven Town Band was permitted to play, at 3 p.m. and 7 p.m., in Letham Glen on summer Sundays. Yet the council protested when, in 1931, the lessee of the putting green in the Glen opened it for play in Sundays. Since the lease had been drawn up when the Glen was still in private ownership, the council was powerless. But, when in 1933 the lease was up, Leven Town Council, now the owners of the ground, terminated the lease. Like most resorts, Carnoustie had a bandstand. The burgh band's Sunday afternoon audiences were people who, as Kate Grimman observed, had been to the Sunday morning kirk service and were still in their Sunday best. She drew a sharp contrast between the formally attired kirk-goers and, quite close by, the folk who had elected to spend the day on the beach and were all casually dressed.

Whereas children might fidget while listening to the band, the younger ones at least sat goggle-eyed when the Punch and Judy man was performing. Some like Fred Willis at Rothesay, 'Uncle Phil' to the weans, were well-loved characters. From 1938 until his retiral in August 1956, he pushed his puppet stand along to the Children's Corner on the town's esplanade. Not just an entertainer,

Dunoon Pavilion and Bandstand. The pavilion was built in 1905 but was destroyed by fire in 1949.

Plenty of wee customers, and some big ones too, in this early postcard view of Kerr's Miniature Railway. Like the mainline loco, the wee locomotives are steam powered. The drivers of the big locos pulled the whistle as their trains thundered past, and their successors do the same today.

Uncle Phil, upset when he saw a little girl knocked down and killed close to his stance, preached to his audience the necessity of road safety, the message contained in a little ditty he had composed. Some of the Uncle Phil-era puppets are on display in the Bute Museum in Rothesay. Inverness Museum also houses Punch and Judy puppets. These were being taken round the villages of the north of Scotland by Duncan Morrison until the 1970s. For this Highland entertainer, Punch and Judy were an integral part of his popular family variety shows. But, by the 1970s, Punch and Judy shows generally were on a downward spiral. Not only had their audiences gone, but in addition some councils banned them on the grounds of political correctness, conceiving them to be too sexist and violent.

Miniature railways were another sure-fire draw and were a popular feature, with all age groups, at Carnoustie, Aberdour, Fraserburgh, Ettrick Bay and other resorts. Eager to acquire what they hoped would be a major asset, Carnoustie Town Council offered steam enthusiast, Harry Ferguson, a site on the beach at a peppercorn rent. The Carnoustie children's railway opened in 1937 and operated successfully till the start of the Second World War. The most famous and long lasting of the wee train systems is Kerr's Miniature Railway, which was started in 1935 by Matthew Kerr senior, when he moved what had begun as a hobby line to the West Links Park, Arbroath. According to his son, Matthew Kerr junior, in a Radio Scotland interview in July 1998, the 1950s and 1960s were the heyday of this railway. In one calendar month, in July 1955, around 27,000 people rode on the train. These of course were, as Matthew Kerr put it, the pre-Benidorm days when on a reasonably sunny day the West Links Park was almost literally black with people. As well as running the railway, his father hired out deck chairs for the beach and, as his son recalled, could easily supply 200 to 300 deckchairs in an afternoon. Sadly, as the holiday crowds dwindled in later years, it was not just the adults' demand for deckchairs that went, but the wee train's wee customers had gone too. When the elder Kerr retired in 1977, the 'wee railway' was continued by his schoolteacher son, Matthew Kerr the younger. But obviously it could no longer be run on a full-time basis. Mr Kerr refurbished the buildings and rolling stock and operated the line, with the help of volunteers, as a non-profit making business and operating only at weekends and at peak holiday times. Sadly, Matthew Kerr died in April 2006, but his wife Jill, helped by many willing volunteers, has managed to keep the trains running.

A fair number of visitors, even when away from home, observed the proprieties and attended one of the local kirks, and the larger seaside resorts at least offered a plentiful choice. Indeed in the 19th century the various Churches established new places of worship to reach out to the summer visitors who might otherwise neglect their spiritual duties. At Strone on the Holy Loch in Argyll, for instance, an 'Alliance' church was built to be used, during the holiday season, by clergymen of different denominations. The availability of a place of worship did not guarantee perfect attendance. Since summer visitors tended to avoid the kirks, the preachers therefore went to the places where holidaymakers did congregate. Thus we have the incentive for the beach missions described in chapter 2. Even as far back as 1899, we find a kirk report lamenting the fact that at Innellan, while the locals were faithful attenders, the church zeal of the visitors was not generally high:

> They come to the place for leisure or relaxation … There is much cycling for recreation on the Sabbath, also a good deal of yachting, and unhappily these forms of pleasure seeking are on the increase.

CHAPTER 6

The Sunshine Years of Suntans and Seawater Swimming Pools

An apparatus for recording the ultra-violet radiation of the sun has been in use at Ardrossan for some time. The most trustworthy records prove that Ardrossan has more sunshine than many of the English resorts and for a long time it had the highest record in Scotland. Sunlight is a means of health. The systematic use of use of sunbaths as a preventative and therapeutic measure in rickets and other diseases has been recommended for many years. Our seaside health resorts offer plenty of the health-giving rays in the visible and short infra red parts of the spectrum, and magnificent air, says Sir Leonard Hill, F.R.S. If that is so, what more could one wish than a holiday in Ardrossan, which statistics prove to be situated in Scotland's sunshine area.

Ardrossan and Neighbourhood, c. 1932

In the Victorian era, west-coast health resorts were favoured on account of their soft, balmy atmosphere and their breezier east-coast equivalents for the bracing and tonic quality of the air. Although resorts might boast of their low rainfall especially in relation to other places, the degree of sunshine, while it might be mentioned in guidebooks, was a secondary consideration. In Edwardian days, large hats, veils and parasols helped keep women fashionably pale. As the quotation above indicates, by the interwar years the climate of opinion had undergone a marked change. The younger generation, enthused by the contemporary cult of sunshine and fresh air, sought the maximum exposure to the sun's rays. For the bright young things of the 1920s and 1930s, a well-tanned skin was no longer a source of shame. A suntan was now fashionable and had sex appeal. It was also considered to be health inducing and could be flaunted on one's return from holiday to gain envious looks from less fortunate stay-at-homes. At Girvan's new Bathing Station, a 1930s Official Guide informs us: 'Sun-bathing is encouraged and numerous canvas shelters have been erected for the convenience of the sun-tan devotees.' Resorts like Girvan with extensive sandy beaches were at an advantage as they were also utilised as a playground for informal sports and games. For the 'youth movement so strong nowadays' Girvan, 'one of the sunniest and driest parts of the West Coast', provided, it was claimed, other facilities for 'healthy sport and fun'. Part of the shore was laid out as an 'outside gymnasium'. The parallel bars, rowing machines and punch balls, we are informed, 'ensure that afterglow on returning from a dip'.

By then, parasols and broad-brimmed hats and all-embracing swimming costumes had been discarded. Swimsuits that would have shocked the Victorians became all the rage. While one-piece suits were still the rule, by the late 1930s fashion-conscious lasses defied the strictures of the small-town prudes and were now sporting two-piece bathing costumes to give maximum skin exposure. Bathing regulations, too, became less restrictive. Bathing machines were phased out or transformed

DIVING PLATFORM AND CHUTE, GIRVAN.   417.

When this postcard photograph was taken at Girvan *c.* 1930, one-piece bathing costumes were the norm. The resort's facilities for 'healthy sport and fun' included a rather dangerous-looking diving platform and chute, both offshore.

into mere stationary changing huts. Increasingly, bathers of both sexes just changed on the beach, with a wrap-around towel to protect their modesty.

Many resorts, particularly those on the sunnier east, began to draw attention to their sunshine records. For example, an Official Guide to Montrose of *c.* 1930, included a comparative list of other popular holiday resorts with their sunshine and rainfall records. Montrose, it concluded, occupied 'an eminent position' for both low rainfall and high sunshine. Nearby Arbroath had an even better claim. According to its 1932 Official Guide, the town had held for two consecutive seasons the highest sunshine record for the mainland of Scotland. The guide was entitled – it comes as no surprise – *Arbroath for Sunshine*. It had to be mainland Scotland only, as in 1931 Lamlash in Arran topped the Scottish table for 'health-giving sunlight' i.e. 'the quantity of Ultra-Violet Ray units'. When, on the other hand, Dunoon's sunshine record came under consideration, the councillors were more circumspect. In 1932, therefore when it was proposed to the town council that a sunshine measuring device be installed, the councillors, fearing that invidious comparisons might be made, declined to proceed with the matter.

Swimming and bathing in the sea also increased in popularity during the 1920s and 1930s, years indeed when in the latter decade, in particular, many new outdoor pools were built. This was a time when there was a flush of enthusiasm for all healthy, outdoor sports and activities. The Strength Through Joy movement in Hitler's Germany was one manifestation of this particular craze. With swimming becoming one of the cult sports of the period, there was, in consequence, a demand for ponds where swimming could be taught in safe surroundings. Added impetus was given by the contemporary sunbathing fad. While you didn't actually have to get wet for this, pools at least provided changing rooms and walls which sheltered dookers and sunbathers alike from snell winds. An outdoor swimming pool was the perfect place for teenagers, in particular, to meet new people, preferably of the opposite sex. It was both a playground and a platform where they could show off their aquatic skills and daring and also to acquire and parade a tan.

Up and down the coast, enterprising town councillors and other individuals saw these new fashions as money-spinners that could help to draw in more day-trippers and long-staying summer visitors and, of course, give the local population a valued facility. In the 1920s, some fifty outdoor ponds were constructed in Britain as a whole. In the following decade, a rough estimate is that nearly four

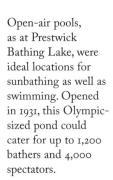

Open-air pools, as at Prestwick Bathing Lake, were ideal locations for sunbathing as well as swimming. Opened in 1931, this Olympic-sized pond could cater for up to 1,200 bathers and 4,000 spectators.

Sun Bathers, Sea Bathing Lake, Prestwick.

times that number were built. They were not all at the seaside. London County Council and other London boroughs were prolific builders of lidos as they were termed down south. Incidentally, the term lido was rarely used in Scotland, where 'pool' or 'pond' were the more usual names. As to which, it depended on local preference. In East Fife, for example, pond was the favoured title. The mining folk of East and West Wemyss, however, put their tiny tidal ponds into their proper perspective by calling them dooking dubs. In Portobello, although it was officially a pool, the man in charge was the pondmaster and in local parlance it was usually referred to as the pond. Going to the baths, on the other hand, meant going to an indoor swimming pool. At any rate, throughout Britain, open-air pools and other amenities were regarded, particularly after the Depression which followed the Wall Street Crash in 1929, as an investment whereby towns could capitalise on what seemed to be the ever-growing visitor industry and, at the same time, use government-aided job creation schemes to offset part of the costs. Arbroath is a case in point. Faced with economic and population decline in the 1920s and 1930s, the town council failing to attract new industries made use of the local unemployed to build concrete promenades along the seafront and a large open-air bathing pool. Costing £22,000, the pond, which was opened in 1934, was the largest in the East of Scotland. Seawater, pumped in and then filtered, chlorinated and aerated, was kept in constant circulation. In consequence, every twelve hours the water was completely changed.

On opening day, 4,350 bathers passed through the Arbroath turnstiles, another 5,200 paid to spectate, and another 3,000 came along for the evening gala. Since the pond was intended to be multi-functional, the designer, who was the burgh engineer, included a platform that could be used for sunbathing, dancing, and gymnastic displays by ladies of the Women's League of Health and Beauty and other groups, and also 'mannequin' parades. These mannequin parades were the forerunners of the later very popular bathing beauty contests. A contemporary press photograph shows that a 1934 Arbroath mannequin parade consisted of a number of comely females displaying bathing costumes for the seaside – all one-piece in those days. So attractive were the pool and other facilities, and maybe the mannequin parades too, that the railways ran special trains and day visitors flocked to the town. Looking back from the perspective of 1950, the Revd W. E. Gladstone lauded the council's enterprise at that time as an act of courage and faith. As proof of its continued success, he informs us that in 1949, there passed through the turnstiles no fewer than 25,000 bathers and

In the 1930s, parades and gymnastic displays featuring nubile young ladies from the Women's League of Health and Beauty were popular attractions at outdoor pools, as here at Portobello.

79,000 spectators. It is noteworthy that there were four times as many spectators as bathers. Open-air pools undoubtedly were places of spectacle. Although there were a few coastal towns with indoor pools, including Nairn (built as far back as 1893), Peterhead, Aberdeen, Arbroath, Rothesay and Portobello, bathing in the open air had, it was reckoned, some special virtue. Witness the Inverness councillor, who, when in the mid-1930s the construction of an indoor pool was under consideration, argued strongly agin this project preferring the alternative option of an open-air saltwater pool, on the grounds that swimming and bathing in seawater was a healthier form of recreation.

The first outdoor pools date back to the late nineteenth century. It was comparatively easy to enclose a rock pool, which could be filled and refreshed by the incoming tides. On the rocky east coast there were quite a few places where outcrops of rock provided a natural shelter and it was therefore a simple matter to build an enclosure that could trap the incoming tide. St Andrews, for instance, already had an established bathing station for males at the Step Rock which the town council determined to enclose. Prior to taking the plunge, however, the council sent a deputation to Aberdeen and Peterhead to view their bathing facilities. Since the council was going to borrow £1,000 for pond construction, it wanted to get things right. To mark the opening of the new Step Rock pond in July 1903, a gala was held which attracted 3–4,000 spectators. A feature of the 'aquatic display' was a demonstration of a 'drowning man' by the fully-clothed 'rescue man' (incidentally, the working day of the council-appointed rescue man started at 6 a.m.). In the following year the council built another simple pool for ladies only. A suggestion that mixed bathing be permitted at the new pond was vetoed. The less adventurous among the councillors argued that 'they were not so far advanced as that in St Andrews.' Basic tidal ponds were constructed at other places too: for example, at North Berwick, Dunbar, and Arbroath (at Whiting Ness on the east side of the town). At Wick a little harbour on the north side was converted into a swimming pool, and then on the south side of the bay a rock pool, the Trinkie, was adapted and enlarged to give the townsfolk an alternative bathing pond. Some of these semi-natural ponds never progressed beyond what the East Wemyss locals called a 'dooking dub'; others were later developed and expanded as at St Andrews and Dunbar. The citizens of that rising place of resort, North Berwick, were also among the pioneers. In 1899, a public meeting was held at which it was decided that attempts be made to raise funds for the erection of a 'Safety Swimming Pond' which was to be available for both sexes, as long as they attended at different hours. In due course, a site near the harbour which had previously served as a rubbish dump, was acquired. The necessary funds were raised by means of galas, concerts, dances and cycle parades. It was later transferred to the town council, which over the years considerably improved the pond. Hygiene, however, was seemingly not a high priority, since complaints reveal that the pond was drained and refilled only once a month.

In the days of Victorian prudery there were, as we have seen, separate bathing places for men and for women. In the pools as on the beaches, mixed bathing did not become common until the 1920s.

Scanty bathing slips were appropriate garb for the all-male environment at St Andrews' Step Rock. The facilities were improved when St Andrews Town Council built enclosing walls to provide a pond that was flushed by tidal action.

By 1922, however, the North Berwick pondmaster was able to testify that in that town, where mixed bathing was now permitted, 'he had never come across anything likely to lead to a deterioration of the morals of the bathers.' In that upmarket resort, even high society ladies, as the local press proudly proclaimed, were to be seen at the pool. St Andrews town councillors were much more circumspect, as it was not till 1929 that they permitted the sexes to mix at their showpiece Step Rock pool and even then, initially, it was only at certain fixed hours.

In the Great Depression years, some government money was available for schemes that provided work for the unemployed. When, however, Inverness Town Council applied in 1929 to the London-based Unemployment Grants Committee for assistance to build an outdoor pool at Clachnaharry, their application was refused (seven years later, however, the council did build fine indoor baths.). Dunbar and Buckie were more successful in tapping government funds for their outdoor ponds. These were two of the towns badly hit by the decline of fishing and other traditional industries. At Dunbar, from the late 1920s onward, the former ladies' swimming pond had been developed step by step into what was in Scottish terms a major attraction. In 1928 the town built a shallow pond where the bairns could wade or play about in wee paddle boats, and two years later it opened a new large seawater pool with extensive changing and spectator facilities. Although the whole scheme had cost approximately £20,000, it made, in its early 1930s heyday, considerable sums for the town. In 1934 the revenue from all sources was around £1,800 a year. The Buckie pool was one part of what was for a small town (1931 population 8,689) an ambitious development. In March 1931 Buckie Town Council decided to purchase a 136-acre seaside estate at Strathlene to the east of the burgh. The town council seemed to have got very favourable terms as it proposed to pay for the estate and its buildings by twenty-five annual instalments of £236, free of interest. The purchase went ahead and the council proceeded to develop the estate as a holiday complex. The small mansion house, which went with the estate, was converted into a council-run hotel with, tacked on to it, a tearoom for the general public. An 18-hole golf course was constructed that same year, for which grant money was available. An outdoor swimming pool was completed in the following year. Other recreational facilities included a putting green and tennis courts and a 77-metre-long wooden chute. So successful were these various amenities that an eight-bedroom extension was built for the hotel in 1933 and the pool facilities were likewise improved in the following year. So impressed was

Strathlene seawater pool was built in 1932 by Buckie Town Council with the stated aim of encouraging swimming and providing a tourist attraction. The author had a holiday job there as pool custodian for two seasons in the early 1950s. With just one antiquated pump available, it required two tides to fill the pond to the brim.

C. A. Oakley in his 1937 survey of *Scottish Industry To-day* that he went rather over the top in his account: 'Buckie has changed so much in its development as a summer resort that I have seen it described as having become "practically a new town".'

As the ups and downs faced by another Banffshire fishing town make all too evident, pool construction was not plain sailing. Macduff (1931 population 3,276) sought to develop its leisure facilities with the construction of a swimming pool, boating pond and paddling pool at nearby Tarlair. Tarlair had long been popular with valetudinarians for the healing qualities of its mineral well and the beneficial effects of seabathing. To start with all went well. By January 1930, local business people had raised £353 which they handed to the town council as a contribution to the costs of the proposed pond. In the following month the Unemployment Grants Committee agreed to a loan in respect of wages paid for a scheme costing £4,000. By that summer the pool, though far from complete, was already in use. In September 1931 the Burgh Surveyor reported to the council that around £2,100 had been spent of which £1,077 was for wages, with 75 per cent of the latter sum grant-earning. To finish the pool, he reckoned that another £2,075 was needed. Unfortunately, however, with a run on the pound, the country was then going through a financial and political crisis. At this time of national emergency, the Labour Government fell and was replaced by a coalition government which slashed public expenditure. These, incidentally, included cuts in salaries for all public servants, thus precipitating a naval mutiny at Invergordon. As for the Tarlair pond, the Unemployment Grants Committee, despite the council's entreaties, refused further help. Consequently, large-scale work had to stop. Schoolboys, however, were enlisted, through the agency of their headmaster, to help prepare for the 1932 season by removing some 15 tons of stones from the pond. The *People's Journal* reported on 11 June 1932 that the pond, though unfinished, 'will provide the finest bathing facilities in the North of Scotland throughout this summer.' Fund-raising continued and a Military [sic] Whist Drive contributed £18 to the coffers (the males ran the whole show, including serving the tea from the 'cookhouse'.). The council too considered imposing an assessment to pay for the remaining work, but in November 1933 decided that it would be inadvisable at that time 'in view of the failure of the English fishing.'

Major work at Tarlair was not resumed until 1934 when an improving economic situation enabled the National Government to authorise more public expenditure. The town council sent a deputation to visit a number of other Scottish outdoor pools and to report back with recommendations. Following this the Burgh Surveyor drew up a list, with estimated costs, of possible improvements. The addition of a diving pit, together with an auxiliary pump to drain it, was one of his recommendations. The provision of high-diving stages could not be too strongly stressed, he declared, 'as recently this form of display has been very much before the public and has proved a bigger draw to swimming pools than even swimming championships.' There were, he added, several professional divers in the country whose services for exhibitions had been booked continuously throughout the season. With the council accepting most of his recommendations, work went ahead. By October 1934, twenty-six men were employed in concreting the bottom of the pond. This stage of work included the building of a tearoom, large enough to seat sixty inside and another twenty on the verandah under cover. The tender accepted was for £2,187, which included building a kitchen and lavatories. To meet all the costs incurred for the pool and associated works, the council managed to secure a loan of £7,000 at 3 per cent over thirty years. To put this figure in perspective, it may be noted that the council obtained another loan of £7,000 that same summer, 1935, to erect twenty three-apartment houses (private houses cost more. New bungalows on a prime site in Prestwick cost from £475.). Nevertheless, expenditure on the Tarlair pond was by no means finished. In October 1935, the Burgh Surveyor informed the council that another £2,000 or so was required for the pool. But he had good news to convey as well. The income from the pond for that

Tarlair swimming pool and boating pond in its postwar heyday. On gala occasions, spectators high up on the slopes above enjoyed a grandstand view of events in the pool.

season, including the rent for the tearoom, amounted to £665, eleven shillings and nine pence. There was no necessity, accordingly, for the council to impose an assessment that year. Bolstered by this success, the town council decided to increase its advertising budget, with photographs of the pool featuring prominently in its promotional material.

The degree of purpose and initiative shown by the burgh councils and people of what were for the most part comparatively small towns was truly remarkable. In Lothian, in addition to Dunbar, there were seawater pools at Portobello (1936), Port Seton (1930), and North Berwick (modernised in the late 1920s). There was quite a clutch in Fife: at Burntisland (1936), Buckhaven (1926), St Monans (1937), Pittenweem (an old tidal pond with extra facilities added in 1935), Anstruther (1927, then doubled in size in 1935), Cellardyke (1933), and St Andrews (1903, upgraded in the 1930s). In addition, there was a small privately owned pond at Kirkcaldy (1936). There was also a freshwater pond at Leven (1921). Going further north, as well as Arbroath and Buckie, there were ponds too at Stonehaven (1934), Rosehearty (1959, a late example), Tarlair serving Macduff (1931–35), Portsoy (1936), Invergordon (1933), Dornoch, and Wick (two pools). On the west coast, too, outdoor ponds were built or expanded at Gourock (1909, then upgraded in 1934), Greenock, Saltcoats (1894 rebuilt in 1933), Troon (1931), Prestwick (1931) and Helensburgh (gifted in 1929 by a local councillor, though with the council becoming responsible for its upkeep). Some of these ponds, Portsoy's for example, would never have been built without the very considerable efforts of local people who raised surprisingly large sums of cash and also did a lot of the hard manual work. It was thanks to local volunteers that the smaller ones were kept going. Portsoy Swimming Club kept that pond going until 1974 when, on the eve of local government reorganisation, it was handed over to Portsoy Town Council.

The degree of proximity of pools in Fife's East Neuk burghs and in Ayrshire suggests an element of local rivalry and emulation. Advocates for a pool in Edinburgh were quick to contrast the city's dilatoriness with tiny Port Seton's achievement in building, in 1930, an Olympic-sized pool which was, it was asserted, 'the only seawater pond in the country to have filtration'. Port Seton then capped this by constructing three years later, for community use, a multi-purpose pond hall. Built largely by voluntary labour, the pond hall was used for dances and other events. The opening of the Port Seton pond, critics asserted, put Edinburgh to shame; the city's pool at Portobello was not started till 1934, and it was another two years before it was ready for use. Up in Banffshire, Macduff's very near neighbour, Banff, also planned to build a pool. Indeed, when a plebiscite was held in 1934, the majority voted in favour. This scheme, probably fortunately, did not go ahead.

In the East Neuk of Fife, with four separate tidal ponds just a few miles apart, local pride and rivalry was a strong element in the mania for pool construction. The Pittenweem pool, which dates back to the early 1900s, was the first. It was described in a 1920s guidebook as 'an enclosed pond, flushed at every tide, where any depth of water may be found up to six feet.' Changing shelters were nearby, 'for which keys may be had.' Local fundraisers and other volunteers played a vital role at all four of the East Neuk ponds: at St Monans, Pittenweem and the two at Anstruther, at Billowness on the west side and at Cellardyke on the east (Cellardyke was not linked to Anstruther till 1929, and fund raising had started before amalgamation.). An Improvements Committee, formed in 1922, raised funds for the initial construction of the Billowness pond and for later additions and enlargement. At all the East Neuk ponds, volunteers helped with some of the basic construction work. Peter Smith, a local poet celebrated, in his poem 'The Pond', the communal effort involved in excavating the Cellardyke pool, which was officially opened on 17 June 1933.

NEW SWIMMING POND, PORT SETON.

A good crowd present at a gala at Port Seton.

> And fegs, they cam frae a' the airts,
> Frae fishin' boats and ploomen's cairts,
> Left joiners' shops and makin' tairts,
> Tae brak up skellies [reefs of rock].
> Clerks, grocers, slaters did their pairts,
> The hearty fellas.

From small beginnings came large outcomes. In August 1935 the Provost of St Monans informed the council that two retired fishermen had given £1 each to open a fund for the construction of a tidal bathing pond. The town council duly went ahead, asking for further donations or loans and starting negotiations with the site proprietor which led to it purchasing the ground known locally as the East Braes for £100. By 1937 the council had a plan, drawn up by architect Mr L. A. Rolland of Leven, and it had secured a loan of £1,950. More money was raised by dances and concerts organised by a Ladies Committee. To save money, the council had already decided to dispense with a concrete floor for the pond. A pool attendant was chosen to be paid £2 per week for the season. The pond was constructed in 'record time' of six or seven weeks. Maybe it was built too quickly as it leaked, and that was a problem that bothered St Monans Burgh Council for some time afterwards. However, on 22 July 1937 some 2,000 people from all parts of East Fife gathered for the opening ceremony, which was followed by a display of aquatic skills, by the Buckhaven Amateur Swimming Club. In the late evening there was another gala, floodlit this time, with races and a treasure hunt which involved diving to retrieve such treasures as tins of canned food. The treasure hunt, the *East Fife Observer* correspondent wrote, continued until a late hour 'bringing to a glorious close a day which will ever be remembered in the history of St Monance' (the name was spelled St Monance in those days.).

Not exactly in the East Neuk but Leven's freshwater, open-air pond was, as the *Leven Advertiser and Wemyss Gazette* reported on 21 July 1921, constructed entirely by the enthusiastic members of the local amateur swimming club 'amid circumstances which were at times depressing.' The newspaper did not need to state what these depressing circumstances were, but just three weeks earlier the Fife miners had gone back to work after a three-month-long, bitter and sometimes violent strike. The swimming club was fortunate in having generous patrons. The laird, Mr Maitland Christie of Durie, had granted the site at a nominal rent, and a good deal of the carting had been done free of charge. Furthermore, most of the tools and materials had been donated, including picks and shovels from the Fife Coal Company and a large quantity of bricks from the Earl of Elgin.

Where councils were the main movers, substantial sums, for those days, were needed, and it was no easy task securing authority for pool construction. Invergordon was fortunate inasmuch as the £2,000-plus cost of its pond was met by a windfall. A private company had taken over the burgh's electric power system and had paid a considerable sum for it. Other councils had to borrow money for such purposes. But this meant that there was plenty of scope for objection from those townsfolk who had to pay rates – the local taxes levied on property. Leven was one council that had to backtrack on a project which the ratepayers considered both unnecessary and too costly. What the council wanted was a seawater, open-air pool to be built on the foreshore. For Leven to go ahead, however, the council, according to the Burgh Council (Scotland) Act of 1892, required first of all a two-thirds majority of councillors. Even if that was secured there was a further obstacle. If seven or more ratepayers objected, a poll could be demanded. As there were plenty of objectors, a referendum of ratepayers was held on 4 February 1931. Since this resulted in a defeat for the council by 739 votes to 619, the townsfolk and visitors just had to be content with the existing freshwater pond in Letham Glen. The council did investigate the possibility of pumping seawater to the Letham Glen pool, but this was considered to be too expensive. A similar poll at Fraserburgh in 1934 also resulted in a defeat for a projected pool.

At Aberdeen, it was the council that in 1938 rejected a £50,000 scheme for an open-air pool and solarium. The Links and Parks Committee had thought it necessary for a beach 'which lacked many necessary attractions'. Some years earlier, Stonehaven Town Council, on the other hand, had considered that its proposed bathing pond would be 'a klondyke', 'a gold mine' and it would bring 'a new era of prosperity' to a town, which had had to endure a decline in visitor numbers. To see what they needed, councillors visited pools at Prestwick, Troon and other resorts. Their architect, R. R. Gall, then designed a handsome Art Deco-style pond measuring 50 x 18 metres. With their ratepayers voting in favour by 656 to 539, the scheme went ahead at a capital cost of just under £10,000. Opened in 1934 the burgh's open-air pool made a substantial profit in its first season. Thus encouraged, the burgh council in the following year installed a filtration system and even more revolutionary a heating system. Not surprisingly attendances soared, with the number of bathers in 1935 going up to 43,262 and spectators to 58,654.

The same process of consultation was followed at Burntisland. In 1934 the town council voted by ten to two 'to proceed with the erection of a Public Open Bathing Place or Swimming Pond at a cost not exceeding £10,000' (this can be compared with the £22,000 estimated cost of Prestwick's Bathing Lake and the £103,240 for New Brighton's enormous pool.). Since ten of Burntisland's householders objected, a poll was obligatory. In the event, 553 householders voted for and 311 against, giving a majority of 242. The necessary finances, however, had still to be procured. As the council minutes reveal, the Kirkcaldy & District Savings Bank provided a loan of £10,000 at 3.125 per cent to be repaid over a period of thirty years. The council then had to secure the sanction of

Dunoon's Lido, though to its critics a white elephant, was a good example of 1930s architecture. The cafe was on the top storey, with terracing and changing rooms below. Observe the rescue boat drawn up on the foreshore. In later years, the building housed the Dunoon Pottery. It was demolished *c.* 1980.

BATHING LIDO, DUNOON

the National Debt Commissioners for this mortgage. To help the council in their deliberations over staffing, wages, facilities, etc., the Town Clerk was instructed to write to his opposite numbers in eight other burghs. In consequence, the council decided to appoint a full-time pool manager (there were twenty-seven applicants) plus seven season-only employees, with additional helpers to be provided at weekends. The season began in May and the pool for that first season was to remain open until Saturday 3 October! One wonders how many were still dooking in a cold open-air pond as late as October. At Dunoon, where proposals for the construction of a bathing pool were repeatedly rejected on grounds of cost, a compromise solution was the answer. Accordingly, the burgh council decided, instead of building an enclosed pool, to upgrade the existing West Bay bathing station. This lido, as it came to be called, was formally opened in June 1937. It provided dressing accommodation for 850 bathers at a time and terraced seating for 2,000 spectators. At Rothesay, too, a similar bathing station was likewise modernised in 1934 and provided with up-to-date facilities that included floodlighting for 'night swimming'. Although commonly used in the south of England for outdoor pools, the term 'lido', as an enclosed pool as opposed to a bathing station, did not have widespread currency in Scotland. Kirkcaldy's wee private-enterprise pond was the one exception. The author of a *c.* 1938 Peterhead guidebook admitted that his town's bathing place was christened 'The Lido' with 'a sense of humour rather than of grandiloquence'.

Rivalry between councils did not stop with pool construction. The different councils were not slow to boost the merits of their particular pond. Prestwick Town Council for one was eager to remind visitors that its bathing lake was the only pool on the Firth of Clyde to come up to Olympic standards. At the opening of the Burntisland pool in 1936, the Provost asserted that they had the most modern open-air pond in Fife. While the Dunbar pool had, the locals boasted, the finest natural setting, the Saltcoats folk asserted that their pond, reconstructed and extended in 1933, was the largest and finest-equipped tidal bathing pool in Scotland. In case of emergency, attendants in boats were in constant attendance. At some pool sites, as at Tarlair and Dunbar, the councils provided added value in the form of adjacent boating ponds where wee rowing boats and paddleboats were available for hire. There the bairns could sail the Spanish Main or row across the Channel, until their hour was up and the dreaded call came: 'Come in Number 9'! Saltcoats went one better, with wee motorboats in a pond adjacent to the bathing station.

A busy day at Saltcoats bathing pond in 1933. Today's health and safety experts might frown on a chute like the one in the foreground.

While many people have pleasurable memories of their dooking days, others remember the more often than not freezing conditions. Mrs Margaret Hunter from Alloa did have very clear recollections of many happy times enjoying the (very cold!) water at Strathlene and other ponds. But she remembered, too, the occasion when her young sons were taken to Tarlair pool and emerged from the water 'teeth chattering, skin turning blue and a downright refusal to go back in to the icy cold'. The joy of outdoor swimming in Scotland in midsummer, she added, is an unforgettable experience. For bairns, emerging from a cold dook, a chitterin bite (maybe a biscuit or sandwich) helped to keep the teeth from chattering. But, in the pool itself, the fact that bathers tended to urinate in cold water maybe had a minuscule warming effect. Councils did, though, take steps to reduce health risks and a few provided artificial heating. Stonehaven's Official Guide (*c.* 1960) stated in bold print: 'Six times in the twenty-four hours of each day the heated sea-water is filtered, sterilised and changed.' The dangers of pollution were only too real, as at Buckhaven, where in 1939 the pool was condemned as insanitary, being too close to a sewage outfall. Heated ponds, like Stonehaven's, were the exception. But, thanks to the availability of waste steam from an adjacent power station, the water at Portobello could be maintained at a theoretical 68 degrees Fahrenheit. Warming the ladies' hearts there, in the postwar years, was a future James Bond, a young man called Sean Connery who for a time served as a lifeguard. When opened in 1936, the 'Porty' pool was one that the city of Edinburgh could be proud of. Built at a cost, according to a contemporary *Scotsman* report, of £80,000, it boasted a 2,000-seat cantilevered grandstand, a café and a restaurant which could also serve as a ballroom. The five-tier concrete diving platform was another distinctive feature. Local man Peter Heatly honed his diving skills there. In the 1950s he won gold medals for the high dive at three successive Commonwealth Games. Portobello also had an unusual attraction for those days – a wave-making plant. But when storms struck pools could have

The water chute and high-diving tower are prominent features of Portobello's modernistic bathing pond, as photographed in 1938.

real waves crashing over the seawall – all very exciting but at the same time always liable to cause damage.

In the 1930s Sunday opening hours were generally restricted. At Portobello, for instance, while dookers were allowed to bathe in the early morning, they had to be out of the water by 10 a.m. The cut-off point at Burntisland was even earlier at 9 a.m. At Invergordon there was no Sunday bathing at all, for which the 'expert and experienced swimmer' who was the Superintendent must have been grateful, since his hours in the peak months from May till the end of August extended from 7.30 a.m. to 9 p.m. These Sabbath day limitations certainly caused some resentment, but for Portobello at any rate they remained until 1947. The Kirk then, of course, complained that whole day opening provided unfair competition to the local places of worship.

Initially, the outdoor pools enjoyed immense popularity. During its first season, nearly 800,000 people paid for admission to the Portobello pond, either as bathers or spectators. Large crowds flocked to their local ponds for swimming competitions. Everywhere midnight galas, fireworks displays, boat races, treasure hunts, life-saving and high-diving displays were popular, as were water polo matches. Community singing was a feature of some galas. There were plenty of comic and other novelty acts too. Old stagers at Port Seton recalled a lady giving an underwater swimming demonstration while wired up with fairy lights. W. C. Bradborn, a Canadian champion log roller, was another star of the touring circuit. One of his tricks involved drinking a cup of tea while balancing on a log. The ineptitude displayed by bathers invited to emulate his feats added to the entertainment. At Arbroath, in July 1948, Dare-Devil Peggy, otherwise known as Peg-Leg Bernard, and his acrobatic diving troupe were a major draw. Bernard was a one-legged diver, who leaped from the high board into a ring of fire on the water. Events of a very different kind were baptisms. Invergordon pool was one that was used, on at least one occasion, for this purpose.

Anita Walker, interviewed on Radio Scotland on 12 July 1998, testified to the popularity of the Arbroath pond:

For a long time it was the focal point for a lot of the seaside entertainment for this town, a place where the whole family could go and the parents knew that the children were safe, as it was a huge pool that went from a very, very shallow end right into a very deep pit for the high diving board.

But then we had 'It's a Knockout', galas, diving displays, as well as the wonderful Miss Arbroath, Junior Miss and children's competitions every Tuesday through the summer time. There were times when we had to admit that it was not quite the day to be in a swimsuit. My funniest and happiest memories are of swimming in the pool at midnight and the rain pouring down on us, and I think that it was because the rain was warmer than the actual pool that it felt good.

Bathing beauty parades like the Miss Arbroath one were held in many of the holiday towns. Open-air swimming pools and lidos, with their changing rooms and large spectator capacity, were the obvious choice for events, which attracted large crowds, as many as 4–5,000 for the Miss Arbroath competition. Long queues to get in were not unusual. In the early days they were small-scale events, but they stepped up a gear when, starting in the 1930s, the newspapers became involved. At Dunbar the contests were organised by the town council, who provided the prize money, in co-operation with the *Edinburgh Evening News*, which supplied the judges and gave the event and the town a lot of publicity. For those days a lot of money was involved. It cost Prestwick £800 in 1948 to kick-start what was to be an annual competition. Not surprisingly quite a few residents were opposed to this kind of 'unwarrantable expenditure'. In the early years, the entrants were either local girls or holidaymakers who were actually staying at the resort. So few had entered for Dunbar's first competition that the Entertainments Manager had to go round the town to rope in some extra volunteers, who duly paraded – clad not in swimsuits but in their best summer frocks. As the prize money increased and, as local success could lead to qualification for regional or national titles, an element of professionalism began to creep in. Some contestants travelled round the country going from one contest to another. By the 1960s, as its Official Guide asserted, Prestwick's competition was quite the most spectacular and famous event of its kind in Scotland and one which added 'glamour to newspaper picture pages all over Britain'. But these increasingly huge events were not just for the nubile young. Since the whole family went on holiday together, they all had a chance to participate. Fathers showed off their knobbly knees, the bairns dressed up for the fancy dress competitions, and even the grannies had their chance to display their curves. And for them there was big money at stake too. In 1958, the *Sunday Graphic* paid out £2,000 in cash prizes for its Glamorous Grandmother of Great Britain contest.

Admiration for the opposite sex was, of course, a two-way process. One mature lady confessed to the spark of excitement she felt as a young lass, when every morning a visiting Boys' Brigade squad was marched down to her local pond. In later years, bathing beauty competitions began to lose favour with the public. They were attacked for being tacky and degrading cattle markets. At any rate, with the masses now heading for warmer climes and the open-air pools being closed down, the holiday crowds and the venues, with a few exceptions, were no longer there. One by one, cash-strapped local authorities put the shutters up on these once so popular pools of shivering delight.

CHAPTER 7

Holiday Excursions:
By Steamboat, Train, Tram and Charabanc

The Rothesay displays [illuminations] of the thirties offered a double spectacle. Apart from the fireworks themselves, Rothesay Bay became a gala of steamers, themselves bands of reflected light twilling with the darkness of the water. The steamers brought people from villages and towns along both sides of the Firth.

From the Ayrshire towns came the 'Duchess of Hamilton'; from Gourock, with the Glaswegians, came sister turbine the 'Duchess of Montrose' and the paddlers 'Duchess of Rothesay' and the elegantly tapered 'Duchess of Fife'; from Kirn, Dunoon and Innellan, the 'Mercury' and the 'Caledonia'; from Largs and Millport, the trim little 'Glen Rosa'; from Arran the sleek and fast 'Glen Sannox'; and from Craigendoran and Helensburgh, the 'Talisman', the 'Waverley', the 'Marmion', and the 'Jeanie Deans' added that aura of romance which accompanied the bearer of names so illustrious whenever they appeared ... well-loved little ships, their mere fortuitous mustering in the one place thrilled the heart of a boy.'

Maurice Lindsay *Clyde Waters*, 1958

The development of mechanised travel in the nineteenth century allowed ever-increasing numbers of town and city dwellers to enjoy the pleasure of an occasional day-trip into the country or to the seaside. From the 1840s onward steamboats and then railways had the capacity to convey huge throngs on cheap excursions. For the 'respectable' summer residents at, say Dunoon or North Berwick, such incursions could be a considerable nuisance. Small villages like Aberdour in Fife were particularly vulnerable. In Victorian days, there had been occasions when great hordes of day-trippers were disembarked, many of them drunk and disorderly. Terrified villagers shut themselves away, scarcely daring even to peep outside so long as their noisy and unwelcome visitors were roaming the streets. On the other hand, as working people had little time or opportunity for leisure, such interruptions were sporadic, peaking at the great public holiday saturnalias. When excursionists came on a works trip or with some other organised group, they could be boisterous but were generally well behaved, good-natured fun being the general rule.

There was one day of the week when excursionists were less welcome – the Sabbath. The operation of Sunday steamers on the Clyde, and on the Forth too, had caused ructions over a long period of time. In 1853 Parliament had passed an Act prohibiting the sale of alcohol on Sundays except to genuine travellers – 'bona fide' was the legal term applied. Some unscrupulous businessmen, however, finding that the Act did not apply to excursion steamers started to run Sabbath-day 'booze cruises'. The local elite in some of the towns and villages affected tried, by strong-arm tactics at times, to stop such Sabbath-breaking excursionists from disembarking. In 1882, the inhabitants of Aberdour tried petitioning the Earl of Morton in his capacity as 'Lord of the Manor' and as owner of the main pier. If this scandalous state of affairs continued, then they pleaded: 'Aberdour as an attractive and flourishing watering-place will soon be a thing of the past'. That same year the sale of alcohol on short-run steamers was made illegal which stopped some of the abuse. But by then the Sabbath day trips were too popular and too profitable for steamer owners to be stopped altogether. Undoubtedly, there was sometimes a lot of drunken rowdiness. On the other hand, for the Victorian working class, Sunday was the only day in the week when they were completely free of toil. Since shop assistants, for example, were kept hard at work till late on Saturday evenings, the one day that they had to themselves was the Sabbath.

The 1882 Act did not put a stop to all Sunday drinking, as excursionists could carry their own supplies or, alternatively, visit a licensed hotel where they could claim to be 'bona fide' travellers and therefore be entitled to buy alcoholic refreshment. Nevertheless, in Highland or semi-Highland resorts like Dunoon, there was still a lot of opposition to Sunday boats. In 1897 the local government authority, the Dunoon Commissioners, drew up byelaws banning Sabbath-breaking steamers from landing passengers. A series of disturbances ensued, most notably on Glasgow Fair Sunday that same year, when, despite a police presence, angry excursionists smashed their way through the locked gates. For bystanders these events were exciting spectacles and great crowds turned out every a time a Sunday steamer was due to appear. This was the case on 15 July 1900 when the first Sunday sailing of the season took place. As the steamer, the *Heather Bell*, neared the pier, several passengers leaped on to the pier and seized a gangway which they ran on to the paddle-box. After a few more excursionists had skipped ashore, the gangway was hauled away and the steamer then pulled away. But the six passengers left behind had still to get themselves and their luggage off a pier, whose gates were locked. Although the five males managed to get over the 10-foot railings with little bother, the sixth, a long-skirted young lady, had more difficulty. With her male companions assisting, she did, nevertheless, manage to clear the obstacle, while the onlookers laughed and cheered. The police, according to the *Glasgow Herald,* stood by and did nothing. Although the Burgh Commissioners, and their successors in Dunoon Town Council, continued to try, with mixed success, to prohibit Sunday landings, they eventually found that the legal position was untenable. They found that, as in an analogous case nearly twenty years earlier, the Court of Session took a contrary view. In that earlier case, the Court had decided that: 'The Harbour Commisioners of Kirkcaldy were not entrusted in any way with a superintendence over the spiritual condition of the town.' In 1902 the Dunoon byelaws were repealed and soon Sunday pleasure sailings became generally accepted.

All resorts offered a choice of day-trips either on land or sea, and no holiday would have been complete without some kind of excursion. On the Firths of Tay, Forth and, above all, on the Clyde, steamer cruises were, in fine weather, a sheer delight. At pre-1914 Rothesay at the height of summer, there were over 100 steamer calls each day, and this gave the holidaymaker a very good choice of destinations. For steamboat travellers, too, there could be an extra thrill – the drama and excitement of races between rival steamers. The crowds on busy steamers, it must be admitted, could be overwhelming at times. Maurice Lindsay, a Clyde steamer aficionado, recalled one 'Glesga wifie's' shrill lament: 'Whit wi' the heat and the sweit [sweat] and the wecht o' wee Wullie, Goad, this is fair awfie.' For his more 'refined' readers, this, he translated as, the woman felt uncomfortable. As he also observed, for many travellers the saloon and its liquid refreshments, as we see from Plate 18, had more allure than the interest and the glories of the passing scene, even the far-famed Kyles of Bute.

Steamers could be hired for private parties as when, on a May Saturday in 1939, the paddle steamer the *Fair Maid* left Leith for a pleasure trip up the Firth of Forth with 600 merry-making students on board. They were a boisterous lot and not at all safety-conscious. The unfortunate crew spent some anxious hours chasing unruly undergraduates who insisted on performing acrobatics on the ship's rails, though fortunately there were no accidents. The students enjoyed themselves by dancing on the deck accompanied by the ship's band. But so great was the crush that the dancing, according to the *Scottish Daily Express*, was 'hardly expert'. The return journey to Leith's West Pier turned out to be exciting in another way. The flag-bedecked *Fair Maid* had to paddle her fastest, so that women students could get back to their hostels before the doors were closed against them at midnight. Luckily for them, the report continued, a train from North Leith Station got them back up town just in time.

Special occasions like the Rothesay Illuminations, described in the quotation that starts off this chapter, must have been marvellous sights. But by the 1950s when Maurice Lindsay penned his elegiac memoirs, the Clyde steamer fleet had been greatly diminished. In 1910 the maximum carrying capacity of the Clyde fleet during the summer months had been around 52,000. By 1950 it had been more than halved – down to some 24,000. Of the steamers that had so excited the young Maurice Lindsay, more than half had gone, some to the shipbreaker's. 'Others,' he lamented, 'like the noble *Waverley* and the plucky little *Marmion* have gone down gallantly after wartime encounters in unfriendly seas.'

ROTHESAY ILLUMINATIONS

EVENING CRUISE

By Saloon Steamer "TALISMAN"
(WEATHER PERMITTING)

TO

LOCH STRIVEN

AND

ROTHESAY BAY

ON

Friday, 29th August 1930

STEAMER TIMES

		Going.	Returning.
		p.m.	p.m.
Helensburgh	... ...	8 0	11 0
Kilcreggan	... ...	8 15	10 40
Kirn ...	... ...	8 30	10 25
Dunoon ...	... ...	8 35	10 20

FARE 1/9

LONDON & NORTH EASTERN RAILWAY

August 1930.   (3-M)   (S.C. 119.)
HUGH PATON & SONS, LTD., Printers, Edinburgh.

The *Talisman*, a First World War minesweeper and one of Maurice Lindsay's well-loved little ships, sailed from Helensburgh and called at three other piers before arriving at Rothesay for the 1930 illuminations.

As the steamer services on the Firth of Clyde declined, and on the Forth and Tay virtually disappeared, some fishermen and boat-owners filled the gap with petrol and diesel-engined craft. From the early 1900s motor boats had been competing with the steamboats on short-run cruises and trips round the bay were available at most resorts. Where they had no suitable landing stage, boatmen used small adjustable wooden jetties to make boarding easier. At Burntisland and Aberdour a favourite trip was the sail to the island of Inchcolm in the Firth of Forth. The Scottish Motor Traction Company (SMT) also saw the potential for cruising on the Forth. From its base at South Queensferry, it began in 1914 to operate pleasure cruises using 'motor yachts'. Some motor-engined boats were quite large and able to sail fairly long distances. At Rothesay, in the interwar years, the *May Queen* was a popular cruising vessel, as was the later and larger *Gay Queen* that could carry 130 passengers. On this vessel you had something that none of the large steamers could provide – a singing skipper who kept the passengers entertained and amused. The *Gay Queen* continued in operation until 1988 by which time it had ceased to be profitable. As the numbers of visitors dwindled, so did the number of motor boats. On the Forth today short summer trips include sails from South Queensferry to the island of Inchcolm and from Anstruther to the Isle of May. On the west coast and in the north-east and in other waters, dolphin-watching and other wild life cruises are very much in vogue. For nostalgia, though, there is nothing to beat the paddle steamer *Waverley*, which provides the kind of cruising that was once such an intrinsic part of the holiday experience of the resorts of the Clyde, Forth and Tay. Completed in 1947, the present *Waverley* replaced her predecessor of the same name, Maurice Lindsay's 'noble' *Waverley* that had been sunk while evacuating British troops from Dunkirk in 1940. That the *Waverley* survives at all is a minor miracle in its own right. When by 1973 Clyde cruising in its traditional form had collapsed, she was withdrawn from service by owners Caledonian MacBrayne, and in the following year offered to the Paddle Steamer Preservation Society for the nominal sum of £1. Restored and assisted with public finance and a great deal of voluntary effort, the *Waverley*, the last sea-going paddle steamer in the world, operates each summer a programme of cruises on the Clyde and other areas round Britain.

It was the vast improvement in road transport that led to first the decline and then, save for the *Waverley*, the complete collapse of steamboat cruising in Scottish coastal waters. There had always

The Beach, Burntisland

Here are two motor boats operating from a crowded Burntisland beach in 1927. This today is one of the few beaches in Scotland that can fly a Blue Flag.

been road excursions on offer with coach hire firms offering trips into resort hinterlands. Local farmers and carters in places like Arran even developed a profitable sideline, meeting visitors off the boats and transporting them to their holiday abodes, and also by using their gigs and wagonettes for excursions. Wagonettes, brakes and other passenger-carrying horse-drawn vehicles were, however, slow and were, therefore, limited in the distance they could cover. At Victorian Dunoon there was a great variety of steamer excursions on offer but only a limited number of coach trips. By the 1930s the opposite was the case. It was the invention of the internal combustion engine that began a process, which for Dunoon and other Scottish resorts was to be revolutionary in its outcome. Even before the First World War, petrol-engined buses were beginning to edge out their horse-drawn equivalents. In 1905, when the SMT company was formed, its prospectus read: 'The Directors believe that the Motor Bus has now been so perfected that it is bound at no distant date to entirely supersede the Horse Bus.' And, with motor buses operated by SMT and many other companies displacing the horse bus, they were soon proved right. Excursions by motor buses soon became very popular. In Arran, for example, the *Glasgow Herald* reported, in July 1914, that: 'A motor tour round the island is now an added attraction for both natives and visitors.' But the big period of development came at the end of the First World War (1914–18) when a lot of ex-military vehicles came on the market, and ex-servicemen who had learned to drive while in the forces purchased many of them and went into business on their own account. A number of them were converted into buses or charabancs (open-to-the-elements tourist coaches). With long, hard bench seats and few springs and originally with solid tyres, they were not the most comfortable of vehicles. But they were flexible and cheap to run and able to reach destinations to which the railways did not go.

Passengers leaving Steamer, Inveraray.

'Spending the day here' is the message on this card posted at Inverary on 19 August 1903. Inverary was a popular place for excursions. The paddle steamer is the *Lord of the Isles* (1891–1928). Notice the horse-drawn brake with its bench seats. During the next decade or two, motor buses replaced the old-style brakes.

As buses and roads were improved in the interwar years, larger numbers of visitors were travelling by road, either in their own cars or by service bus or, with a group, in a charabanc. Both for travel to a resort and for excursions while there, holidaymakers were opting for the greater flexibility and variety of possible destinations that increasingly more comfortable and reliable buses, and motor cars, now afforded. As early as the 1920s, resorts like Largs had to provide municipal car parks to cope with the great increase in road traffic. It is clear that more and more middle-class holidaymakers were abandoning train and steamer and were opting instead for a touring holiday either in their own car or in a motor coach. There is no question that, from the 1920s onward, the ever increasing number of cars and motor coaches led to a wider dispersal of the tourist 'cake' and that ultimately affected resorts like Rothesay that were heavily dependent on traditional means of transport. Some locals, nevertheless, refused to see the writing on the wall, arguing, for instance, that the absence of a vehicular ferry to Bute didn't really matter. The Provost of Rothesay was quoted, in July 1929, as asserting that hundreds of motorists who had been touring the mainland ended up at Rothesay at any rate, only minus their cars. In Provost Maclachlan's rather optimistic opinion: 'They come down here after a motoring holiday to tune up their nerves again. The strain of driving tells on them, and the amenities of Rothesay act like a pick-me-up.' It is fairly certain, nevertheless, that the local hoteliers would have much preferred to have touring motorists drive straight up to their doors.

Until buses eventually superseded them, the tramway systems of Aberdeen, Dundee, Edinburgh and the Isle of Bute carried huge numbers to their respective beaches. As we have seen (in chapter 4), the tramcars of the Rothesay Tramway Company linking the town to Port Bannatyne and Ettrick Bay were for many years a great success. With the line to Ettrick Bay largely on its own private track, the company could guarantee that there would be 'no disagreeable road dust or dirt' on their 'scenic electric railway'. In 1936, though the SMT company, which had taken over the system five years earlier, replaced the trams with buses.

The Edinburgh trams, first horse then cable and lastly electric, carried large numbers to Portobello and Joppa and eventually, by the independent Musselburgh system, along the coast to Port Seton. It was in 1909 that Cockenzie and neighbouring Port Seton were linked to the Musselburgh Tramway Company's network. Prior to that date, visitors to these villages had to travel by train to Prestonpans station where a horse-drawn bus ran to the coast in the summer months. But, with the Musselburgh electric trams connecting end-on to Edinburgh's cable cars, more visitors and day-trippers were attracted to the two fishing villages. In 1922 Edinburgh's cable cars were converted to an overhead system, making it compatible with Musselburgh's, so within a year you could board a tram in Edinburgh's Princes Street which took you right through to Cockenzie and Port Seton. The system was cut back to Levenhall on the east side of Musselburgh five years later, but by then a cheap and cheerful motor bus service had been competing successfully with the trams. In the meantime, the tramcars had helped to establish the joint burgh of Cockenzie and Port Seton as a viable holiday location. By taking in summer visitors, the fisherwomen of these communities were enabled to make a valuable addition to the family income. In their turn, their summer visitors, many of whom came back year after year, delighted in watching all the activity at the harbour and in seeing the womenfolk selling the fish that their men had landed at the harbour. Another fishing village-cum-seaside resort, Buckhaven in Fife, also benefited by being connected to a tramway network. At that time, Buckhaven, like the nearby golfing resort of Leven, was connected by the Wemyss and District Tramway to mining towns like Methil and East and West Wemyss and ultimately to Kirkcaldy. This system lasted from 1906 to 1932. Another once busy route, from

In this postcard, which bears a postmark date of 1928, we see a row of touring charabancs lined up ready for departure in Castle Street, Aberdeen. The destination boards are prominently situated. Many visitors would have used these trams to go to the beach and prom.

Dundee to Broughty Ferry and Monifieth, was terminated in the previous year. That line had once been advertised as 'Scotland's most beautiful tramway'. Dundonians still had the option, though, of using the train for the journey to Broughty, and 7,000 of them did just that on a very hot summer day in 1934. With many tramway systems being shut down, the 1930s was a bad decade for trams. Portobello and Musselburgh, however, kept their trams till 1956, when Edinburgh's entire system was closed down. In Aberdeen the Sea Beach route, a highly popular one in the summer months, was also withdrawn in 1956 and the rest of the system two years later.

Although trains and steamers could transport far greater numbers, the bus had the advantage of flexibility. In all resorts, bus companies offered a variety of 'land cruises' including evening excursions. Aberdeen Corporation Transport ran short excursions in the town and country to give visitors a flavour of the area. Other operators went further into the surrounding countryside, with 'Royal Deeside' a popular choice. In its publicity material, Aberdeen made the most of the royal connection with:

Balmoral Castle, the autumn residence of H.M., The King, chosen for the healthiness of the climate, splendid scenery and sporting facilities, only a short distance inland.

A 1930s visitor remarked on the array of tourist coaches destined for places with attractive names like Stonehaven, Inverness, the Linn of Dee, and Braemar, 'each and every name suggesting that a journey to it would afford the visitor with a further wealth of interests.' Some southern bus companies combined a city hotel break with a visit to the Braemar Highland Gathering and the considerable inducement of a peek at the royal family. Just as Aberdeen was the gateway to Royal

Deeside, Dunoon was promoted as the 'Gateway to the Western Highlands', thus rendering it more attractive to tourists from outwith Scotland. Writing in the early 1930s, J. J. Bell noted that the town was receiving visitors from all parts. This situation he contrasted with his younger days when in the summer Dunoon seemed to belong to Glasgow and Paisley 'when even an Edinburgh voice sounded strange, and an English one attracted attention'. As a touring centre, Dunoon had a clear advantage over Rothesay as the anonymous author of the town's 1939 Official Guide emphasised. Displaying an element of one-upmanship, he drew attention to the large contingents arriving by steamer from Rothesay and other coast towns 'not so favourably situated' to take advantage of the wide variety of tours available at Dunoon. In contrast to the ten pages devoted to steamboat excursions in the guide, no fewer than twenty-three pages, not counting advertisement pages, were given over to motor and coach tours. Aided by the 'recent road-making activities, improvements and extensions by the Ministry of Transport', the Dunoon bus companies offered 'long tours of adventure into a region steeped in history, tradition, and romance'. Motorists too had the option of covering large expanses of most interesting country 'without the inconvenience of daily changing their abode'. 'Close upon 2,000 miles of highway,' the guide claimed, 'traversing what is practically a virgin country are available to motorists.'

The author of the above-mentioned guidebook waxed lyrical on the subject of evening 'Mystery Drives':

> When often as many as 40 large coaches with venturesome spirits will set off to unknown destinations, probably a lonely lochside inn, where there will be music and dancing in the moonlight, amid a weird environment of beetling crags, mysterious woods and ghostly shadows, with the skirl of the pipes re-echoing through the mountain pass. One can readily imagine the spirits of a vanished race peering through the shadows amazed at the strange ongoings of a strange people.

Jack House, a Glaswegian journalist, who was given the task of writing the *c.* 1948 Official Guide, was more cynical on the subject of mystery tours running from Dunoon in the evenings. Although

GLENDARUEL HOTEL, ARGYLL.

It is clear from this 1930 postcard that the hotel and tearoom at Glendaruel made a favourite stopping place for 'chara' excursionists and motorists. The Glendaruel circular tour was a sixty-mile trip from Dunoon. While the hotel is still there, the adjacent tearoom is no more.

he admired the bonhomie and camaraderie on the buses (some of which carried a band with them), he facetiously pointed out that the mystery would not have occupied Sherlock Holmes for long. 'After all, there is a limit to the number of places you can reach from Dunoon in an hour or so's drive. You're pretty sure to land at some lochside hotel.' As with the earlier guide, there are far more pages of text devoted to what Jack House terms the 'bus tour country' than to steamer trips and an almost incredible thirty-one photographs of Highland scenery including views of Loch Lomond, the Trossachs, Oban, Glencoe, and Loch Linnhe.

Evening excursions into resorts also became increasingly popular. As industrial workers and employees in the retail trade were now enjoying a shorter working day, trips to the seaside or into the country were a feasible and pleasant way of spending a summer evening. Both train and bus companies exploited the novelty of trips to towns both familiar and unfamiliar. Writing, in 1959, on the social changes that had impacted on the burgh of Johnstone, the local contributor to the *Third Statistical Account of Scotland: Renfrew and Bute* remarked on how the horizon of the ordinary citizen had been widened. 'The fleets of motor coaches have altered the scope and scale of holiday and weekend travel ... Even the Sunday school excursion, which yesterday travelled in gaily decorated horse-drawn lorries to nearby farm or country estate, has succumbed to the lure of the bus and takes the more sophisticated modern child to the coast at Ayr, Troon or Prestwick.' While the seaside resorts benefited from this increased traffic, historic inland towns like Dunfermline were a popular alternative. The special trains put on by the railway companies attracted huge numbers – like the 4,000 Dundonians who descended on Dunfermline on a wet July evening in 1933. Catering for excursion parties gave retailers good trade, especially those owning licensed premises. In the post-Second World War years, resorts found that summer visitors were not staying for such long periods as at the beginning of the century. A steady stream of day or evening visitors, accordingly, helped to compensate for the decline in the number of long-stay visitors. For North Berwick, it was estimated in 1953 that, on any day at the height of the season, the population increased fivefold. Here and at nearby Dunbar, the character of the town was changed thereby. Until the 1920s Dunbar was considered to be a rather select holiday resort. By the 1950s, while it still attracted many visitors who stayed for a week or ten days, it had developed into a town where 'innumerable day trips come from most parts of Scotland and Northern England'. The beneficiaries from this kind of tourist stream were cafe owners, newsagents, souvenir sellers and such like.

For resort residents, though, noisy and rowdy excursionists were still a bone of contention and complaint. On the Forth, although the steamer fleet had gone, there was, in the 1950s, an increase in the number of coach parties arriving on summer Sabbath days. This led to complaints in the press and heated discussions at Kirk Presbytery meetings. Although the pubs were closed on Sundays, so-called 'bona fide' travellers were still demanding access to hotel bars. At St Andrews, where on some Sundays around 100 buses arrived, a small minority of 'drunks, rowdies and litter-louts' was held to ruin the day for other visitors and locals alike. Further west in Fife at Aberdour, the Sunday invasions were also deprecated. In addition to the noise and litter, it was considered 'that a desirable class of longer-staying visitor is kept away during the months of July and August'.

On the other hand, for the miners and their families from the grimy coal towns and villages of West Fife, Aberdour was a precious place – the 'lung' of West Fife they called it. For communities like Cowdenbeath, Kelty and Lochgelly, it was the natural place to go for picnics and day outings. When times were difficult, many folk from that area saved their pennies by walking there and back. Septuagenarian, Nellie Seivewright from Cardenden, recalled her childhood days in the mining village of Crossgates. On fine Sundays her parents put their picnic materials into the pram and the

May Day rally at Aberdour's Silver Sands around 1950, with Willie Gallacher, the Communist MP for West Fife, preaching the gospel according to Marx. The function of the naked-lady lamp-standard on the Co-operative lorry is obscure. A prize for the raffle? No red flag flies at the beach nowadays, only a much prized Seaside Award flag.

whole family walked the 3 miles to Aberdour. For their meal, her father lit a fire on the beach. After their day at the seaside, they walked back again, a stiffer 3 miles as they were now going uphill. So important was Aberdour that the Coal Industry Social Welfare Commission purchased the land adjoining the Silver Sands beach on the east side of the village. The original idea was to build a rehabilitation-cum-holiday centre at the Silver Sands. But by 1955 the Commission had dropped that plan in favour of constructing a tearoom and shelter, on the understanding that Fife County Council provided a car park, road access and other amenities. The beach shelter and shop were built but not the more fanciful suggestions, which included proposals for an open-air swimming pool. The council, for its part, did go ahead with the very considerable cost of providing access roads, car park and 'adequate sanitary facilities'. The deciding factor for the council were the traffic hazards caused by the great number of buses and cars arriving in the village. Aberdour was by no means the only seaside resort where the arrival of large numbers of motor-borne excursionists necessitated expensive change and adaptation. Nowadays, at all resorts fewer come by bus but on a fine summer day the car parks can be very busy.

CHAPTER 8

Outdoor Pursuits:
Sailing, Boating, Golf and Other Sports

The squadron of the Royal Clyde Yacht Club is a great attraction during the season, and numerous regattas are held, at which some of the finest racing by yachts of all sizes and rig is witnessed. The anchorage is crowded with as fine a pleasure fleet as is to be seen anywhere, and the place presents quite a gay and lively appearance.

Guide to Dunoon, c. 1906

The anchorage so described was at Hunter's Quay on the Holy Loch near Dunoon. In July during the early 1900s fashionable society gathered there and at other sailing centres for the so-called Clyde Fortnight. At this time, for the jet set of the day, the Clyde was a centre of yachting second only to Cowes. With some 1,000 members and over 400 yachts, the Royal Clyde at Hunter's Quay was one of the prestigious clubs. Even more upmarket was the Royal Northern, based at Rothesay. To be eligible for membership of this most exclusive of clubs, your yacht had to weigh at least eight tons and, like all similar vessels would be crewed by professional sailors. Obviously, only the very wealthy could indulge in this kind of sporting contest. For example, at the 1901 Clyde Fortnight, the large yachts included the *Meteor* and the *Shamrock*, the first owned by the Kaiser Wilhelm II and the second by multi-millionaire grocer Thomas Lipton. Lord Dunraven and the cotton magnates, the Coats and Clarks of Paisley, were other prominent yachting figures.

Some benefits percolated downward to the more humble sections of society. To handle the vast spread of canvas needed for the big yachts, a crew of at least twenty was required. For crofters from the Hebrides and local fishermen, crewing on the yachts was a valuable ancillary source of income. Yacht building and maintenance, too, was a fairly important local industry. With newspapers carrying results and detailed accounts of each event, yachting had developed into a spectator sport. Although the Clyde Fortnight was the highlight of the yachting and social season, during the summer months regattas were held at different centres and these attracted the interest of onshore and offshore spectators. These regatta races and the ostentatious display of wealth provided an unrivalled spectacle not just for the enthusiasts but also for Maw, Paw and the weans 'doon for the fair'. Not only did crowds watch from the shore but also many holidaymakers packed into steamers to follow the course of the races. Indeed in those days the starting and finishing lines were determined, in part at least, for the benefit of the onshore spectators. Some Rothesay boarding houses listed among their attractions their excellent views of the Firth and the 'Yacht Racing Course'.

For many decades the royal yacht *Britannia*, a Clyde-built cutter, was a favourite with the doon-the-watter cognoscenti. Owned by the Prince of Wales, as he was then, in 1894 it outclassed the

Vigilant, one of America's most famous yachts, in a series of races. An English journalist viewed one of the contests:

> Yacht-racing caught on in the South of England last season more than ever before but it is doubtful if a match of any sort would ever attract such a multitude of people as lined the shores on Saturday last from Kirn to Dunoon and filled the steamboats … It is true that the racing was stirring enough to have galvanised a mud engine into life, but such unbounded, delirious enthusiasm as was displayed when Britannia won we should never have expected from sober Scots folk.

Another but smaller centre where great wealth was conspicuously displayed was Tighnabruaich in the Kyles of Bute. This small summer resort, reckoned to be the most beautiful on the Clyde, had been built virtually from new by West of Scotland professionals and businessmen. Prosperous Victorian and Edwardian villa owners, served by a phalanx of servants, could relax there in comfort and comparative seclusion yet, thanks to frequent and regular steamer services, could reach their offices in under two hours. Tignabruaich formed part of a ribbon development of villas by the western shores of the 'far-famed' Kyles of Bute. In the golden age of the Clyde steamers, there were no fewer than three steamer piers along a strip, which measured a little over 2 miles. At Tighnabruaich Pier alone there could be up to twenty calls a day. In the pre-1914 days of economic wellbeing and middle-class financial confidence, yachting was, for these villa owners, thanks in part to royal patronage, a prestigious form of recreation. In the early 1900s the annual Tighnabruaich Regatta brought a large assemblage of yachts into the Kyles. Robert Ingham-Clark, the owner of Glen Caladh, the big hoose of the area, officiated as Commodore. On his 148-ton yacht *Maruja*, which was dressed overall with bunting, a band entertained his guests who included some of his important business clients. *Para Handy* author Neil Munro, writing in more conventional mode, described the stuffy formalities that were still in play at that time.

> The off-hand manners of the present day [1907] have cut a little into the reverence due to the Commodore of the fleet, but there is still a penalty for the owner so reckless of the proprieties as to join or leave the fleet without a salute to Commodore, or disregard the sunset gun with which the Commodore vessel signals the lowering of all flags and the hoisting of anchor lights.

In the harsher economic climate of the post-First World War years, the beautiful but ruinously expensive J-Class sailing giants began to disappear from the Clyde. In 1937 the Royal Northern moved to Rhu on the Gareloch nearer to Glasgow and more accessible by car and eventually in 1978 it merged with the Royal Clyde Club. The great steam yachts had long gone, too. The blast of the 1930s economic depression had sunk too many fortunes and with them these rich men's toys. For the cruising fraternity, the sheltered waters of the Clyde estuary still had many attractions. Cruisers, both motor- and sail-propelled, gave a small but welcome source of income to resort hotels and shops.

As we see from this postcard of 8-metre yachts at Tighnabruaich Regatta, racing on a smaller scale continued. Yachts of this class were 15 metres in overall length, weighed 10 tons, small beer though compared to the J-class, which weighed some 143 tons. Joyce, evidently a sporty type, who sent this card in 1938 from Tighnabruaich to a friend in Glasgow, wrote: 'Having a topping time, sailing, boating, bathing, walking, fishing, playing tennis, etc. The weather is marvellous so far, and we have all got "Riviera complexions".'

Tighnabruaich Regatta, as with many other small-town and village galas, was held during the Glasgow Fair, then the busiest time of the year for Scottish resorts.

Nevertheless, the interwar years of economic depression and the post-Second World War world of very different aspirations brought development to a halt. As in other resorts, some of the Tighnabruaich residences were converted into boarding houses. Post-1945, Glen Caladh, like many another great mansion, was demolished and the estate broken up. The house site, once the hub of a great sporting estate, became a wildlife centre fitted with hides, the camera replacing the gun. Commenting on the immediate postwar years, George Blake took a less than optimistic view of such marginal communities as Tighnabruaich and its adjacent settlements of Auchenlochan and Kames.

> These are sub-Highland places in which the urge outwards from the dark, satanic mills prompted the building of seaside villas and cottages. They have remained primitive so far as shopping facilities and all the other accepted services are concerned. They rest in lovely surroundings. In relation to the forces that created them they are, however, exhausted and remain rather as memorials to a communal urge now, not so much spent, as diverted.

Other forces, however, had come into play. Right round the shores of Scotland, on the east coast no less than the west, small boat sailing was flourishing at, for instance, North Berwick where dinghy racing had been introduced in 1929. Dinghies provided a relatively low-cost means of access to the sport. After the Second World War factory-built boats made sailing cheaper, and thus widened the spectrum of ownership. New people came into the sport, many of them quite happy to sail dinghies and other small, low-priced craft, and this brought new vigour to resorts that were feeling the challenge of overseas competition. Carnoustie is a case in point. Founded in 1960, Carnoustie Yachting Club was just one of a rash of new Scottish clubs. In 1972 it was able to obtain a lease from the town council for the former Beach Pavilion – a revealing change of function. With this building converted into a clubhouse, the Carnoustie club was able to develop facilities which enabled it to host championships and to welcome visitors 'who roll up with their dinghies in tow.' Significantly, a late Victorian guide *Carnoustie and its Neighbourhood*, while describing a number of forms of recreation available to visitors, made no mention of sailing.

Yachting holidays offered by hotels, and encouraged by organisations like the Scottish Youth Hostel Association (SYHA), helped to introduce young people to the delights of sailing, canoeing and other water sports. In addition, the Tignabruaich Sailing School, then running in co-operation with the SYHA offered a variety of courses ranging from elementary to advanced. Young people eager to take up the sport benefited from the cheap accommodation available at the village youth hostel. Although the SYHA pulled out of the area in 1998, the sailing school continues today, but now has windsurfing as an optional activity. In pre-war days the Royal Hotel at nearby Auchenlochan had supplied visiting yachtsmen with water, oil and petrol. By the 1960s the Royal too had a sailing school offering, as well as cruising options in a 12-ton sloop, sailing instruction with the chance of racing in the thrice-weekly regattas of the Kyles of Bute Sailing Club. Of the steamer piers, though, only Tignabruaich now survives. Served by local volunteers, it is an occasional port-of-call for the *Waverley*, the Clyde's last paddle steamer. In compensation, a new road by Loch Riddon, opened in 1969, made Tignabruaich more accessible for car-borne visitors and provides spectacular views of both the loch and the Kyles.

In the last decades of the twentieth century marinas and sailing schools (at Oban, Largs and Cumbrae, for example) proliferated, although in the case of Largs many residents had thought that a marina would have a detrimental effect on the area. Cumbrae hosts Scotland's National Water Sports Centre which was opened in 1976. Nor did you need to own a boat in order to sail. In the 1970s grant and loan assistance from the Scottish Tourist Board brought an increase in the number of sailing craft for charter. 'Yachties', whether cruising enthusiasts or racing buffs, help to bring new life and vitality to coastal resorts and many otherwise moribund small fishing ports in all parts of Scotland. Yet, exciting to them as their races are, they lack the drama and spectator-appeal of the big yacht contests of days of yore.

Other water-sports, like diving, water-skiing, canoeing and wind-surfing, have gained their devotees and bring a welcome modicum of trade to our seaside resorts with Largs, for example, holding the World Windsurfing Championships in 2002. The marine life and sparkling clear water have for some years enticed the diving fraternity to St Abbs in Berwickshire. At nearby Eyemouth a late 1950s guidebook informs us that water-skiing 'has also been attempted in the sheltered bay and may develop into an organised sport in the future'. From Portmahomack in the north to Portpatrick

Lochranza Pier on Arran was served by the steamer *Kintyre* en route to Campbeltown.

in the south-west similar observations, around the same time, confirm that this was a sport of recent development. Canoeing was also becoming fashionable at this time. While kayak-style canoes had been a Victorian innovation, it was only when more portable designs came on the market in the interwar years that canoeing began to enjoy a measure of popularity. At some resorts, enterprising boat hirers were quick to add canoes to their fleets. Interestingly, an abandoned outdoor bathing pool at Cellardyke in Fife now serves as a training pond for trainee canoeists.

Traditionally, for the multitude, rowing was the most popular water sport. Inshore fishermen, as well as offering trips round the bay, saw boat hiring as a lucrative form of income. While long-stay visitors might take a boat for a week or longer, Paw would hire a rowing boat for an hour or so and demonstrate his nautical skills to a wary Maw and hopefully happy weans. Board of Trade regulations ensured that boats were inspected as to their suitability, otherwise no licence could be issued. It was the Harbour Trustees who bore the responsibility for licensing Rothesay's boats (no fewer than 207 in 1886). In 1893, Burntisland Town Council, empowered by the Burgh Police (Scotland) Act, 1892, allocated licences for twenty-three rowing boats plus two sailing vessels. The conditions set down by the magistrates of Burntisland, according to the council minutes, included banning intoxicated persons and the use of boats by 'persons of both sexes for bathing together or at the same time.' Well into the twentieth century, boating remained a highly popular activity at all the resorts. At Rothesay, according to the *Bute County Directory*, there were twelve boat hirers in the town in 1923, and another four a few miles along the coast at Port Bannatyne and an equal number across the Firth at Millport. With so many hirers there was a considerable degree of competition and rivalry. For the masters of the Coast steamers, rowing boats and small motor boats, which could also be hired, were a perennial menace. Some holidaymakers played a form of maritime chicken by deliberately rowing across the bows of the steamers, forcing them to heave to or to take evasive action. In the early 1900s there were reports that, at Rothesay, some reckless young men were even gambling on the outcome, betting their friends that they would be able to stop the steamers by rowing across their course.

Angling also had its devotees and guide-books gave information as to suitable inland lochs and rivers, and, of course, at seaside resorts youthful enthusiasts could be found fishing with rod or hand-line off every pier and rock outcrop. Local seamen catered for sea anglers by providing

Sinclair's Boating Station at Dunoon.

them with lines and bait, and by taking them out to sea. Lads, whose parents had hired a boat for the holidays, fished for fun. Maurice Lindsay, in later life a notable figure in the Scottish literary scene, recalled his youthful ploys, when he and his friends spent evenings fishing in Dunoon's West Bay in the days when mackerel were still plentiful: 'It was no uncommon thing for two of us in a boat to bring back 20 or 30 mackerel as the last light sank behind the hills.' For contemporary youngsters, it would be difficult to find a rowing boat to hire not to mention there being a lot fewer fish. In the 1960s, the Scottish Tourist Board, conscious of competition hotting up, began to publish brochures giving information and charts on the best places to fish. Some seaside places began also to hold sea angling festivals including, but not exclusively, traditional resorts like Largs, Lamlash and Eyemouth. Mention, too, was made in the Scottish Tourist Board's Annual Report for 1973–74 of 'a growing provision of sea angling boats on the Moray Firth and on the Galloway coast.' Largs was described thus:

> Largs is a very popular boating centre and a gay little holiday town which caters for sea anglers. Situated on the Clyde estuary it is easily reached either by road or rail. It is within easy reach of several good fishing banks, including the Piat Shoal and the Skelmorlie patch. The local boathirers now run a comprehensive service for sea anglers.

Scotland for Sea Angling, 1972

Between the wars, hiking became something of a craze, and the resorts tried to capitalise on this new enthusiasm and an older one for cycling. Montrose guide-books of this period highlighted its convenience for cycling tours or 'pedestrian rambles' in the Grampian glens. Technological improvements and affordable bikes meant that by the 1890s cycling and touring by bike had become increasingly popular. An Argyllshire traffic census for the week beginning 8 August 1911 gives us an idea as to how numerous the cycling fraternity had become. In the Dunoon area alone, 1,807 were recorded at Innellan and 2,645 at Sandbank. Not everyone found this development to their taste. A correspondent to the *Glasgow Herald* in 1900 complained that his stay by the shores of Loch Long had been spoiled by 'furious' cyclists. These men, he bemoaned, rode in bands, scorching round

Stances for boatmen providing services for sea anglers, photographed at Ayr by the author in 1986.

corners at great speed and monopolising the narrow Highland roads. Large numbers of women took to cycling, although medical opinion was divided as to its suitability. Some American medical experts maintained that saddle pressure combined with rapid leg movement could arouse 'feelings hitherto unrealised by the young maiden'! The solution on a horse was to ride side-saddle, but on a bike that was definitely a non-starter. Some restaurants and cafes, and of course cycle shops made a point of catering for this developing market. In 1897, the proprietor of one of Stonehaven's two bike depots advertised that for cycle clubs visiting the town he could store for the day 100 cycles. Visitors arriving by public transport were always able to hire bicycles. In some resorts, cycle shops did a lot of business by hiring out bikes. A 1968 tourist survey reveals that, in the island resorts of the Firth of Clyde, there were some seventy bicycles available for hire at Rothesay, around 290 on Arran, and a rather incredible 1,000 at Millport on Great Cumbrae. Though the tourist numbers in Millport have slumped as elsewhere, in 2003 there were still three cycle hire firms operating in the town. Hiking and walking has soared in popularity. In 1970, 29 per cent of holidaymakers in Scotland listed hiking and walking as one of their activities but it is fair to assume that the traditional resorts were not major beneficiaries in this respect.

Pony trekking was a postwar innovation, which enjoyed its greatest popularity in areas like Strathspey and Badenoch where the first experiments had been carried out in 1952. But it also proved to be a popular activity in coastal resorts like Stonehaven, Dunbar and Innellan and in the tourist islands of Arran and Bute. With its spectacular high peaks and rocky ridges, it was the island of Arran, which had most appeal for outdoor enthusiasts. This varied island, 'Scotland in miniature' as some like to call it, was probably the only seaside resort which dared to produce a guide-book with, on the front cover, not a bathing belle but a picture of a hiker. This was a time when there was a craze for walking right round the island, all 60 miles of it in twenty-four hours! In the foreword to this 1930s guide, issued by the Isle of Arran Publicity Association, visitors were exhorted to bring their golf clubs, tennis things, bathing suit and walking boots. 'You will use them all,' the readers were informed. The author continued: 'We have no swing-boats but plenty of rowing-boats. We have no giant wheels or towers for seeing far. But we have hills – higher than any wheels and towers.'

Nowadays there is a round-the-island Coastal Way with specially produced map and guide and four to five days the recommended time for walking it. As, however, with an equivalent route round Bute, some of the Arran walk has to be on roads.

In some resorts, youngsters with a nautical bent but too young or unwilling to venture out to sea could indulge themselves on artificial ponds. Girvan was one resort that took pride in the extensive provision it made for holidaymakers. These included a model-yacht pond and a boating lake with dashing-looking motor boats. While they may have looked like imitation speed-boats, their speed was restricted. Nevertheless, for bairns of all ages they required less effort and were a lot more exciting than rowing boats. Some sixty years later, the boating lake remains but the motor boats have gone, replaced by pedal boats and rowing boats. As in many another resort, the Girvan ponds are situated in a park area close to the seafront, specially developed for recreational use. Dunbar Town Council, gifted a suitable piece of land, constructed sports facilities including tennis courts and putting greens, also a multi-purpose pavilion and shelter. In case of inclement weather, the pavilion's 'ample' verandahs offered sitting accommodation for sixty and standing room for at least another 100. As at other towns, Dunbar's public park was the focal point for works excursion parties who were as often as not organised into line to march from the railway station to the park. Montrose, the locals could boast, was exceptionally well-endowed with public parks and

The Boating Lake, Girvan.

There were 5,000 present at the opening event for the new Girvan Boating Lake in May 1938. Despite some Sabbatarian opposition, the council sanctioned Sunday opening. The lake, designed by a local artist, was laid out in a Willow Pattern design.

gardens, which gave it 'a colourful Arcadian appearance' and almost entirely relieved the town of 'the industrial ugliness too common in most places.' Resorts with links lands, like Burntisland and Nairn, were blessed with a natural sports ground, used most obviously for golf but also for other sports events. In both towns the links remain the arenas for their Highland Games. To ensure that the Nairn Games attracted posh visitors as well as the plebs, the date was set as the first Saturday after the 'Glorious Twelfth'. Well-to-do individuals who had come north for the grouse shooting would thus be free to attend this prestigious event. Highland games, like the Cowal Gathering in Dunoon and the Burntisland Games, had, and still have, considerable popular appeal, and thus boost the resorts' tourist economy.

Bowling greens, putting greens and tennis courts were facilities that even wee resorts sought to provide. For Cullen in Banffshire, faced with the decline of its fishing industry, the establishment in 1902 of a bowling and tennis club was of great importance in its subsequent development as a holiday resort. These facilities were subsequently extended with a new pavilion added in 1925 and two years later an extension of the tennis courts. A busy resort like Stonehaven did things on a grander scale with, in its circa 1969 heyday, able to boast of its fourteen 'well-kept hard tennis courts'. Even where clubs were private, they made a point of welcoming visitors and this was not just a consequence of financial need. Inappropriately shod visitors could cause problems at bowling greens, though. One group was spotted at Aberdour in August 1912 playing in drizzling rain in hob-nailed boots. Not surprisingly the green was reported to be in a terrible condition. Bowls then appealed mainly to the older generation, but tennis had special significance as it was a game, which brought young men and young women together and thus gave opportunities for social interaction, even better if it led to a romantic relationship. Some of the larger resorts ran tournaments which

Lady tennis players at Lundin Links in 1925. Though created as a golfing resort, tennis became popular there too.

attracted not only outside competitors but also sizeable crowds of spectators. A publicity-conscious council at St Andrews brought the Scottish Hard Courts Championship to its new Kinburn Park in 1923 and continued to support this tournament for many years thereafter. Most resorts also had to have a putting green. St Andrews Town Council built one of the earliest public courses in 1914. When the council first proposed to lay out a putting green on a site which hitherto had been used by seaside entertainers, it encountered resistance. Even though St Andrews was a golf-mad town, there were complaints, to no avail ultimately, about the 'merry pierrots' being displaced. Other towns followed suit and so popular were these facilities that, in some resorts, several putting greens were required to cope with demand. In the 1930s, Ardrossan on the Ayrshire coast for example, could boast of having no fewer than four greens. Towns held weekly putting competitions with scores and prizewinners often published in the local press. The game's popularity may be gauged by the fact that when, in June 1929, the Pittenweem green was opened for the season, a large crowd gathered for the official opening. Despite the introduction of 'crazy golf' and other novelty courses, putting greens don't attract the same number of customers nowadays and many have been closed.

With the number of golfers on a worldwide basis ever increasing, Scotland's reputation as the 'Home of Golf' is a major asset. Once a minority sport, golf had, by the 1880s, become very fashionable. One of the prestigious centres was North Berwick where, according to a Victorian guidebook: 'the Speaker of the House of Commons, the Lord Mayor of London, statesmen, archbishops, bishops, doctors of divinity, ministers of all denominations, judges, lawyers, merchants, all go to the Links when they come to North Berwick, and from spectators they almost inevitably become themselves players.' For golfing shrines like North Berwick and St Andrews, the game's popularity was a major boost, and still is, to the local economy. To meet increasing demand, additional courses were constructed. The benefits filtered down the social scale. In the 1920s unemployed men, anxious to secure casual work as caddies at North Berwick, slept rough in tents and touted for custom at the railway station.

Other places benefited from the new craze. For Lossiemouth, a guidebook author asserted that its rapid development was 'due mainly and, in the first instance, entirely to the Golf.' At Lossie such was the seasonal demand that new hotels were erected and villas to let were built next to the links. Gullane by 1912 was well on its way to becoming a miniature St Andrews. A. G. Bradley marked how Gullane had been transformed. In 1871 it had been a secluded village with a single inn, which sufficed for its handful of visiting golfers. It was 'now [in 1912] a town with a long street of shops, several hotels, and a neighbourhood covered with private houses.' After the opening of the Gullane station in 1898, a regular Saturday morning special train arrived from Edinburgh – the 'Golfers' Train' – and 'streams of motors from everywhere' brought players to the three neighbourhood courses of Gullane, Luffness and Muirfield. The holiday seasons brought stir and excitement and extra employment for young and old. Young boys ferried visitors' luggage and caddied for them on the links. Gullane also became popular with West of Scotland golfers. When in 1900 a new course was added, the *Glasgow Herald* printed a detailed hole-by-hole description of the Gullane course. From 1912 to 1930 the 'Lothian Coast Express' carried holidaymakers from Glasgow to the Lothian golf resorts. But the depression years plus the impact of the 'streams of motors' brought retrenchment which included the closure of the Gullane branch line in 1932.

When he first saw Machrihanish's 4 miles of sandy beach, dunes and machair links of springy turf, Old Tom Morris, by then a legendary figure in the world of Scottish golf, exclaimed, it is said: 'Providence meant this for a gowf-coorse.' Laid out by the St Andrews professional in 1876, this Kintyre course was within twenty years acknowledged to be 'almost world-famous'. A light railway connecting it to Campbeltown was an advantage. It was a mere twenty minutes' journey and the trains were frequent. Special trains could be arranged 'on moderate terms'. To accommodate summer residents a hotel and some villas were added. Murray's *Handbook for Scotland* (1894) considered the hotel to be good, but tourists were warned that it was 'crowded with golfers in summer'. In 1932, three years after closure of the colliery it was built to serve, the Machrihanish line was shut down. Appropriately enough, the coaches were converted into beach huts. Away to the north, another light railway had been opened to link Dornoch to the main Highland line. To further exploit the town's tourist potential, the Highland Railway Company opened a hotel. The bait, as set out in the company's adverts, was 'the most fascinating golf links in the kingdom'. By 1909 about one-third of the club's membership (by then it was the Royal Dornoch) came from London. Royal Dornoch remains, like Machrihanish, a course for golf connoisseurs.

Other railway companies sought to capitalise on the golf boom by developing their own resorts, complete with luxury hotel. Significantly, these railway company speculations were built not at any of the major resorts but instead were developed on what was, as far as tourists were concerned, virtually virgin soil. For the Glasgow & South Western Railway (GSWR), Turnberry in Ayrshire was the choice. In 1903 the company purchased a recently built course and three years later opened a luxury hotel and to serve it constructed a light railway (the Maidens and Dunure). According to *Black's Guide to Scotland* (1907), the railway ran right past the back of the hotel 'so visitors can be deposited at the very door'. The fact that this railway hotel included a garage as well as stables was a pointer to future trends. Although it never paid, the line survived until 1942, when, with fewer customers owing to the war, the branch was closed. The hotel and golf course nevertheless flourished, and Turnberry like Carnoustie, Largs, St Andrews and Troon hosts the Open Championship on a regular basis. Currently Japanese-owned, Turnberry, like other prestigious hotels, features a spa and leisure area. Not all railway company ventures succeeded, however. For the Great North of Scotland Railway (GNSR), Cruden Bay, located by Port Errol in Aberdeenshire and just thirty miles from Aberdeen, seemed to be the ideal site. In 1896 the company had opened a branch line from Ellon to the fishing village of Boddam, and this branch also served their new Cruden Bay Hotel (completed in 1898). The GNSR even provided an electric tramway meant originally to transport patrons from the station to the ninety-four-room hotel, but in the event was relegated to

Cruden Bay Hotel from the South.

Mary, who posted this postcard view of the Cruden Bay Hotel on 7 August 1915 to a lady friend in Insch, exclaimed: 'I can hardly believe myself I'm here. This is the place for mixed bathing.'

carrying luggage and laundry. An 18-hole golf course for men and a nine-hole one for ladies were the hotel's prime attractions. Like similar grand hotels, there was a wide choice of other activities on offer – bowls, tennis, croquet, boating and fishing. Then there was, of course, bathing on the beach and rather daringly for the time – mixed bathing too. The hotel, the management boasted, had not just the finest golf course in the kingdom, but also the finest air. To emphasise the resort's health quotient, hotel adverts gave the telegraphic address as 'HEALTH, PORT ERROL'. While the air may have been bracingly healthy, the same could not be said for the hotel's financial status. In 1932 the branch line was closed to passenger traffic. Occupied by the military during the Second World War, the hotel was afterwards put up for sale but finding no buyer this white elephant of a building was demolished in 1953. The golf course, nevertheless, survived as did the holiday homes in the village, which was seemingly destined to become, according to one optimistic scribe, the Brighton of Aberdeenshire. Currently, on the same stretch of coastline but nearer Aberdeen American tycoon, Donald Trump, is developing a luxurious golf resort on the Menie Estate by Balmedie. Controversially sited on a site of special scientific interest, at the time of writing only one of the two promised courses has so far been completed.

The GNSR, as did the other railway companies, played a significant role in popularising other town and village resorts. Its advertising material promoted the towns and villages of the Banff and Moray coast as the Moray Firth Riviera with the golfing facilities available among their prime attractions. In the south-west, the GSWR played a similar role with the Ayrshire golf resorts, as did the Caledonian and North British and their post-amalgamation successor companies, the LMS and LNER, in their catchment areas. The various companies made fare concessions, opened conveniently located rail halts, and put on early morning golfers' trains. As well as offering special cheap tickets, the North British Railway agreed that, when there were big tournaments at Kinghorn, express trains would halt for players. Golf club members did their bit, as at Cullen where they stressed their wee town's accessibility – just six and a half hours' train journey from Glasgow and fourteen from London. Generally, private clubs at resorts welcomed visitors. At Girvan 'you will not be long before you feel thoroughly at home', but if you sought a sterner challenge the Turnberry championship links were a mere five miles away. And there was a good motorbus service, which delivered you right to the clubhouse door. But this was the 1930s when the motoring section in the Official Guide of this 'Atlantic resort' was addressed to 'the fortunate possessor of a motor car'!

AT THE GOLF COURSE, WHITING BAY

Lady golfers at Whiting Bay golf course in Arran. While the card is dated 21 July 1919, it is an Edwardian-era photograph. Compare the skirt lengths with the shorter tennis-styles popular in 1925.

Ayrshire today can boast of the number and quality of its links courses but, in comparison with the east coast, golf was a late development. When in 1851 Old Tom Morris was enticed to Prestwick from St Andrews to be greenkeeper-cum-professional, he thought that he had made a great mistake, there being 'very little play' then. Gradually golf began to take root among the business and professional classes of the West of Scotland. By 1890 there were seven courses in the county with another seven added in the following decade. Troon, now renowned for its championship links, was comparatively late on the scene, with its first course opened in 1878. By 1910, though, there were four courses in Troon, three of them municipal. In addition to being 'the Land of Burns', Ayrshire could now lay claim to being 'the Land of Golf'. One consequence for the county, as CA Oakley remarked in 1937, was 'the establishing of many excellently equipped hotels, of a type not previously known in Scotland.'

On the Isle of Arran (population in 1891 a mere 4,766) no fewer than seven courses were constructed, most of them in the golfing boom of the 1890s. Shiskine, a 12-hole course, which dates from 1896, is on a list of the top 100 British courses.

By the early years of the twentieth century golf's popularity had expanded to a remarkable degree, so much so that we find even the *Girl's Own Paper* giving advice on the care of golf clubs. To keep rust off a man's golf clubs, young readers, patronisingly regarded as wives of the future, were instructed to rub the steel heads with Vaseline! One hopes that golfers remembered to remove the Vaseline before striking the ball. By that time, a resort without a decent golf course was at a considerable disadvantage. All over the country, course construction was virtually a growth industry, with big centres and tiny villages all competing for the custom of the golfing tourist. When the golfing visitor was male, then the gains were compounded since invariably the married man was accompanied by his family who, if they didn't take to golf themselves, found alternative means of entertainment.

Aberdour in Fife was one resort where development lagged because, unlike so many other Fife and Lothian seaside resorts, it lacked its own course. A club was formed in 1896 for, it was claimed, the benefit of residents and summer visitors alike and, with funds raised through a bazaar, a 9-hole course was constructed. Unfortunately, after a few years, the farmer from whom the ground was leased needed the land back, thus taking the club back to square one. By 1905, though, the club had found another site on part of the estate of the Earl of Moray. The Moray estate stipulated, however,

1 The Concert Hall at Portobello's Marine Gardens had been built originally for the Scottish National Exhibition of 1908. This was just one of the site's many attractions.

2 Doon the Watter by train – a typical example of the down-to-earth humour favoured by Glasgow postcard publisher Millar & Lang.

I AM COMING HOME FROM DUNOON

3 The cartoonist has depicted a 'Summer Girl' departing, leaving behind many distraught suitors.

4 Elie was from early days, and so remains, a favourite resort of the Edinburgh bourgeoisie. Donkey and pony rides on the sands had a long tradition there.

5 The comic postcards of the day reflected the more free-and-easy sexual climate to be found at popular resorts. In some towns the more suggestive ones were banned. But there was no problem with this card posted at Saltcoats in August 1919 by Mary, who informed Delia in Maryhill that there were 'plenty of clicks (boyfriends) here'.

6 In this artist-drawn card posted in 1926, a bathing belle displays a stylish costume, while the ogling gents queue to hire bathing costumes and towels. One shilling for the hire of a bathing machine would have been rather expensive.

7 Annie who posted this card in Millport in July 1923 simply wrote, maybe disappointedly, 'Some hopes'! This is the kind of postcard that could be used for any seaside town by just stamping on the appropriate name.

8 Aberdeen Corporation publicity brochure of the early 1950s confidently pronouncing that it was Scotland's leading holiday resort.

9 While this Peterhead guidebook of *c.* 1938 has a stylish cover, its contents are uninspired. One wonders how many holidaymakers really wanted to know the names of the town's Provost and Bailies.

10 The Shell Bus at Leven, here shown in a 1935 Valentine postcard, was put on site in 1927 along with buildings that were covered with buckies (shells). In later years, this old Leyland bus was almost entirely encrusted with shells. A small menagerie in the grounds added to its curiosity value. A bungalow now occupies the site.

11 An Edwardian period view of the al fresco tearoom at Ettrick Bay, Isle of Bute. Note the extremely solid furniture. The brick building was the toilet block.

12 Donkey carriage at Ettrick Bay. The hooded girl on the left was tending the donkey. This card was posted on 27 July 1914. Eight days later, Britain went to war with Germany.

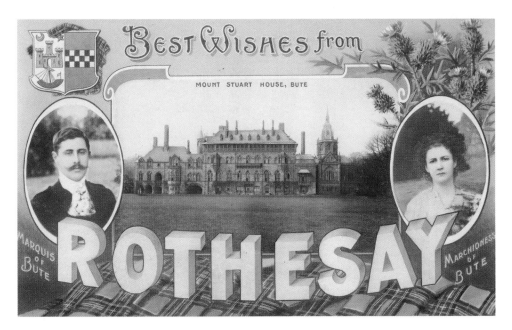

13 Mount Stuart, the Bute family residence, was featured on many postcards. Also portrayed here are the 4th Marquis and Marchioness. Mount Stuart is now open to the public.

14 In the days when cars and motor lorries were few, cycling became incredibly popular.

15 Young prizewinners at a North Berwick swimming gala in 1958. One of the winners is holding her prize – a briefcase! Once the race had been completed, the competitors had to parade round the pool. It looked to be just the night for a chitterin bite and the obligatory mug of Bovril.

16 Cover for the 1908 guide *Caledonian Excursions*, featuring a yellow-funneled 'Caley' steamer and the company's two mainland termini, at Wemyss Bay and Gourock.

a lady was looking at Mrs A's rooms to days for Mrs Dixon for September

Old Stone Pier, Aberdour. *April 15th 1906*

17 The crowds on the pier and on the steamer, the *Lord Morton*, show how popular Aberdour was as a destination. It was a regatta day, which explains why a crowd is lined along the harbour wall. The rowing boats in the harbour were hired out by the hour.

SCENE: The dining-saloon of a steamer on the Clyde.
Voice from above: "Come up, Jock, come up! Here's the Kyles of Bute!"
Jock: "Deil tak' the Kyles o' Bute! D'ye think I'm gaun tae spoil ma holidays wi' scenery!"

18 The caption from this card reads as follows:
'SCENE: The dining saloon of a steamer on the Clyde.
Voice from above: "Come up Jock, come up! Here's the Kyles of Bute!"
Jock: "Deil tak' the Kyles of Bute! D'ye think I'm gaun tae spoil ma holidays wi' scenery!"'

19 This postcard is another example of the kind of cheeky cartoons published by Glasgow firm Millar & Lang. Overindulgence in alcohol did lead to a lot of trouble in the resorts.

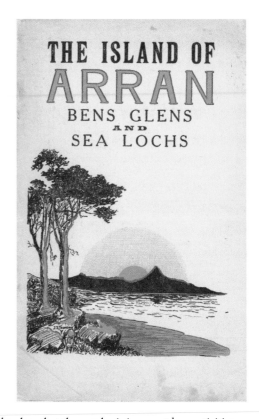

20 These covers from 1930s Arran guidebooks make clear that the emphasis is on outdoor activities.

SOUVENIR PROGRAMME 1957

21 At its peak, Dunoon's Cowal Highland Gathering attracted around 30,000 spectators. After a shaky start, the games were re-established in 1900. In that year, the highlight was the jump, from a balloon, by a lady parachutist. As a spectator event, it continues to enjoy great popularity.

22 Passengers landing from the steamers at Campbeltown Pier could go right into the carriages of the Campbeltown & Machrihanish Light Railway – an integrated transport system they call it nowadays. The railway opened on 25 August 1906 and in the first three weeks no fewer than 10,000 passengers were carried.

23 Kinghorn was only one of many courses in Fife that proved to be popular with visitors from Edinburgh and elsewhere.

24 This kind of jokey postcard (posted at Carnoustie in July 1913) was very popular, maybe because there was a germ of truth in them.

25 At the beginning of the twentieth century, a frequent and fast steamer service meant that holidaymakers going to Arran were well served.

26 St Andrews Grand Hotel as it was in 1906. As the Hamilton Grand, it now houses luxury apartments for visiting golfers. This was an advertisement card informing potential customers that the hotel was now under new management and had undergone extensive alterations. There was an electric lift and electric lighting throughout.

27 It's thumbs up for Aberdeen – ideal for a family holiday, with the sun shining on its golden sands and blue sea and obligatory Scottie dog, otherwise known as the Aberdeen terrier.

28 For this 1958 Scottish railway guide, British Rail featured a young couple of the age group who, more informally dressed, would soon be forsaking domestic holiday haunts for more exotic locations.

29 Stonehaven outdoor swimming pool, photographed by the author on a warm day in July 2003.

30 Cartoon – We are just leaving.

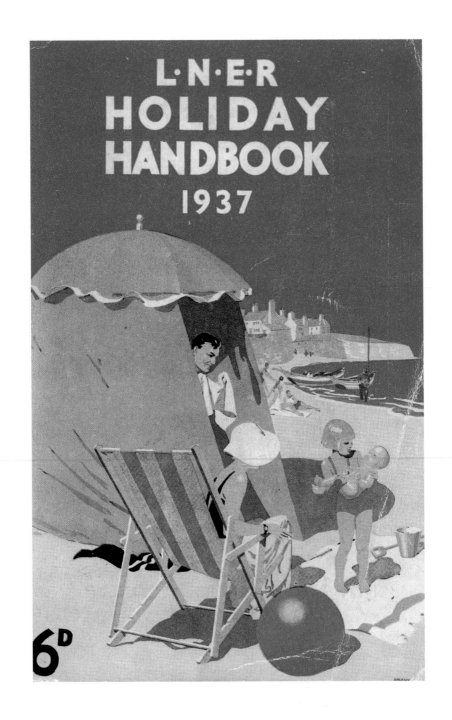

L·N·E·R
HOLIDAY
HANDBOOK
1937

6ᴰ

that the fairways be at least 50 yards from the carriage-way that led to Donibristle House, the earl's mansion. Nor could any member venture on to this carriage-way to search for a lost ball. A local newspaper nevertheless commented, 'The course will add greatly to the attraction of Aberdour as a holiday and health resort.' Since once the new course was in operation a very large proportion of the membership came from Edinburgh, it proved to be an accurate forecast. It was the same at the nearby Burntisland and Kinghorn clubs, which also drew many of their members from the capital, their access eased by the better rail connection following the completion of the Forth Railway Bridge in 1890. In the following decade, there were 234 applications for membership of the Kinghorn Golf Club. Of the applicants, no fewer than 135 had addresses in Edinburgh.

It was a similar pattern in the west, where we find that Millport Golf Club was actually established in Glasgow in 1888. Significantly, women from the middle and upper classes were taking to golf in ever increasing numbers. At Aberdour, when the club was formed in 1896, the membership comprised sixty-two men, sixteen ladies and three youths. Sixteen years later the women, ninety-four of them, outnumbered the combined total of men and youths by two. Lundin Links in Fife was one of the places where a ladies' course was constructed, mainly it seems to reduce pressure on the links where men played. The Lundin Ladies Golf Club, formed in 1891, continues to this day, maintaining its policy of banning men from its admittedly constricted clubhouse but welcoming them to the course itself.

In Victorian Scotland, playing any kind of sport or game on the Sabbath day was deeply deprecated. Sunday play only began to creep in very gradually. In the Kyles of Bute in the 1930s, there was no golfing, or boating either, on the Sabbath and even taking the car out for a Sunday run was frowned on by the stuffier locals. On private courses, however, well-heeled golfers could cock a snook at Victorian conventions. As we see from these extracts from an Aberdeen businessman's diary, one such course was at the railway-owned Cruden Bay Hotel.

Sunday 12 March 1899.
We played golf, and shocked the natives a bit I expect. I started well but did not keep it up and was over 90.

Sunday 15 April 1899
After the people had gone to church Jas Duncan and I started our great match for £1 ... After lunch Henry and I played James Duncan and George Simpson and halved after a splendid match. Good golf. We played poker in the evening and I kept up my victorious career.
[*Great North Review* Vol. 40 No. 156 Feb 2003]

Such desecration of the Sabbath was criticised by the unco guid. One newspaper reporter retorted that people would be 'just as well employed in playing golf on Sundays as loafing about church doors and annoying worshippers as they are complained of doing in Aberdeen'. When a few bold golfers also broke the Sabbath at the Shandon Hydropathic course on the Gareloch, there were more complaints. One critic, a regular visitor to hydros, declared in the *Glasgow Herald* in 1900 that he 'wouldn't dream of going to one where the Sabbath is openly desecrated'. The Sabbath-breaking golfers were defended by another correspondent, who pointed out that the course was on a hillside well away from habitations and that, at any rate, it was a 'wholesome, harmless game'. At nearby Helensburgh, the local club introduced Sunday play in 1926 and, as elsewhere, had to face a storm of Sabbatarian protest. There were similar denunciations when, in 1932, the members of Prestwick

Golf Club voted to introduce Sunday golf. However, by that time there was Sunday play at a large number of courses. Burrow's *Guide to the Scottish Highlands, c.* 1930, gives a list of 'Some Highland Golf Links'. In this list, covering roughly Scotland north of the Forth, there were no fewer than thirty-three golf courses where Sunday play was permitted, three, admittedly, in the afternoons only. Aberdour, Banff, Lossiemouth, Monifieth, and Stonehaven were among the seaside places listed.

Where courses were municipally owned, change was a lot slower. The situation at Prestwick exemplified the split between municipal and private. The town's 1936 official guide lists five courses. At the three private ones Sunday play was permitted, but it was the opposite case at the two municipal courses. At Kinghorn in Fife the town council rejected a plea for Sunday golf. As one councillor said, 'The golfers have it for six days in the week; let the public, who want to walk on it, have it for one day.' The council had a point as the land had been bought by the council as public parkland. It took another seventeen years for the veto to be reversed. St Andrews Town Council reluctantly sanctioned Sunday golf in 1948 but only after a plebiscite and for the peak summer months only. Two years later, following pressure from local tourist interests, all-the-year-round play was sanctioned, but for only one of the town's four courses. At North Berwick, hotel interests also pressed for Sunday play but seemingly there were legal difficulties and Sunday golf did not arrive there till 1958. The local defenders of the Sabbath, long bothered by the unwelcome presence of Sunday trippers, regarded Sunday golfers 'as an aggravation of an already unsolved problem'. But the barriers were coming down and, as attitudes changed, Sunday play became generally acceptable.

In the early twentieth century the railway companies played an important part in promoting the game, but now that role has fallen to Visit Scotland and local tourist bodies, with assistance from the Scottish Golf Union and commercial sponsors. From its earliest days, the Scottish Tourist Board promoted special interest holidays. In 1970 it published *Scotland Home of Golf* and that duly became an annual publication. While inland centres, like Gleneagles, also benefited, seaside resorts gained a great deal from the burgeoning interest in golf. When, for instance, the Open Championship circus arrives in town, quite ordinary properties can be let for outrageous sums. With the Open held more often than not on Scottish links courses, the benefit, both short-term and long-term, to towns like Troon and Carnoustie cannot be underestimated. A number of new courses have been built to meet increasing demand, especially from overseas. Not all these new ventures have met with local approval. A large-scale golf, leisure and hotel development, the St Andrews Bay Golf Resort and Spa, was criticised by locals for being intrusive and spoiling an area of great landscape value. Ramblers, following Fife's vaunted coastal path, were also opposed. They pointed not only to the loss of amenity but also to the hazards posed by wayward golf balls. Despite fierce local opposition, Fife Council gave it the go-ahead. Local hackles were raised again when, in 2003, the St Andrews Links Trust announced plans to construct a seventh course. According to one critic, St Andrews was becoming 'Disneyfied'. However, at the same time golf tourism was estimated to be worth £100 million to the Scottish economy. Although the resort beaches, the rare heat wave excepted, have been deserted, the golf links have usually been quite busy. Although other countries like Ireland and Spain are providing real competition, Scotland can still boast of being the Home of Golf.

CHAPTER 9

Rooms To Let:
From Seaside Landladies to Grand Hotels

In search o' ludgins we did slide
Tae find a place whaur we could bide.
There was eighty-twa o' us inside
A single end in Rothesay-o.

This comic verse from a Glasgow street song is obviously a caricature, but there is an element of truth in it. For post-Second World War Saltcoats, we are told: 'There are stories (no doubt exaggerated) of as many as 12 persons of both sexes crowding into a two apartment house, and possibly sharing a single lavatory with the occupants of other overcrowded dwellings.' City folk, accustomed to living in a single-end (a one-roomed dwelling), were content to squeeze into equally cramped accommodation, which usually meant one room or maybe even just part of a room with a sheet hung up as a divider. Coast landladies, moreover, needing every extra pound they could make, were ready to squash them in. Mrs Mary Miller lived in Rothesay in a flat with one room and kitchen plus an outside toilet but, like many another local, let part of her house each summer. In *Rothesay's Yesterdays* she related:

Each summer we moved into the room and let the kitchen. We hung a printed card up on the window. This read 'Kitchen to let, one bed'. A couple was preferred and they had to supply their own sheets. It was £5 for the [Glasgow] Fair fortnight. We also got the same for the Paisley Fair, which was the first fortnight in August and we could get maybe £4 for the first fortnight in July which was the Greenock Fair; if lucky we might get £2 for a fortnight in June. An errl [a deposit] of £1 was taken which was non-returnable. Wicker hampers were sent in advance with clothes and foodstuffs for the fortnight.

Since their visitors had sole occupancy of the kitchen, the owners were not supposed to enter it. This entailed the Millers having to fetch their water from the washhouse. If, however, their visitors were out, they would fill their pail from the kitchen sink. For cooking, all they had was a small gas ring in their room. It was vital to keep a sharp eye open in case their visitors tried to sneak in friends who would then sleep on the kitchen floor. Luckily, in the outside lavatory door there was a small hole, which was, Mrs Miller added, a good vantage point for spotting strangers. It was common, during the Glasgow Fair, for folk to arrive off the steamers and find nowhere to stay. But for them, as we have already noted, there was always the Skeoch Wood as a last resort (first choice, however, in some cases). At busy times, the 'Hotel-de-Skeoch' or 'Coast Hotel of the Beautiful Star', as it was facetiously called, could be filled with men, women and indeed whole families.

For more affluent holidaymakers, there were, in many holiday towns and villages, villas and blocks of flats built by speculators for summer-letting, the best of them, as a late Victorian guidebook asserted, 'filled with the most ample appliances for health and comfort'. In the early 1900s such dwellings were usually let for a month and even two or three months at a time to middle-class visitors, whose names and addresses were printed in the local newspaper's weekly Visitors' List. Well-to-do families sent a lot of luggage in advance: spare clothing, towels, tablecloths, sheets and pillowcases. Taking your own bedclothes ensured that they were clean and lessened the chance of acquiring fleas. While mother and her children, and household servants if any, stayed for the entire holiday period, the father, except for a short break, generally stayed on in the city, returning to the resort for weekends. While visitors may have taken a lot of linen with them, they purchased their foodstuffs locally. That could mean good business for local shopkeepers. Some also diversified into providing lists of furnished houses and apartments to let.

When the summer visitors arrived, the house owners who had let out their properties moved in with relatives or crammed themselves and their families into one room or into their 'back house', which could be a garden hut or annex. At Kames in the Kyles of Bute, when the summer visitors arrived, the Tarbet family moved into their 'Wee Hoose':

> This was a one-room building with a porch. There was a fire at one end where there was a cupboard and a table. At the other end was a double bed and bunk beds and I think there was a curtain which could be pulled across. We used one of the outdoor toilets and water had to be carried from the wash-house to the porch where it was kept in white enamel pails. Lighting was by oil lamps and cooking was done on a primus stove. This was no different from the main house, except that in the winter a lot of the cooking was done on the kitchen fire or in the oven.

In the *Scots Magazine* (April 1980), Ravey Sillars gave a graphic picture of the hard work involved in 1930s Lamlash for the annual flitting of the family's household goods from the front house to the back house. The letting house and its furnishings had to be thoroughly cleaned, scrubbed and polished. The rooms were papered and painted and 'new rugs were bought (to be paid for in the autumn) and windows embellished with fresh net curtains'. The reward was the grand sum of £8 or £10. 'For the loan of a seaside cottage, cleaner than clean, in the month of July – just two fivers!'

Ravey Sillars was describing a period in the history of Arran when the landowners had a more liberal attitude to house letting. Due to feudal restraints imposed on estate tenants by the main landlords, the Hamilton family, there had been a shortage of holiday accommodation on the island. A mid-Victorian tourist was shocked. 'Such a place I never saw. The Duke of Hamilton, who is proprietor of the island, will not let the people build houses for strangers. Nearly all the present dwellings are huts, and yet they fetch enormous rents, the accommodation is so very scarce and so many strangers resort to the island in the summer.' Occupants of estate properties were not allowed to take in holidaymakers and other tenants had to ca canny over the number of visitors they could accommodate. Only, when some tenants had become so poverty-stricken that they would probably have had to go on the hated poor roll, and the scanty payments that they might have received would have been at the landowners' expense, were they at long last allowed to take in lodgers. Even then there was a catch, with the tenants finding they had to pay extra rent for the privilege.

The death in 1895 of the 12th Duke of Hamilton inaugurated a new era in Arran. Although the last limitations were not removed till 1913, from 1895 tenants met with fewer restrictions. With feus more readily available, wealthy outsiders, and some locals too, built new houses or improved existing ones. Boosted by the building of new steamer piers and, in consequence, much better and more frequent services, east coast villages like Brodick, Lamlash and Whiting Bay enjoyed a period of rapid growth. Though the overall population was declining, new shops, holiday villas and hotels were erected. Even so, much of the accommodation available was of the most basic type. Nevertheless, Arran enjoyed a large measure of social prestige and was particularly popular with outdoor types, some of whom perhaps, like H. V. Morton, an early 1930s English travel writer, approved of the Hamiltons' 'firm hand' and wanted the island to remain a place for 'discerning' visitors. If, Morton wrote, the island had 'fallen into the clutch of speculators whose idea of beauty is a swing-boat and a full till' the island would then have been a place to avoid. 'So many harsh things,' he added, 'are said now and then in Scotland about landowners that I think it only fair to suggest that all those who love the beauty of Scotland owe gratitude to the owners of Arran for their policy of undevelopment.' The 'undevelopment' of the island did not include the safeguarding of the Gaelic language. Whereas in 1911, 20.7 per cent of the Arran population spoke Gaelic, the proportion by 1951 was as low as 3.4 per cent, a mere 107 of the then population of 3,158.

For the West of Scotland bourgeoisie the island was a cult resort and for the younger generation, the 'Arran set', a potential marriage bureau. Although there was a considerable element of snobbery (Whiting Bay was for many years regarded as having more social tone than the other villages), simple, indeed often primitive, Arran villages had their own devotees. Many visitors returning to the same place, often to the same accommodation year after year, developed relationships with the local residents and with other regular visitors. In the less populated west side of the island, George Blake noted how the regular summer visitors formed what amounted to a local improvement association – a club more powerful than anything that the natives could muster. Come the end of the season, though, the native Arranites were able to reclaim their island.

For holidaymakers, finding good accommodation was a bit of a lottery, except for folk who were happy to return to the same place and the same lodgings year after year. Prospective visitors would have studied the newspaper advertisements or would have written to an agent, usually a resort shopkeeper, for a copy of his letting lists or, if living close at hand, go on a reconnaissance trip. Some guidebooks included accommodation lists – as, for example, the 1904 edition of the *Pictorial Guide to Aberdeen*, which provided a 'Descriptive List of Private Lodgings'. There are sixty-five names in the list – all women, the archetypal seaside landlady! Most were, or had been, married with just 26 per cent unmarried, and they had over 270 bedrooms to fill. Having a piano was a plus point, with six of the lodgings supplied with that amenity. Nearly half the lodgings on this list had bathrooms, but the largest establishment, with twenty-one bedrooms, had neither bathroom nor a sitting room. It is certain that Aberdeen, like other resorts, would have had a lot of back street lodgings with no bathroom and just a basic outside loo. It is not stated but

Carnoustie High Street; observe the house agent's sign.

some of these Aberdeen landladies would have confined themselves to letting. Others would have given a fuller service, either 'full board' or what was termed 'attendance', which included cooking the food their visitors had purchased for themselves. After the First World War, in all resorts, quite a number of the large letting houses were put up for sale. As more affluent holidaymakers were now opting for full board, many of these large residences were converted into boarding houses. In Ayr (*c.* 1936) the Official Guide listed thirty-two boarding houses, including two girls' hostels, and ninety-one private apartments (hotels were individually advertised). Whether boarding house or private apartments, virtually all were seemingly run by women. One of the Ayr boarding establishments served kosher food only.

Unfortunately, the traditional seaside landlady had a poor public image. A favourite subject for seaside humour, she was the butt of the comic picture postcard artist and of the variety show comedian. A favourite old gag with the stage comics tells how the posher visitors always took their holidays in June because the sheets in the bedroom were still clean at that stage. Evelyn Cowan tells the story of the Rothesay landlady who bought new blankets for her cats' baskets. The old ones she removed from the baskets and put them on the beds of the holiday lodgers. No wonder that the comic song, which introduces this chapter, continues 'and woke half a million fleas in a single end in Rothesay-O'. One customer who had encountered some mean and grasping landladies got her revenge with an article headlined 'Holidays I'd Like to Forget' (*Sunday Mail*, 23 May 1937). While she accepted that they had their problems, the writer, a Mrs D. L. Murray, assailed the 'Coast Landladies' for providing uncomfortable and sometimes verminous beds and utterly foul meals. 'The butter is the cheapest,' she complained, 'the bread is tough ... the soup is made of stuff that tastes of cardboard, the meat is tough and the fish gluey.' On the other hand, some visitors were more trouble than they were worth, their peccadilloes causing all manner of grief. It was not uncommon for city folk to book rooms for maybe four persons then turn up with a large tribe of weans.

Catering for holidaymakers could indeed be a desperately hard occupation for women who were often elderly widows. *The Trials of a Seaside Landlady*, although a work of fiction, gives pointers to the precarious nature of this occupation. 'Mirren Tate', the fictional Clyde Coast landlady of this *c.* 1900 comic story, offered her 'saut-water' (salt water) summer visitors her parlour and adjacent bedroom and a wee closet for one month for £6 and 10 shillings, providing attendance but no board. A widow, she hoped to make enough over the summer season to maintain herself and pay her rent. If she failed, the alternative, she averred, was the workhouse. The point is jokingly made, but for some elderly widows the poorhouse was a real enough threat. It was often a struggle to survive. For Mirren, 'Hoose-lettin to saut-water folk' is 'naithing but toil an' trauchle, trauchle an' toil, wi' niver a look-up, or a meenit to ca' yer ain ... Crack aboot public servants! I wad like to ken wha's a better servant o' the public nor the coast lan'lady. She belangs to a patient, thrifty, hard-workin', an', as a rule, sober section o' the community, an' ane wham it cud ill affoord to dispense wi'.'

Boarding house landladies who ran their premises on semi-military lines were jokingly likened to concentration camp commanders. Nevertheless, in establishments operating, for reasons of economy, with limited space and few staff, some degree of organisation and regimentation was perhaps necessary. Inadequate facilities meant that the morning queue for bathroom and loo was one of the drawbacks of 1950s boarding-house life. During the 1930s and 1940s, however, washbasins were installed in the bedrooms of the better houses. By the 1950s some proprietors were adding a cocktail bar for their guests and upgrading to licensed, private hotel status, and increasingly they were being run by couples. Even the name boarding house went out of fashion, with guesthouse becoming the preferred alternative. Whatever it was called, a good establishment drew its customers back year after year. For seven successive years from the 1940s into the 1950s,

Walter Hutchison, now of Dunfermline, went with his pals from Glasgow to the same boarding house in Stonehaven. Miss Napier, the proprietor of 'Garron View', his boarding house, could, he told the author, provide three meals a day for some ninety people by using a three-sitting system. Since 'Garron View' couldn't accommodate all ninety, some of the diners had to 'sleep out' in nearby private houses. For the evening meal, high tea was the norm with biscuits and tea served at late supper. Only the larger hotels where the toffs stayed served dinner in the evenings.

Since most guests arrived by train, they didn't move far from the boarding house, so, except maybe for the odd bus excursion, they returned for all their meals which, incidentally, meant hard work for the staff. Walter Hutchison and his Glasgow companions spent their days playing football, golf, tennis, and swimming. Evenings they spent at the dances 'checking out the local talent'. The midnight swimming galas at the open-air swimming pool were other 'must attend' occasions. Since guests usually stayed for a week or longer, there was time for a degree of camaraderie and group solidarity to develop. If there was space for a putting green on the lawn, house competitions were held and hotly contested. Walter Hutchison and his pals also used to challenge the older guests at their favourite sport – bowls. At the end of the holiday, in many boarding houses a group photograph was taken and that became a valued holiday souvenir.

Catering for summer visitors was usually done for financial reasons. Mrs Nancy Burgess got into the trade because having a large house (six bedrooms, two public) facing the sea at the Argyllshire resort of Machrihanish meant she had to endure a constant stream of friends and relatives wanting a cheap holiday. Staying with relations and distant friends, it may be said, was the only way very many people could afford a holiday. But, feeling that she was being taken advantage of, Mrs Burgess decided that she might as well make a business of it, as she did very efficiently from the late 1940s till *c.* 1958. Fortunately, she was very sociable and loved cooking since like many landladies in those days, she provided full board. The guests enjoyed a cooked breakfast, dinner at midday (the main meal), high tea including home bakes, and supper at 9 p.m. with more home bakes. At seven guineas (seven pounds seven shillings) a week, daughter Carol McNeill reckoned it to be very good value and, as most of her visitors came back year after year, they must have concurred. Everything was very informal. There were no rules, though late coming for meals was not encouraged. There were no keys for the bedrooms and no front door keys issued either. Mother did all the cooking with two

Like this Arran boarding house, quite a few of these establishments had a putting green for the use of their guests. The cigarette machine would have been a little money-spinner for the proprietor. In the postcard, which is dated 13 June 1939, the writer was having a great time. The forty people in the house were 'a cheery crowd'.

local ladies coming in to do the cleaning. Young Carol helped too and the money she earned during her school holidays bought her a typewriter – very important for a budding writer. To free up the bedrooms for use by visitors, Carol moved into a maid's room, which adjoined the kitchen, while her parents occupied the second of these tiny rooms. For such a large household, there was but one bathroom plus a toilet/cloakroom beside the front door. As in other golfing resorts, while the males went to the links, mother took the children to the beach. When it was very wet, they stayed inside and played cards and board games. One visitor, Carol recalled, entertained them with card tricks. There was also putting and crazy golf on the front lawn. With most of her school friends living in Campbeltown, Carol enjoyed having the visitors' children to play with. She made money off them too, she confessed, by buying dolly mixtures in bulk and selling them to the other children in small bags of ten! As for her father, who held down a very responsible post, he complained, perhaps only semi-jocularly, Carol said, that he didn't get a civil word from his wife till the season ended.

In earlier days, various voluntary bodies and organisations, like Churches and trade unions, had established holiday and convalescent homes in a number of resorts. For high-minded young people there were the Young Men's Christian Association (YMCA) camps and holiday homes. Their feminine equivalent, the YWCA, had a holiday home in Rothesay where, just before the First World War, young working women could be accommodated at prices which, from 15 shillings per week, were considerably cheaper than most boarding houses. The West of Scotland Convalescent Homes in Dunoon was a fairly typical charitable foundation. Founded in 1869 through 'the energy and philanthropy' of the people of Glasgow, it was established 'for the purpose of affording sea-air, bathing, and repose to invalids whose circumstances prevent them regaining in any other way the health and strength necessary to resume work'. Applicants, though, had to be recommended by a donor or subscriber. There were quite a few organisations catering for sick and needy children. In Edinburgh, in 1905, the Directors of the Free

Group photograph, all male except for the matron, at the Railway Convalescent Home at Ascog by Rothesay. The home was a substantial building set in its own grounds and had the obligatory putting green. It was one of a number of similar establishments set up by the Railway Convalescent Home Society, which was formed in 1899. One patient, writing home in July 1931, had been given a week's extension, but he felt that his stay was doing him some good.

Breakfast Mission opened holiday homes in Kinghorn to give the children of the Mission a fortnight's holiday by the sea. They were later taken over by the Church of Scotland for the same purpose, but are now privately owned. With homes at Prestwick, Rothesay, Saltcoats and Maybole, the Glasgow Poor Children's Fresh-Air Fortnight was one of the largest of these organisations. Each year thousands of needy children, and many mothers too, were sent to their convalescent and hospital homes. For the stunted, undernourished weans of the early twentieth-century Glasgow slums, these 'fresh air fortnights' afforded a welcome respite. A stay at the homes, wrote a *Glasgow Herald* correspondent in July 1900, 'with their cool and invigorating ocean and upland breezes, nourishing food, and good medical care and nursing has saved many a little life that would have succumbed in the foul and stifling air of our city slums, beside furnishing to many a poor, tired mother a brief season of rest'. This charity survived until the 1970s, a time when many of the old-style holiday homes were being closed. The West of Scotland Convalescent Homes in Dunoon, for instance, were demolished in 1973. Nevertheless, a number of charities still maintain seaside-based convalescent homes. The CLIC Sargent Cancer Care for Children Fund, for instance, upholds this worthy tradition. This charity's Malcolm Sargent House in Prestwick, opened in 1989, gives families from across the UK the experience of short breaks away from the stress of a hospital environment. In their seafront play garden young cancer victims can whizz round the home's pedal car racetrack and indulge in other holiday joys. Also, the Glasgow Children's Holiday Scheme maintains the Fresh-Air Fortnight tradition. As well as having family caravans at Wemyss Bay, the organisers of this scheme rely on volunteer families taking children into their own homes. Other volunteers escort the children to their holiday destinations.

From the 1960s onward, changed holiday patterns – with holidaymakers opting for touring holidays or self-catering flats or caravans – heralded the end for the traditional boarding house. Some proprietors changed with the times, applying for drinks licences and, helped by loans and grants from the Scottish Tourist Board and Highlands and Islands Development Board, installing ensuite facilities. Their guests, now much more mobile, were travelling out and about much more during the day and therefore coming back later in the evening. Proprietors switched from providing high tea at 5.30 or 6 p.m. to serving dinner at a later hour in the evening. More owners, with the difficulty of finding domestic help an additional burden, preferred to confine themselves to the Bed and Breakfast short-stay market. Extra taxation burdens didn't help. Taxes like SET (Selective Employment Tax), introduced in 1966, and then VAT in 1973, which replaced it, were found to be onerous. New fire regulations introduced in 1971, though necessary, were an even greater burden. Many owners, already losing trade, just could not afford the cost of upgrading their accommodation. While some guest houses owners just closed their doors, others divided their property into self-catering flats, since the Fire Precautions Act did not apply to that sector. At any rate, holidaymakers valued the greater freedom of self-catering and the end of confining restrictions. You could even live on the cheap by cramming into a little room or attic in a backstreet tenement. There, you might find, as Anita Walker said of Arbroath, a few young lads sleeping on a floor, who 'probably existed on a tin of beans for the week' but still had a whale of a time. As the numbers slump continued, hotels and boarding houses were shut down. In Lundin Links in Fife the last big boarding house closed in 1980. The 1970s enthusiasm for cheap foreign holidays, we are told, was the last straw. Those who still opted for the traditional week- or fortnight-long holiday now preferred to stay in a flat or chalet or static caravan. Since, however, motoring holidaymakers tended to carry their own supplies, the switch to self-catering did not necessarily help local traders.

The accommodation situation has changed in other ways. In many small towns and villages, outsiders now own an undue number of properties. This is by no means a new phenomenon as, between the wars when houses were going cheap, a number of people in Central Scotland bought up holiday houses, mainly tenement flats, in towns like Rothesay. In *c.* 1951 Millport, for instance, there were 1,500 rateable properties, and over 500 of these were used solely for holiday purposes. In the post-war years from the 1950s onward, in moribund fishing villages, like Pennan and Collieston in Aberdeenshire, derelict properties were purchased and renovated for use as holiday homes, and likewise some good properties too. Arran and the East Neuk of Fife are among the other areas so affected. Elie, with 942 inhabitants in 2001, possessed no fewer than 765 dwellings but 261 (34 per cent) of them were either second residences or holiday accommodation. The result is that a large number of houses stand empty for a great part of the year. Such a marked increase in the number of second homes can mean a population imbalance and can create conflicts of interest. Too often the indigenous working population simply can't compete when house prices begin to soar. Also, the character of the more desirable small towns can change very markedly according to season. While during the holiday months they may come to life, in the off-season some places risk being turned into ghost villages.

As for the grand hotels, the post-war years saw many of them close their doors. In St Andrews, the Grand Hotel, once patronised by the upper echelons of society but now in a decrepit condition, was put up for sale. An offer by the Roman Catholic Church to buy it for conversion into a Training College outraged ultra-Protestants. A successful counter offer by the University of St Andrews, which resulted in the hotel becoming a students' hostel, also aroused local ire. The local Hotelkeepers and Boarding-House Keepers Association opposed this and similar purchases by the University since they would be to the detriment of the town's appeal as a holiday centre. The wheel is turning again, however, as the University has sold this hostel and the former Grand Hotel has been converted into luxury timeshare apartments, designed to appeal to wealthy visiting golfers. At the time, though, the loss of large hotels, like Port Bannatyne's Kyles of Bute Hydro, which closed in the 1970s, had a detrimental effect on resorts' ability to cater for the increasingly important conference market. The surviving large establishments depend very largely on the trade provided by the big coach companies. The hotels serve as a base for their short three- or four-day coaching holidays. As part of the package, guests are provided with post-dinner dances and other forms of entertainment, with traditional 'Scottish nights' a particular favourite. Guests who have been out all day on coach tours tend to stay in their hotels after their evening meal and that benefits the hotels' bar trade. Unfortunately, in the holiday trade as a whole, a poor standard of service has been one of the perennial complaints levied against the industry. The best are very good, but as a House of Commons report stated in 1999 'the lower and middle ranks of the market have a considerable way to go before it reaches the standard of parts of Europe and North America, for example'.

There is no doubt, though, that the holiday business has come a long way from the far off distant time when Stonehaven landladies got into a stir and state of excitement as they prepared for the onset of Glasgow Fair.

> The housewives will be in a state,
> An' fleein' in despair,
> For they'll a' be gettin' lodgers
> On the first day of the fair
> A' their roomies will be croodit [crowded]
> What an unco stir 'twill be
> When the Glesca folk come trippin'
> Tae Stonehaven by the sea.

'The Glesca Fair' by Walter Donald

CHAPTER 10

The Call of the Wild:
Holiday Camps, Shanty Towns and Caravans

And all around us were trees, hayfields, meadows, running water, tall purple grasses and flowers of many hues, patient animals feeding, little chaffinches gathering crumbs, the scent of the woodfire, the blessed winds, the great white clouds, sunsets behind the mountains, and at night the full moon and the stars. 'Till one has lived with Nature one has not lived.'

This poetically penned account of a Girl Guide camp in the countryside during the 1920s epitomises the need many felt to commune with Nature and to answer 'the call of the wild'. Camping was the obvious way to achieve this end – a goal that tended to take adventurous young people into the countryside and away from towns. Some holidaymakers, though, opted for a campsite in the proximity of a resort, thus enjoying, on the one hand, the simple life and, on the other, ready access to the amenities and entertainments of the traditional resort. For many, older people no less than the young, it was a means of getting a holiday on the cheap. We find, therefore, camp sites, official or otherwise, springing up in or close to a number of seaside resorts. In Prestwick, for instance, in 1926 the Ayrshire police noted the presence of a large number of tents spread over five sites. There had been no problems, the Chief Constable reported, with the Boys Brigade camps which were 'more or less under military discipline and were properly conducted' or with the sites occupied by 'respectable people of the working class'. At one site, however, there were 'young men of an undesirable class'. In response, the Prestwick Burgh Council enacted byelaws to control such undesirable visitors.

Although in the country as a whole there were a lot of 'No Camping' signs, nevertheless, in the interwar years when farming was in depression, quite a few farmers and crofters saw campers as a valuable source of extra income. In the LMS Railway Company's 1934 edition of *Camping Grounds in Scotland*, a number of resorts were featured. In the Firth of Clyde, Arran could offer a large number of fields, most of them in or close to the villages of Brodick (seven), Lamlash (three) and Whiting Bay (four). In Bute there were seven sites at Kilchattan Bay, including one for which the contact person was the Factor of the Bute Estate. In the latter case, and probably with a number of others too, consent was given only for specially organised camps like Girl Guides or Scouts. According to the LMS list, there were only two sites, both on farms, in the vicinity of Rothesay and none at Millport or anywhere else on Great Cumbrae. Yet, the *Rothesay Express* noted, in July 1934, the presence of crowds of campers, with one farmer having 100 tents in his fields, housing around 500 occupants. It is evident that camping had caught on, since a contemporary Gourock guidebook tells us that 'in recent years', during the months of July and August, as many as 3,000 to 4,000 people were setting up camp at Lunderston Bay, near Gourock. This area was popular because it was the nearest sandy beach to Glasgow. To serve this 'canvas town' wooden huts had been erected as temporary shops to supply the needs of the campers. The AA (Automobile Association) also

A mostly formally dressed group of campers at a site near Dunoon – presumably not of the 'undesirable class'. The casually dressed trio in front were 'on duty' – cooks for the day. The older man and the boy were, as the message on the back of the card explains, visitors down for the day. Were they a Quaker party, as the sign on the music stand would seem to indicate?

provided a list for its members, *Caravan and Camp Sites*. In the 1937 edition, members were warned with regard to one of the Ayr sites: 'Site is not recommended during the Glasgow Fair holidays, the second and third weeks in July.' They were also cautioned that Mr Donald Macrae at Gairloch in Wester Ross did not permit arrivals and departures on Sunday.

Elsewhere, according to the LMS 1934 list, campers were welcome at Broughty Ferry, one of the sites being the esplanade – application to the Park Superintendent of Dundee Town Council. Montrose and Stonehaven were two other burghs where the local authority allowed tents to be pitched at a fixed charge. In the AA's list, three coastal authorities were included: Oban, Lossiemouth and Leven. The decision to provide a camping ground at Leven was taken in 1930. That year the burgh council decided to clear and level the ground and sow grass at the old Durie pit, then put up suitable lavatory and washing facilities and 'advertise this ground for a holiday camp'. Nearby residents objected, but the council, deciding to try the camp for one year 'under proper supervision', appointed an attendant at £2 and 10 shillings a week.

A step up from the campsite in the wild was the fixed-site holiday camp, which began to appear in the years before the First World War; some were provided by organisations like the Young Men's Christian Association. The Glasgow YMCA, for example, had its own permanent campsite, including a substantial main hall, at Lochgoilhead. The Healtheries at Rothesay was one of a number of privately owned holiday camps which were coming into vogue at this time. The first holiday camp as such was Cunningham's Camp in the Isle of Man, opened in 1894, and it set the pattern for the Healtheries and other such establishments. The Healtheries, developed round a boarding house, with its 'liberal table' – four meals a day – attracted young men who favoured the healthy, outdoor life but wanted a modicum of comfort with it. Campers, attracted by the adverts 'the jolliest, cheapest and most comfortable way to spend a summer holiday', could choose between bell tents fitted with wooden floors and spring beds, and small canvas covered, wooden-framed huts. In the mid-1930s new facilities and buildings were added, including extra accommodation at the ladies' camp. These buildings proved to be of great value from the government's point of view. Starting in 1935 the Healtheries, along with Butlaw Camp at South Queensferry, was used, under a government holiday scheme for Special Areas, to house unemployed workers and their families. In 1938 some 3,250 families were given the kind of holiday that otherwise they could not have enjoyed.

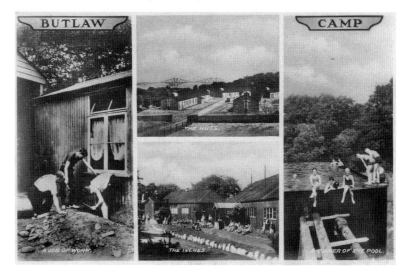

Elma, who sent this postcard in July 1936 from Butlaw Camp, a former naval barracks and fixed-site camp at South Queensferry, was not enamoured with it. 'Camp is lousy' was her bitter comment. The tank swimming pool looks highly dangerous.

At the start of the Second World War some of the more difficult evacuees were housed at the camp, evoking this waspish comment from the Town Clerk: 'The proprietor is well up in managing this class of person.' Later in the war the camp, like others of its kind, housed military personnel.

In 2002, M. Margaret McQueen Bounelis provided Rothesay Museum with an account of camp life in prewar days which was perhaps not all that different from the formula that Billy Butlin developed for his camps, except that Butlin's camps were more self-contained.

> When the Healtheries were in full swing, the holidaymakers arrived on Friday afternoon. They were assigned their cabins, and the life of the camp became busy. Picnics to Ettrick Bay were scheduled, as were nights at the Rothesay Entertainers. Sports days, with football games, three legged races and other sports for men and children were held. At night there were dances and talent shows in the large entertainment hall and on Thursday evening, the campers' last night, a fancy dress ball was held with prizes given out for the best costumes, and for the winners of the games on sports days. It was a very active full life from June till September, and I believe there were as many as 500 people a week spending time at the Healtheries just before the war.

There was another holiday camp located at Rothesay: the Roseland Summer Camp, better known as the Co-op or 'Store' Camp. Founded in 1911 by the United Co-operative Baking Society, this was a popular establishment until it closed in 1974. A caravan park now occupies the site. Butlin's camp at Ayr was a more substantial enterprise. Built for the Royal Navy by Billy Butlin at the start of the Second World War, Butlin took up his option of buying the camp back when the war was over. Opened by comedian Sir Harry Lauder in June 1947, Butlin's camp at Heads of Ayr attracted a lot of interest. While some snooty individuals looked down on what they thought was the Butlin's camps' regimentation combined with over-hearty mateyness, the customers thought otherwise. At the height of the season, over 4,000 'campers' arrived at the Ayr camp from all parts of Britain, most travelling by train. Indeed, until 1968 Butlins had its own dedicated railway station. In 1954, up in the north-east, Banff Shopkeepers' Association, bewitched by the success of Butlin's seemingly magical formula, suggested that a holiday camp be built on the burgh's links. Banff Town Council approved of the idea and went so far as to write to the famous entrepreneur-cum-showman,

The camper who sent this postcard from the Healtheries in August 1913 marked his tent with a cross. The kitchen staff are lined up in front of the house, and the campers on view look to be wearing their Sunday best. It was formally named as Boarding House and Young Men's Holiday Camp. The bell-tents had wooden floors and spring beds.

but perhaps fortunately to no avail. Even the *Saltire Review* thought that the Ayr camp was a phenomenon that would be of interest to its high-minded readers. Certainly A. L. Taylor, visiting in 1958, saw no evidence of regimentation. He commended too the behaviour of the campers, which he thought was 'quite decorous, even rather circumspect'. Appropriately for a writer in the *Saltire Review*, Taylor noted the Scottish flavour, which was imparted in a variety of ways that included thistle-shaped decorations, tartan carpets and ablutions labelled Lads and Lasses instead of Ladies and Gentlemen. On Saturday changeover day, a piper piped the campers into the camp on their arrival and again when they were heading to the railway station. At Friday night finale, the Redcoats and other staff serenaded the campers with 'Ta Ta the Noo', and then everyone joined in with 'Auld Lang Syne' followed by the Butlin anthem, 'Goodnight Campers'.

> So we say Goodnight Campers,
> Don't sleep in your braces,
> Goodnight Campers, put your teeth in Jeyes's.

In later years the Ayr camp was revamped and renamed Wonderworld West. The intention was to give the camp a more family and child-friendly atmosphere but wild-partying youths gave Wonderworld West a bad name. Accordingly, in 1998 the site was closed and a new owner, the Haven group, took over. The old chalets and once popular ballroom were demolished and replaced by a new caravan holiday park. The name was changed also to Craig Tara and, like Seton Sands, now also another of the company's properties, it is promoted for its family-friendly facilities and forms of entertainment.

Between the wars more downmarket settlements appeared in some areas where, for a modest rent, simple huts could be erected or old buses and vans converted into rather basic holiday abodes. While some were fittingly described as shanty towns and earned the planners' disapproval, others, like a settlement of picturesque bungalows at the hamlet of Lendalfoot 6 miles south of Girvan, were better regarded. The *Third Statistical Account: Ayrshire* (1951) states: 'It has blossomed out in recent years as a holiday resort for townspeople, who have built substantial wooden bungalows for themselves along the narrow seaboard.' This community was part of the so-called hutting movement, which blossomed in the interwar and early postwar years but which in some areas has foundered when ground rents were increased to a level which the hutters regarded as exorbitant.

The link between Butlin-style holidays and camping in the great outdoors was somewhat tenuous. Billy Butlin, though, insisted on calling his customers campers. These happy campers on a cycle built for three and dressed for the Scottish climate were at least enjoying some physical exercise.

Quite a few of the former 'shacklands' sites survive but, having been taken upmarket, in very different form. In the 1940s, working-class families enjoyed a cheap and cheerful holiday in old buses and ramshackle huts at Kinghorn's Pettycur Bay site. Today the Pettycur Bay Holiday Park boasts a hotel, restaurant, function suite and an all-the-year-round leisure complex which embraces a swimming pool, sauna, fitness suite, and games areas. Another site that has been transformed out of all recognition is Port Seton near Edinburgh, where a farmer expanded a simple campsite into a sizeable chalet park. City dwellers took leases on small plots where a hut could be built, an old railway carriage installed or a caravan parked. With a frequent bus service from Edinburgh, the Port Seton holiday camp proved very popular and by 1953 there were some 660 huts 'of varying size and appearance' on the site, crammed into a comparatively small area. There was a small store and a dance hall 'for social activities'. In the immediate postwar years, quite a few owners were families with young children who, due to the then housing shortage, were obliged to live with their in-laws. Their holiday hut gave them the chance of a welcome break on their own. From the 1970s onward, mobile homes replaced huts and shanty-type dwellings. As at Pettycur and a number of other places, the present-day Seton Sands Holiday Park bears no resemblance to the original.

Caravans, initially horse-drawn, provided another way of getting to the great outdoors. In the 1920s the motor car supplanted the horse and thus widened the caravanners' range. Caravanners, who were then mainly middle class, generally opted for the quiet of the countryside in preference to the stir and bustle of the traditional seaside resorts. The AA's *Caravan and Camp Sites* guide, 1937

1039   THE BUNGALOWS, LENDALFOOT.

The bungalows at Lendalfoot in Ayrshire were comparatively upmarket.

edition, listed a mere three sites in coastal Fife and none at all for the East Lothian coast. In rural Perthshire, on the other hand, there were forty-three. After the Second World War, though, there was a boom in the use of static caravans as holiday abodes. For working-class people, especially those with families, renting a static van for a week or a fortnight became increasingly popular. It gave them holiday accommodation that was both free-and-easy and cheap. Some working people could now emulate the middle-class commuters of prewar years. Jane R. Handley recalled how her father acquired a caravan in the 1940s and, paying a small rental, parked it at Kilmun by the Holy Loch in Argyll. 'We moved there from Greenock for the summer season, my father and in later years myself commuting by steamer and rail to Greenock.' Ordinary families, she pointed out, especially those who had enjoyed steady employment during the prewar slump, could now afford to become increasingly independent of the vagaries of landladies. Some even became landlords themselves by letting out their caravans.

Businessmen and some public bodies now began to fill a need for sites with at least basic sanitary facilities. Some were small, like the privately owned Lundin Links caravan park, which started in 1951. Although there were only eight vans on the site, it nevertheless had flushing toilets. As for the municipalities, it was the town council of doucely sedate St Andrews which showed the way. By the early 1950s, its Kinkell Braes camping ground, which had been purchased just before the war, had been transformed to such a degree that it was regarded as an exemplar for other local authorities. A visiting journalist praised the town's model caravan park, where the vans were laid out in streets and the camp wardens, as well as collecting fees, gave 'reminders on camp hygiene to those who may be needing a little guidance on such matters'. Presumably, offenders were directed towards the ablution benches and flush lavatories 'grouped at convenient points'. The Kinkell Braes caravan park was at its busiest in July, when the big cities' trades holidays were held. Come August, though, the golfing enthusiasts had arrived and, as the *St Andrews Citizen* noted in 1953, there was 'a noticeable change in the type of visitor now in the town'. The July visitors, on the other hand, were obviously not golfers. That summer the number of Glasgow Fair visitors, overwhelmingly from the manual working class, was estimated at around 3,000, many of them based at the Kinkell Braes caravan park. Some residents insisted that the local authority should be 'severely reprimanded for encouraging this trade'. By attracting 'a new class of visitor' the council, it was argued, had changed the character of the town, thus rendering it less attractive to its traditional type of visitor. But others welcomed the influx of more plebeian holidaymakers. One noted approvingly how these July caravan dwellers and campers had banded themselves into a distinct community, organising their own camp sports and weekly galas. During the 1955 Glasgow Fair holiday, the onset of the gala day was marked by the children of the caravanners, headed by a Boys Brigade bugle band, marching round the site. For the sports' prizes, we are told, the camp residents had raised 'substantial sums'.

Many local authorities, though, still regarded caravan-park residents with suspicion. In some places where provision was made, councils, as the Scottish Tourist Board observed in 1954, spoiled the effect by cramming too many people onto an inadequate site. The board, nevertheless, commended the efforts made by such resorts as Montrose, Banff, and Nairn and pointed to the business engendered for local shops. In Aberdeen that same year a local newspaper assailed the civic authorities for lack of initiative. Aberdeen, its editor argued, would not keep its proud claim to be Scotland's leading resort 'until the needs of the fast-growing army of caravanning holiday-makers have been met'. In Arran, although the car ferries introduced in 1957 made the carrying of caravans easier, they were, nevertheless, banned for a number of years.

CARAVAN SITE, LEVEN. (28)

Leven Town Council opened their Shepherd's Knowe caravan park on a prime site, right by the beach, in 1953. Unlike the mobile homes found in most contemporary sites, the vans seen in this postcard were proper tourers. Following the example of many other councils, the local authority sold the park to a private operator in 1990.

Between 1950 and 1970 there was a five-fold increase in the number of cars in Britain, and this led to a considerable rise in the number of people taking a caravan holiday. Holidaymakers preferred the flexibility that caravans, and self-catering flats, too, for that matter, afforded. To meet this demand, large new caravan parks were built on virgin sites, some near to resorts, others in more isolated locations but all accessible to the new, greatly-extended car-owning population. Of the new sites, some were under municipal management, others were privately owned. The largest of these parks were, in effect, purpose-built self-contained holiday villages. A 1960 Act of Parliament ensured that such sites had to be licensed by the relevant local authority, except ironically those that the authorities ran themselves. In the following year, the Scottish Tourist Board published the first edition of a booklet, *Scotland for Caravan Holidays*, listing the various touring and static van sites. By then there were pitches for nearly 15,000 caravans in Scotland. Five years later there were 20,000 pitches spread over 400 sites – a phenomenon of considerable economic and, indeed, social significance. The impact of the town's caravan site on the small Angus resort of Monifieth was noted in the *Third Statistical Account: Angus*. The development of this site, it was argued, had given the town a new-found and welcome holiday atmosphere in the summer months.

There were drawbacks, though. The Solway coast became a boom area for caravan parks, the largest capable of holding more than 2,500 people. But the consequent huge influx of tourists meant problems for the medical practitioners in the area. So much so that in 1973 the executive council for the National Health Service for Galloway pleaded for assistance for the local doctors who had to cope, during the holiday season, with vastly increased numbers. In other respects, caravan parks could be a mixed blessing. For the Scottish Tourist Board and similar agencies, visual blight and the 'hydra-like nature' of the caravan parks was, and still is, a serious issue. The serried, and only too visible, ranks of mobile homes on some large sites are regarded by some as a blot on the landscape.

The Call of the Wild at the Ganavan Sands, near Oban.

CHAPTER 11

From Wartime Exigencies to Post-War Boom

From 1937 the ageing *Fair Maid* was the Forth's only excursion steamer. Her service was terminated by the outbreak of hostilities [on 3 September 1939] and when she left the Hawkcraig Pier [at Aberdour] for the last time, a small crowd of locals turned out to wave goodbye. She sailed off bravely, siren blowing and her orchestra playing 'Polly-Wolly-Doodle, Fare thee well, Fare thee well.' She never returned and in 1940 went back to the Clyde for duty as decontamination vessel.

Steamers of the Forth by Ian Brodie, 1976

With aerial attacks and the threat of invasion, the Scottish resorts were affected by war to an unparalleled degree. Huge quantities of sand were removed from beaches to fill sandbags, 7,000 tons from Broughty Ferry beach alone in the first week of the war. As in the First World War, excursion steamers, like the *Fair Maid*, were requisitioned for military use. Whereas prior to the outbreak of the war there were some twenty-five major steamers plying in the Firth of Clyde, a year later there were only seven and they were mainly operating as ferries rather than as excursion vessels. The Clyde paddle steamer *Waverley* was one that was called to war. In the First World War she had been used as a minesweeper, and now for the second time this veteran ship was converted to fill that role again. In May 1940, she, along with another four Clyde steamers, crossed the English Channel to help evacuate British troops from Dunkirk. Unfortunately, HMS *Waverley* was attacked by German aircraft and was sunk with the loss of some 300 men. At Rothesay, with so many of the steamers called up for war service, the launch owners did profitable business until their vessels were requisitioned too. The *Gay Queen*, for instance, was sent north to Orkney to serve as tender vessel for the fleet in Scapa Flow. Following the post-Dunkirk invasion panic, all along the east coast fortifications were built. At especially vulnerable points, minefields were laid, concrete anti-tank blocks constructed, and wooden posts stuck into areas, like Fife's Pettycur Sands, where German gliders might be landed. Later in the war, beaches, on both the east and west coasts, were cordoned off and farms and villages evacuated so that they could be used as training grounds for the Allies' D-Day invasion of Europe. This meant considerable disruption and some hardship, but it was accepted as a contribution towards winning the war. Virtually everywhere hotels and public halls were taken over by the military. The Beach Pavilion at Leven, for instance, was used as a mess hall by Polish soldiers stationed in the town.

The Firth of Clyde, in particular, became a war zone of immense importance, with, for example, the establishment of naval bases at Faslane and Rothesay. Bute, as well as providing a base for training submariners, was a training ground for commando operations. Inverary, too, played a key role as the training centre for combined operations. The Clyde was, in addition, the main assembly point for Atlantic convoys. Yet, although resort proprietors lost much of their usual holiday business, they compensated by providing billets for evacuees at the beginning of the war and, more profitably, for service personnel and their families. As in the First World War, Dunoon and Lochgoilhead profited by being unaffected by the anti-submarine boom, which kept the remaining Clyde pleasure steamers penned in the upper waters of the Firth of Clyde. There were even some unexpected benefits. At Lundin Links in Fife the greater part of the ladies' golf course was put to the plough, but, in return for their sacrifice, the ladies were permitted not only to play on the men's course but to do so free of charge.

As we have seen in the case of Rothesay, many folk still wanted to spend time and money on holiday pleasures. Accordingly, in holiday towns some amenities were kept going. Aberdeen's magnificent new Bon-Accord Baths were completed despite wartime shortages. Opened by the Lord Provost on 30 August 1940, this centrally located, indoor pond, claimed to be among the finest in the country, was kept open for the duration of the war. At Prestwick the town council also kept the bathing lake open, providing an admittedly curtailed programme of swimming galas and band concerts. Stonehaven open-air pool was likewise kept open, but the heating was reduced and ultimately discontinued. The army took over the showers for the use of troops in local military camps. Attempting to cut back on what it considered to be unnecessary travel, the government exhorted councils and voluntary bodies to organise amusements and events to keep people at home during the local holiday weeks. For its 1943 Holidays at Home week, Elgin offered fancy dress parades, sports, football matches, gymkhana, and ladies' ankle and bathing belle competitions. At Glasgow, the Scottish Ramblers' Association was asked to organise rambles for the Fair Week. Overall though, the government's plan was not a success. Although there were no special trains as in prewar days, people packed into the ordinary trains and buses and travelled to other towns. In this time of great food shortages and rationing, city folk took trips to holiday towns and, employing the emergency ration cards issued to people who were away from home, searched for scarce foodstuffs to take home with them. The residents of the Fife holiday resorts complained, according to the *Fife Free Press* of 18 July 1942, that visitors were emptying their local shops.

When war with Germany came to an end in 1945, victory was celebrated with a national holiday, VE Day (Victory in Europe), on 8 May. Although the war with Japan continued until 14 August, that summer the British people, tired of war and the concomitant shortages and sacrifices, sought

A CORNER OF THE BATHING BEACH, ABERDOUR.

This Aberdour postcard from prewar stock reads: 'We are enjoying our VE weekend here.' Like everything else, new postcards were in short supply in 1945. The diving board has long gone and only a few bits of rusted stanchion remain today.

solace in holiday jaunts, sometimes for the day and sometimes for longer-stay periods. Finding accommodation could be a problem, as many hotels and boarding houses were still occupied by military personnel and there were still some areas where access was limited. At Dunbar, there was no putting at the prom until trenches dug by the military could be filled in and the ground returfed. Rationing, too, remained in force. As during the war, the government issued pleas for holidays to be staggered and so hopefully ensure that there would be transport facilities and accommodation for all prospective holidaymakers. Headteachers, however, complained that staggered holidays, particularly during the months of May, June and September, had an adverse effect on school attendance. At any rate, the mass of the public took no heed and stuck to the traditional holiday months of July and August. As with the wartime 'stay-at-home' holiday schemes, attempts were made to provide more choice of entertainment for those who couldn't get away. Thanks to the Corporation Parks Department, Glasgow weans, for instance, were able to enjoy the age-old beach treats of pony and donkey riding without going near the seaside.

With a clapped-out railway system and worn-out buses and, in 1945 at least, even a shortage of bus conductresses, travelling, too, was still far from easy. Nevertheless, people were determined to get back to normal. After five years of war and as many years again of post-war austerity, there was a considerable pent-up demand for recreation and a change of scene, and, accordingly, people were ready to put up with all sorts of obstacles. They formed long queues at the railway stations and suffered being packed in like sardines. Since the effects of the war and post-war austerity made travel abroad and even to the larger English resorts difficult to achieve, it was for the Scottish seaside towns and villages a boom time once more. At the start of the 1945 Glasgow Fair holiday, for instance, 257 trains left the city for a variety of destinations. From the Central Station alone no fewer than 105 trains ran to Gourock over a three-day period. Nor was the effect confined to the more popular or close-at-hand resorts. Up in the north-east, Buckie had, according to the *Banffshire Advertiser* of 6 September 1945, experienced a big year for visitors. Rail arrivals, including a surprising number from England, had increased by 100 per cent, and there could have been many more as the local hoteliers reported that their rooms could have been filled many times over. It was the same in nearby Macduff, where the town's Tarlair seawater pond was a considerable asset. At the conclusion of the 1949 season, Macduff's Tarlair pond, the *Banffshire Journal* reported, had had its best year ever. 'In the past summer thousands of visitors seeking a change from austerity have found pleasure and relaxation in this large and splendidly-equipped enclosure.' Tickets sold amounted to 50,228 and the drawings came to £1,278 6s 9d.

By then the accommodation situation had eased somewhat. Many more hotels had been returned to their civilian owners. Hoteliers and boarding-house keepers were now, though, complaining of an insensitive Catering Act, which imposed working time regulations that may have been suitable for large London hotels but were completely inappropriate for small rural and seasonal establishments. Even Tom Johnston, first chairman of the Scottish Tourist Board and onetime fiery socialist, railed against this Act pushed through by the postwar Labour Government. Though it was still an age of austerity (sweets were now once again rationed), many more workers were now receiving holidays with pay. By 1945 some 80 per cent of the British workforce were enjoying at least a week's paid leave, and some had longer. And the trend was upward. In the very next year, the members of the Scottish Typographical Association secured an extra week's holiday with pay. By 1949, at the start of the Dunfermline Trades Holiday, textile workers were being given holiday money covering eight or nine working days. In 1953 miners, for the first time ever, were given two weeks' summer holiday with pay. Previously, when they got an extra week off, there was no pay to go with it. 'The miners,'

GANAVAN SANDS AND MORVERN HILLS, OBAN.   B.1919.

By 1949, when this photograph was taken, campers and caravanners had returned to Oban's Ganavan Sands. The large hangar on the beach was a relic from wartime days, when Oban Bay was a base for anti-submarine flying boats.

the *Dunfermline Press* commented on the eve of the local trades holidays, 'have a fortnight in which to recoup their energies, and, with fat pay packets, will carry the West Fife accent into all parts of the country.' All miners over the age of twenty-one had been paid the munificent sum of £18 15*s* for their two weeks away from the pits. In addition, the savings and other local banks had paid out large sums of money 'obviously intended for holiday spending'.

A moderate rise in the standard of living and extra time for leisure allowed more working class families to savour the delights of extended holidays. In the mining town of Cowdenbeath, there was a big increase in the number of those who had decided on 'a fixed venue' for the 1949 trades week, and consequently there was an exceptionally large exodus' by rail and by bus. Contemporary newspaper reports give some indication as to the favoured destinations. In Dunfermline, although some holiday-goers were off to London and the south coast of England and the Continent, long distance travellers were, nevertheless, in a minority. Aberdeen was in favour, as were the Fife resorts, the latter still the most popular destinations. As for the situation in Glasgow that same year, it seems, according to the *Scotsman*, that Scottish destinations also took first place. On Fair Friday for instance, around thirty special trains were heading for Aberdeen. In contrast, eight went off to London and five to the north-west of England – for Blackpool, Morecambe and the Isle of Man. Aberdonians in the meantime headed south to Glasgow and other West of Scotland destinations. Buses too were packed, both going from and returning to Glasgow. The *Ardrossan and Saltcoats Herald* reported, on 29 July 1949, that the Ardrossan SMT Bus Station had handled a record number of passengers on the previous Sunday. Between 5 p.m. and 10.30 p.m. over forty buses, including thirty specials, left for the city fully laden.

With more people opting for extended holidays away from home, traditional festivals like the annual summer fair at Johnstone ceased to be held. By the 1950s the town was now deserted at the annual holiday period. From the *Third Statistical Account: Renfrew and Bute*, we learn: 'Travel facilities, more extended holiday periods and lately holidays with pay have established the custom of the annual summer holiday and made possible for the many a period of recreation for mind and body which was once the privilege of the few.' Not surprisingly, there was an explosion in demand for holiday accommodation. From June to September the Ayrshire coastal towns, so accessible by train or bus, were flooded with visitors. For Saltcoats, a 1951 report tells us: 'Especially during the

Glasgow, Kilmarnock and Paisley Fairs crowds pour in by bus, rail and car, some to lodge for a time, many just for a day. A large proportion of these who come are working-class people.' These working-class folk didn't want, and couldn't afford at any rate, anything too posh. They chose to stay in private houses, sometimes with attendance, sometimes without.

It was the same in Girvan. Since its five hotels were on the small side, as were the town's fifty boarding houses, most visitors found accommodation in private houses. All these establishments required extra staff, as did the local laundries and other service industries. The laundries' biggest customers were hotels and boarding houses and in the more affluent towns like Ayr and Troon 'the better-off coast residents'. The fact that 'yacht and shooting lodge washings' were a specialty at the Oban Steam Laundry tells quite a lot about that town's holiday trade. All resorts were well-off for shops too. In relation to its 1961 population, Millport, in these pre-hypermarket days, had, as calculated by Isobel Robertson, about eighteen food shops in excess of the needs of its then 1,470 inhabitants. With the burgh's toy, fancy goods and bicycle shops totalling eleven, it was again far above the Scottish average. In this little offshore town practically everyone was involved, one way or another, in the tourist industry. Not every resort was quite as dependent on the holiday trade as Millport. But, with their summer visitors spreading their cash widely, it is hardly surprising that the townsfolk and the governing councils of the principal Ayrshire resorts – Largs, Saltcoats, Troon, Prestwick, Ayr and Girvan – had come to accept that tourism was one of their major industries. Accordingly, the elected councils in these burghs were quite prepared to cater for visitors by providing an extensive range of leisure facilities. Saltcoats, for instance, had its entertainment pavilion, park with bandstand and putting green, model yachting pond, and a commodious tidal bathing pool partly rebuilt in 1933. Ayr offered even more, as we can see from the 1956 official guide, *Ayr for Health and Pleasure*. In addition to its two miles of 'safe, sandy beach', the catalogue of its attractions included tennis, bowling, boating on the River Ayr, an amusement park on the foreshore, horse racing and golf courses in and around the town in abundance. And, of course, Ayr was right in the heart of the Burns country – then as now a steady draw. Nor was there any need, as the guide put it, to fear the worst the weather man might do, since there were no fewer than six cinemas, two theatres, an ice rink, and two 'first-class ballrooms'.

A feature of the coastal towns was the great number of cafés selling ice cream and fish and chips with, in the holiday period, long queues outside. Many landladies in those days (and they paid a

Boating lakes with rowing boats for hire were fairly common, but some, as here at Ayr, had petrol-driven motorboats. The towers of the Beach Pavilion are just visible in the distance.

reckoning in the long run) turfed their lodgers out in the street after breakfast. In bad weather, bright and cheerful cafés were a welcome refuge and were cheap eating-places for day-trippers and for holidaymakers who were not on full board. Many of these cafés were Italian-owned: in *c.* 1950 Troon, ten out of eleven. In their early days the unco guid of the Protestant establishment had cast a dubious eye on Italian cafés, the more especially since they opened on Sundays and were popular with the young. In 1901, for instance, the members of the kirk session of Montrose strongly condemned such establishments for their 'baneful effect on the morals of the many young persons who frequent them'. In time, though, they and their owners became accepted as part of the community. With their Vitrolite glass and other Art Deco features and, not least, their beautifully arranged selection of chocolates, candies and sweets, some like Giulianotti's in Stonehaven, Nardini's in Largs and Togneri's (Togs) in Troon became tourist meccas in their own right. Cafés and restaurants provided a lot of employment too, as did shops, hotels, boarding houses, and laundries. The drawback was that it was mainly lowly-paid seasonal work. But, without their local casual employees and an annual influx of seasonal workers, the resorts couldn't have functioned.

Busy though they still were in the late 1940s and 1950s, the Scottish resorts couldn't sustain their near dominant position for ever. Once the postwar travel restrictions were eased, the ordinary man and woman began to look elsewhere. Portobello was one resort that was beginning to lose trade. To remedy this, the Portobello Traders' Association was formed in 1949 to promote the interests of their distinctive part of Edinburgh. Since these business people felt that the city's own guide was insufficient in this regard, they produced their own guidebook 'to encourage people to spend their holiday here and to make it easy for them to find accommodation'. The doon-the-watter resorts, likewise, found that their appeal was on the wane. The decline in long-stay visitors was most apparent in towns like Gourock that were just too close to the city. Despite good facilities – putting greens, outdoor swimming pool (modernised in 1934), boating pond, pavilion, public park, etc. – Gourock was on the slide. The days when its summer population doubled and sometimes trebled were coming to an end. The railway station was certainly busy but, except for some day-trippers, most visitors just headed to the steamer pier. With Dunoon and Rothesay too, there were signs of disaffection. One explanation, as quoted in the Glasgow *Evening Citizen* in July 1947, was: 'People remember the too-heavy charges they often had to pay during the war years when they couldn't get

Now gone, but in its day the Largs Moorings restaurant and café provided a welcome refuge on cold, wet and windy days. With its modernistic, 'ocean liner' styling, the Moorings was a notable seafront landmark. The replacement building semi-imitates the architectural style of the old.

to other parts of the country. Now they would rather go to Ireland and at least be sure of getting good food.' Blackpool by this time had become increasingly popular with Scots everywhere. Even as early as the 1920s what John K. Walton describes as 'Glasgow's love affair with Blackpool' was well under way – 'a sometimes violent relationship', he pungently adds. In West Fife, the 1953 trades holiday saw a big exodus to Blackpool and, but for a shortage of buses, even more would have gone. So heavy was the demand that bus bookings were stopped a fortnight prior to the commencement of the holiday. An advertisement in British Rail's 1952 holiday guide points to the scale of attractions available there: they included no fewer than thirteen 'live' shows. Nor was it just the number of shows. Blackpool could attract the top stars of the day. When it came to entertainment provision, Scottish resorts just could not compete with the likes of Blackpool.

Nevertheless, at peak holiday times the demand for accommodation remained at a high level. In their post-Second World War housing policy, Millport Town Council set out to encourage the tourist trade by its choice of types of houses that were to be built. By 1955, eighty-four houses had been built, each with four or five apartments and, according to the *Third Statistical: Renfrew and Bute*, large enough to accommodate summer visitors. Millport's tenants were positively encouraged to take in visitors, benefiting not only themselves but, in addition, the community at large. In the 1950s, the proms and beaches seemed as busy as ever. Locals going about their normal business were crowded off the Dunoon and Rothesay proms by the sheer weight of visitor numbers. There are no exact figures, but local estimates were that, at the holiday peak, Dunoon's population trebled, Troon's went up by some 20 per cent, and Ayr's and Girvan's more than doubled. Rothesay during the 1952 Glasgow Fair was reported to be full up, with some holidaymakers travelling down on the chance of getting accommodation through cancelled bookings. Having a short and very concentrated holiday season compounded the problem. The vogue for staggered holidays was now over. In July 1952, the *Buteman* reported that June was becoming, as it was in prewar days, a month favoured chiefly by day excursionists. Consequently, boarding house keepers and other providers had to make the best of a very short season – basically just July and August. Boarding houses and apartments, the *Buteman* asserted, had to develop 'elastic sides' to meet the demand from 'July-only' holidaymakers.

But the need to develop 'elastic sides' had a long-term impact. Too often, holidaymakers were expected to tolerate conditions infinitely worse than their normal. The Revd John P. Crosgrove, Convener of Housing at Rothesay, stated in 1950:

> It seems to me almost incredible what vast numbers of our citizens will put up with because sea-breezes are being thrown in free. It is psychological blindness to imagine that this inertia will continue.

The experience of poor accommodation and overcrowding in Rothesay had already induced many Glaswegians to head east for their holiday. There, resorts like Carnoustie, Leven and Dunbar were booming. For North Berwick, and it was true of other east coast towns as well, everything possible was done for the 'comfort, attraction and welfare of the visitors who, in the main, provide the wealth of the community'. As on the west coast, the benefits were spread right through the community. At North Berwick, we are told, there were more shops and a greater variety in the type of shop available and in the quality of their 'purveying' than in comparable towns. Practically every household provided lodgings for summer visitors and 'this supplement to the family income is further augmented by boys, during the summer school vacation, carrying clubs on the links'.

THE PROMENADE AND SEASIDE.
BROUGHTY FERRY.

Broughty Ferry beach in the interwar years, and for long thereafter, was very popular with Dundonians.

It was a similar picture with the Fife coast resorts. At Leven, where at peak holiday times the estimated population increase was some 12,000, there were considerable profits to be made. According to the 1951 *Third Statistical Account: Fife*, the Town Council drew in 'appreciable sums' from the letting of refreshment rights on the prom and from the lease of the Beach Pavilion to concert parties. At Kinghorn, we are told, the provision made for summer visitors also brought a considerable sum of money to the town. According to the 1951 account, this 'new industry' had come to the fore 'in recent years'. It was not in truth a new industry for Kinghorn, for as far back as 1862 there were twenty-four proprietors of furnished lodgings in the town. But what was probably true was that the tourist trade was now relatively more important, especially compared to other industries. While Kinghorn and neighbouring Burntisland, both handily situated for Edinburgh folk, had a long history as holiday towns, for more distant East Neuk fishing towns like Anstruther tourist-related developments were of more recent date. With little prospect of attracting new industries or of expanding existing ones, that town needed holidaymakers to ensure its future prosperity and accordingly 'has turned its attention increasingly to the potentialities of the summer holiday traffic'.

On the other hand, at neighbouring Pittenweem, where the fishing industry in 1951 was still comparatively buoyant, the tourist trade was not considered to be 'so fully developed as in the neighbouring burghs, though it is commonly held that Pittenweem is supreme in picturesque appeal'. It must have been different in the 1930s since, according to the *East Fife Observer*, no fewer than 1,199 visitors arrived by train for the 1935 Glasgow Fair week, plus an estimated 200 to 300 by car and bus. There is no doubt though that, at the joint burgh of Elie and Earlsferry, folk there had been making money out of tourists since the eighteenth century. Moreover, since the town's industrial decline went back a long way, their twentieth-century successors, rather unusually, did not actively seek new industries. This golfing resort, according to the 1951 account, had always attracted the well-to-do type of person 'who was prepared to come for a long stay and to live as part of the community'. The burgh's entire reliance on a tourist economy had its disadvantages, though. It had an ageing population and few employment opportunities for young people. Lundin Links and the adjacent village of Largo were other upmarket resorts, favoured in the main by 'the well-to-do person who has come in his retirement to make his home in the parish, or has brought his family there for the summer months'. In the 1951 parish account, however, there is a hint of alarm, inasmuch as in recent years bus loads of day-trippers had been arriving 'with increasing frequency', though not on the scale known in Aberdour. The benefits of the tourist economy for the East Fife communities were not to be denied. The *Third Statistical Account*, however, stated that in the ancient royal burgh of Crail, in addition to seven hotels, four boarding houses and a 'holiday camp', there were 'few houses where accommodation is not available.' 'House-letting, in the holiday season, may be said,' the account continued, 'to be almost the keystone of Crail's economy.'

It was the same story in other counties. The Banffshire and Moray fishing towns also benefited from this somewhat unexpected post-war bonanza. In 1950, according to the *Banffshire Advertiser*, the Provost of Portknockie reckoned that the income from that year's record number of visitors had completely dwarfed the earnings from fishing. During the 1952 Glasgow Fair, Buckie alone entertained at least 600 visitors and when they had departed, the streets were 'strangely quiet after the merriment and gay holiday spirits of our southern friends'. In those days, a favourite gift for visitors to buy were boxes of herring, posted to their friends and relatives. Many visitors went back to the same small towns year after year. In the small burghs, like Portknockie (1951 population 1,456) and neighbouring Findochty (1951 population 1,490), it was possible, as the following newspaper report indicates, for locals and visitors to develop a surprising degree of camaraderie.

Findochty gave a right royal send-off to its annual Glasgow Fair fortnight visitors when they set off on their homeward journey from the Town Hall on Saturday. To the accompaniment of cheers from a large number of local folk who had assembled, that grand old lady Mrs Deckers provided a song and dance turn, while it was amusing to see Andy McDonald sprint down the road in true Olympic style to shake hands with a friend as the bus was about to leave. Perhaps Thursday provided the highlight of their stay when a match and social evening took place at the bowling green. [Once] the game was over, everyone made for the pavilion where a thoroughly enjoyable evening was spent. These popular visitors have certainly found a place in the hearts of their Findochty friends who will be looking forward to giving them a welcome next year again.

Banffshire Advertiser, 7 August 1952

This post-war tourist boom left some north-east folk bemused. As one correspondent to the *Banffshire Advertiser* in 1952 remarked: 'It is still rather a mystery why Aberdeen and our district in general are becoming holiday meccas, closely rivalling the Clyde coast resorts in popularity. Are our hoteliers and landladies less "hardened" than tradition attributes to their Rothesay counterparts? Does the freshness of our climate and the lack of amenities on the southern scale appeal to the folks who "want to get away from it all"?' The lack of amenities did not go unnoticed, however. Visitors to Buckie were dismayed by the complete lack of organised holiday events, some 'nondescript' dances excepted. Wee Findochty, with its gala week, fancy dress parade, swimming competition and dances, did much better. Findochty, like other small fishing communities at that time, needed the boost that the holiday trade provided. It is interesting to note that the burgh was 'dry' at that time, having no pub or licensed hotel. For visitors, though, Buckie's Strathlene swimming pool and golf course were no distance away and its pubs readily accessible by bus.

Further east into Aberdeenshire, the small burgh of Rosehearty converted a harbour, which had ceased to have much commercial value, into a tourist asset by building a small open-air swimming pool within its walls. Opened in 1959, this pond was for some years a decided boon to the community. In the same county, Collieston, as we have seen, was yet another picturesque but decaying fishing village which gained new life from the new tourist economy. The population sank from 419 in 1891 to an estimated winter population of 116 in 1952. As the *Third Statistical Account*: *Aberdeenshire* (1960) tells us:

> Yet Collieston was not destined to become a deserted village. The chalybeate springs which once helped to attract visitors may be forgotten, and the harbour wall may be beginning to crumble, but it still furnishes a safe bathing and paddling pool. Many houses which stood derelict for years, or changed hands for as little as £20, have been rebuilt, and are used as summer residences or for holiday lets; in the holiday season also tents and caravans appear.

Aberdeen, too, profited from the post-war tourist explosion. To ensure that the boom continued, the council created, in 1948, a publicity department to advertise the city's attractions. The redoubtable Colonel Harry Webber, Director of Publicity, could boast that there were over 700 addresses in the list of hotels, boarding houses and guesthouses. According to the city's 1953 *Third Statistical Account*, the tourist trade 'may be accounted as one of Aberdeen's major industries'. A new publicity slogan was coined. The stodgy 'Silver City by the Sea' became 'The Silver City with the Golden Sands'. With a council which had 'systematically developed the city's amenities to attract visitors', Aberdeen had quite a lot going for it. Golf, tennis and other sports were well catered for. In those cinema-going days, there were, as we have seen, plenty of picture-houses too. The city could boast, too, of a rather unusual attraction – the fish market. To help visitors to make the most of this 'memorable experience', the Fish Market Publicity Association provided guides to show visitors round and to explain the workings and extent of that then vital local industry. There were even cash prizes for the best photographs taken in the market. Its drawback, though, was that in order to see the market when it was really busy, visitors had to get up very early in the morning. Peterhead was another town where visitors were encouraged to go and savour the stir and bustle of the fish market. In prewar days, that burgh offered another curiosity – parties of convicts from the local prison, under surveillance of guards and warders, moving about their duties outside the prison walls. As a 1938 guidebook effused: 'This is always a special thrill for the stranger.'

Aberdeen's tourist economy continued to boom. In the mid-1950s the number of visitors was still soaring, many coming from south of the Border and overseas. Exceptionally fine holiday weather helped. In 1955, Glaswegians had the unusual treat of a Fair Fortnight free from rain. What was equally significant was that it was a time of high employment and rising incomes. In that same year the number of unemployed in Britain was the lowest since the war. Two years later, Prime Minister Harold Macmillan gave his famous 'never had it so good' speech. Aberdeen's tourist numbers at that time were also boosted by the city's participation in a British Railways (BR) holiday venture. Under this 1950s 'All-In' Holidays scheme, organised by BR and leading travel agents, holidaymakers paid the costs of travel, hotel accommodation and excursions up front. There was no hurry on the council's part, though, to remove Sabbath restrictions. A very long-standing municipal byelaw banned the playing of games on the Links: 'No person shall play at any game on any part of the Links on Sunday.' In the early 1950s the author, when a student at Aberdeen University, was chased by 'parkies' for playing football on the Links upon the Sabbath day. Nevertheless, Glaswegians were still arriving in large numbers, bringing colour, life and laughter to the city streets and seafront. Shirley Cunningham, who in the early 1960s was a journalist in the city, recalled: 'Despite few facilities, such as cafés at the beach and a long walk to get there, they seemed irrepressibly cheerful, even if they had been chucked out of their digs at 9.30 a.m. for the day. I still have a mental picture of a small group and their dog, sheltering from a downpour under a bridge at the beach, singing away happily to a guitar.'

Regrettably, features that were part of the city's seaside heritage were removed. In 1954 the Victorian bandstand was demolished, as were the last bathing coaches. The latter might still have been used, as they had been for many years and, as still happens in some Continental resorts, as static changing huts. However, the completion in 1959 of the long-awaited Beach Boulevard improved access. Dookers and sun-worshippers could also rest assured that their comforts were looked after. The council employed four lifeguards, four play park attendants, six beach leaders and a nurse. There were also twelve beach attendants, usually students, to look after the 1,500 deckchairs that were available for hire. In 1963 these, along with twenty-six family huts, thirty bathing tents, and 300 'suntraps', earned the corporation some £2,500.

As an alternative to the beach, there were, as we have seen, many bus tours on offer. The Corporation Transport Department operated a wide variety of tours within the city and immediate neighbourhood, lasting in duration from half an hour to two and a half hours. Reaching out to a much wider area were independent operators who offered day and weekend tours to: 'Rugged mountains, pine-clad hills, fertile valleys and plains, castle and cottage famed in story and ancient ruins steeped in the history of Scotland's greatness all within easy run from the Silver City by the Sea.' For the ever-increasing number of motoring visitors, Aberdeen City Police Force issued a guidebook with helpful hints and a map showing parking places. Motorists were reminded that on the most popular section of the Beach Esplanade, the speed limit was 15 mph. They would, it

The Colintraive Ferry at the Kyles of Bute, which came into operation in 1950. This vessel, the *Eilean Mhor*, was Bute's first vehicular ferry. This former tank-landing craft had a very limited capacity and ran, as we see in the postcard, right on to the beach.

was also assumed, 'wish to drive slowly in order to benefit from the sea breezes and experience the atmosphere of gaiety on the beach.' By 1967 the booklet was into its 22nd edition. In 1971, too, the city's publicity department issued a guide, *Around and About Aberdeen by Car*. Well before then, though, the city's change in role to a touring centre, particularly as the 'gateway to royal Deeside', was evident. Whereas in older guide books guest house advertisements stressed proximity to tram and bus routes, their 1960s equivalents laid more emphasis on the availability of car parks. New, too, were adverts for motels, including in those more innocent days one called the Gay Gordon Motel.

Unfortunately, the ever-increasing number of cars was beginning to cause gridlock. A 1955 Glasgow Fair census of traffic recorded in one hour 1,300 vehicles passing, or rather crawling, through Prestwick. But, at least, the doon-the-watter resorts were now becoming more accessible for motorists. The long-awaited Kyles of Bute car ferry, operated by the Bute Ferry Company Ltd, had been opened in 1950 and the more direct Wemyss Bay to Rothesay route was ready in October 1954. The Gourock to Dunoon service had been inaugurated earlier that year. Ardrossan to Brodick followed in 1957 and Largs to the Isle of Cumbrae in 1972. Except for the short-distance Kyles and Cumbrae routes, there were no roll-on roll-off ferries, the boats then using a slow and costly hoist-loading system. The car ferries, however, had their downside, namely the closure of a large number of subsidiary piers, and the scrapping of a number of excursion steamers and the consequent curtailment of the number and variety of excursions. For some visitors to Arran, too, the number of cars on the island affected the quality of their holiday. Arran, they complained, had lost much of its traditional, peaceful island quality. Others, on the other hand, may have found small islands, even with a car, to have but limited appeal – like the visitor to Rothesay in 1959 who wrote on a postcard that when it rained he had hired a car and went for a drive, and that he had now been round the island six times! One wonders whether he ever returned to Bute.

The new car ferries, though convenient, were perceived to be expensive and now the ever-increasing car-owning population had, as the next chapter will demonstrate, even more options than hitherto. The ties that had bound them to their traditional resort destinations were breaking, and they were broken the more readily when they found that, as in Dunoon, the Sabbatarian shackles were still in force, with Sunday golf and cinema shows still banned. In 1949 a local plebiscite had resulted in a substantial majority for the status quo. However, towns like Dunoon had to face strong competition from resorts in England, and now also overseas, which enjoyed a much more relaxed attitude to Sabbath observance. And these overseas resorts had, at least, the considerable benefit of a much kinder climate. But too many people seemed blissfully ignorant of the foreign threat. Among them was the compiler of *The Buteman Guide to Rothesay* (*c.*1965 edition), who thoughtlessly repeated material from earlier editions, and thus wrote, after mentioning how other, older industries had failed: 'Rothesay, therefore, has for some years been left very much to its own natural resources as a watering place and health resort, and never has it been so prosperous.' This by 1965 was just not true.

CHAPTER 12

New Threats and Challenges:
The Flight to the Sun

The herd can change direction as quickly as the tide can sweep away the sand of the shore.

John P. Crosgrove on 'The Psychology of the Seaside Resort' in *Transactions of the Royal Sanitary Association of Scotland, 1950*

The above shrewd observation made by a Rothesay Town Councillor was certainly prophetic. That same year, 1950, saw the start of foreign package holidays using chartered aircraft. Admittedly, that first trip to Corsica in an old wartime Dakota made little impression, but the organiser, Vladimir Reitz and his tour company Horizon Holidays, went on to greater things. However, for some years to come, the holiday crowds, the 'herd', still headed, if not necessarily to Rothesay in particular, to one or other of the Scottish or English seaside resorts. When the weather was good, St Andrews, Aberdeen, the Clyde Coast towns and other resorts did very well. Within a few years, however, the situation was beginning to change for the worse. By the late 1950s the decline in domestic tourism was causing alarm in the industry. It was a time when the standard of living was rising and many people truly believed that they 'never had it so good'. Between 1952 and 1964, average wages rose by over two-thirds and despite the effects of inflation working folk had much more money to spend, and more of them could now afford to buy a car. In their choice of holiday destinations, working folk were now more ambitious. The now more affluent and, also more mobile, working class regarded their former favourite places as just too accessible and, what was even worse, dull and uninspiring. They were suffering from, to use a current vogue term, 'destination fatigue'. Broughty Ferry, Portobello and Saltcoats and such like were okay for a day out but were now too familiar, too commonplace and the range of available activities too limited. Once people from grim industrial towns could look upon the likes of Rothesay and Ayr as exciting and even exotic destinations, but these days were passing. The large English resorts, on the other hand, had a range of fairground thrills, theatres, cinemas and other entertainments that Scottish resorts could not match. The growth in the 1950s of car and coach travel widened choice, and working-class holidaymakers were now going much further afield. In the 1950s and 1960s, car-owners, and more of them too were towing caravans, thought nothing of venturing as far south as Devon and Cornwall or, if staying in Scotland, heading for the remoter Highlands.

One of the signs of the times was the shelving of some local rivalries. In an endeavour to stimulate tourism, the Banffshire resorts, which in the early 1950s had enjoyed an unexpected tourist boom, combined to publish a county brochure. The Clyde resorts had also adopted a joint advertising campaign. But much more was required. In 1958 the Scottish Tourist Board, using its house magazine *Take Note*, issued a wake-up call to municipal authorities. The increased mobility of the modern holidaymaker

THE BEACH, HOPEMAN   D 5589

The number of beach huts testifies to Hopeman's popularity in 1960, when this photograph was taken. Hopeman is one of the many Moray Firth coast villages, with a sandy beach and golf course, which appeal to city folk who want a quiet holiday.

and the limited financial resources of many local councils meant, the Board argued, that more co-operation and better funding were essential. As it was, it insisted that large areas of Scotland were fast asleep. Some resorts, though, did begin to stir themselves. To attract more golfers, Nairn Development Association held in 1959 the first of its special off-season Golf Weeks. Top professionals like Henry Cotton ran golf clinics and demonstrations, and the hotels co-operated by offering an inclusive tariff embracing course entry fees and tuition, also talks and social events. Golf during the daytime was followed by entertainment like concerts, dances and film shows in the evenings. So successful were these golf weeks that the idea was copied by other resorts. By the early 1960s many hotels in Rothesay, Dunoon and other resorts were offering special off-season rates for senior citizens.

Resorts began to recast their image in other ways, seeking, for one thing, to attract visitors by producing more colourful and less didactic guidebooks. For instance, a 1968 official guide for once-staid North Berwick featured on the front cover three glamorous water-skiing maids in acrobatic pose. As their guidebook illustrations and titles show, resorts put a lot of emphasis on their family holiday facilities. *Carnoustie ideal for the family* is a typical late-1970s title. Similarly, we find a 1960s guide for nearby Monifieth stressing that it was a quiet town, one that was 'unspoilt by those distractions which are found in larger holiday centres' and that with no slums it was also an attractive residential centre.

As for resort promotion, this previously was just another of the myriad duties performed by a town clerk or burgh chamberlain or, in the case of Peterhead, the burgh surveyor. In the post-war years, some burghs – Arbroath, Dunbar, and Fraserburgh for example – appointed tourism-cum-publicity officers. Their role was to promote and publicise their town and to organise events and entertainments for visitors. In 1956, Bill Cumming was appointed as Publicity and Entertainment Manager for Carnoustie. Giving the people what he thought they wanted, he organised talent competitions, beach games, and beauty contests. One event, which showed how more affluent holidaymakers had become, was a follow-my-leader chase by cars. Bill Cumming, driving the town's publicity van, led the procession, taking the visitors to places in the district which they might not otherwise have found. At Stonehaven, too, the town appointed an entertainments officer for the summer months. In addition, the burgh chamberlain (the town finance official) served as publicity officer. From his office some 10,000 promotional postcards were sent to factories all over Britain. In all communities, however, there were some to whom the whole notion of tourist development was anathema. When an amenities group to improve tourist facilities was formed in Gardenstown, one of the councillors of this Banffshire fishing village (and stronghold of the Brethren religious sect) objected, as he did not wish to see his village turned into a miniature Scarborough.

As always, some seasons were better than others. The 1964 season was marred for Aberdeen, an outbreak of typhoid giving the city the wrong kind of publicity. Good weather was a boon, as when in 1955 and 1966 the weather was particularly fine. The very good summer of 1966 saw Aberdeen bounce back, with a record number of visitors That year too, as *Take Note* tells us, bookings for Arbroath's hotels, boarding-houses, lodgings and many caravans were sustained over the whole summer and not just for the Glasgow Fair. It was the same at Dunbar, where the swimming pool takings soared and hoteliers were even turning customers away. At that time most visitors were still spending at least a week, many a fortnight, in their resort of choice. Bill Stratton, a Burntisland shopkeeper, recalled how, in the 1960s, Glaswegians were lavish in their spending. The other trades holidays were quite good for trade. But, he said, 'everybody was waiting for the Glasgow Fair because when they came, by train, by bus, whatever it was, they stayed for a fortnight solid. They came with 20, 30 pounds. In those days, that was a lot of money, you know. And they said, "Well, I brought it, get something for my missus, something for my daughter, something for my son." Putting 10 pounds on the counter, he says, "Get them something each."' But the trend overall was downward and it was most marked in the traditional peak holiday month of July. Eventually, too, the decline spread to the August (mainly English) market. In the 1950s the Scottish seaside resorts, boosted by British Railways holiday schemes, had still attracted substantial numbers of English visitors. But the 1960s Beeching-era cuts in the railway network meant that many resorts were deprived of their rail link. The East Neuk of Fife fishing communities and the Buchan and south Moray Firth coast towns (Nairn only excepted) were among the resorts affected. The days of summer specials to the Fife coast and other holiday hotspots were well and truly over. Traditionalists like David Daiches mourned the passing of the south Moray Firth coast line. Describing family holidays at Cullen in Banffshire, he wrote in *The Listener* (13 December 1973): 'We used to take a pram for the baby, bicycles and a large quantity of luggage – all of which travelled effortlessly in the luggage van.'

Like Cullen, Banff was served by rail until this branch was closed to passenger traffic in 1964. The number of parked cars and buses testifies to its erstwhile popularity.

When this Visit the Clyde Coast poster was issued by the Scottish Tourist Board in 1965, the golden age of the Clyde excursion steamer was well and truly over. Here we see in the foreground one of the last, the turbine steamer *Queen Mary II*, crossing the path of one of the Dunoon–Gourock car ferries. Both vessels are in the original Caledonian Steam Packet Company colours. (*Image reproduced by permission of VisitScotland*)

The lady who posted this card at Dunbar in September 1947 wrote that the weather had been not too bad. By the 1970s, however, holidaymakers who went abroad would expect to find weather that was a lot better than not too bad.

The Firth of Clyde resorts were badly affected by the slump in domestic tourism. For the County of Ayr, a study reckoned that the economic value of tourism had dropped by around 23 per cent between 1959 and 1964. The Scottish Tourist Board was forced to concede that the resorts faced problems. In *Take Note*, in the February 1964 issue, the editor admitted: 'It is no secret that in the past couple of years the Firth of Clyde resorts have not had the same number of visitors.' The decline in Scottish holiday visitors was due, he considered, to the ever-increasing number of families who now possessed motor cars and enjoyed a much wider choice of destination. For holidaymakers coming to Scotland, Dunoon, Rothesay and many other Clyde holiday centres were regarded as dead-end routes. They were, the editor argued, 'not on the trunk road from anywhere to anywhere'. As the years passed, there were even more motorists on the roads. By 1973, according to Scottish Tourist Statistics, 76 per cent of British tourists in Scotland were travelling by car, with a mere 10 per cent going by train and another 8 per cent by regular coach or bus.

The hoteliers and merchants of Prestwick followed the example of other towns and formed their own Tourist Development Association. However, attempts made there and elsewhere in the Clyde area to attract visitors from south of the Border met with but limited success. In the late 1960s the Clyde resorts, for example, depended far too much on their traditional, and by then declining, catchment areas. According to David A. Pattinson's 1965 survey, only 15 per cent of holidaymakers came from south of the Border. Saltcoats and Brodick, it was reckoned, drew 86 per cent of their 'resident visitors' from West Central Scotland, and Girvan even more at 88 per cent. Only Dunoon and Largs had a more diversified clientele, with Largs having 30 per cent of its long-stay visitors coming from England and 3 per cent from Northern Ireland. Over in the east, it was a similar situation with the Angus resorts, for example, appealing to native Scots rather than people from abroad. Optimists, however, hoped that the new road bridges over the Forth (1964) and the Tay (1966) would bring Continental caravanners and campers flocking to Arbroath!

Nevertheless, the age of easy prosperity was coming to an end. Over-reliance on their traditional, seemingly captive markets had tended to engender complacency. Much of the resort accommodation and other facilities were not up to modern standards. During the easy years when competition was limited, many tourist providers had become complacent and so did not move with the times. They failed to recognise that the new generation had more sophisticated needs and, with new and more varied leisure interests, were unwilling merely to follow in their parents' footsteps. British holidaymakers were looking outward and were widening their horizons. In the 1960s and 1970s foreign holiday packages became cheaper. Holidaymakers enjoyed the novelty of new destinations and modes of travel – a whole gamut of new experiences and, what was even more novel, more or less guaranteed good weather. Holiday packages and cheap flights offered a comprehensive service for an all-in price. Travel company reps smoothed the way for nervous travellers, guiding them from airport to resort and back again. To meet increasing demand, travel agencies multiplied. A Dunfermline newspaper noted, in 1963, the increasing number of people heading for a place in the sun on the Costa Brava or Majorca or even further south to 'little known resorts' on the Costa del Sol. Between 1951 and 1970 the number of British people going abroad for a holiday almost quadrupled. But they were still predominantly from the middle class and at that time, as the British National Travel Survey indicates, the great majority of Britons were still holidaying at home. It was not till the late 1970s that the great explosion in package holidays and the consequent slump in the domestic market began to make a major difference. More modern, and larger capacity, jet aircraft helped to bring prices down by a substantial degree and this was very much to the favour of lower-income groups.

With Britons heading for foreign shores in increasing numbers, the UK government began for the first time to take a really serious interest in developing and exploiting Britain's tourist potential. To this end, in 1969 it set up as a statutory agency the British Tourist Authority, with the reconstituted Scottish Tourist Board also now a government-financed statutory agency, as were its English, Welsh, and Northern Irish equivalents. The original Scottish Tourist Board (STB) had been formed in 1945, with Tom Johnston, the outstanding wartime Secretary of State for Scotland, as its first chairman. Though established with government approval, it received no grant of any kind from central funds. Thanks to Tom Johnston's astute leadership, the STB, created at a time when Scotland was rightly described as 'a small and struggling starter in the tourist business', had more leverage than its miserly-treated precursor, the prewar Scottish Travel Association. So casual had been the prewar attitude to the tourist trade that even such an acute observer as C. A. Oakley when writing on Scottish tourism put inverted commas round industry. Tom Johnston for one thing ensured that his board, though self-described as predominantly a consumers' association, managed, unlike its predecessor, to keep control of all the money it raised. Although the STB had limited powers and was funded rather inadequately by local authorities, it did some very valuable work in the way of guidebooks and brochures and accommodation lists. In addition, the reconstituted Scottish Tourist Board was now empowered to invest in effective research – to discover, for instance, what tourists were actually doing and what their needs were. It was now also enabled to help finance projects such as new hotels, building extensions and heritage trails. The STB, however, marketed Scotland as a whole, and the traditional coastal resorts merited only a share of a cake, which had to be very widely distributed. On the other hand, the Highlands and Islands Development Board (HIDB), formed in 1965, was funded on a comparatively generous basis and, right from the start, could spend money both at home and abroad on advertising the scenic and other attractions of the Highlands and thus boosted the numbers going to that region. Arran and some of the smaller Highland resorts, though, did come into the HIDB's sphere of influence and so benefited from its largesse. With the STB, on the other hand, to the Board's chagrin, the overall body the British Tourist Authority retained responsibility for all overseas publicity. It was 1984 before the STB before gained the right to market Scotland overseas.

The Hotel Development Incentive scheme, established under the Development of Tourism Act of 1969, did provide large sums of money for new hotels, extensions and modernisation. As far as the traditional resorts were concerned, however, the benefits were limited. STB grants and loans did enable hoteliers and guesthouse proprietors to carry out extensions and make other improvements. But these, on the whole, were small-scale projects. The large international hotel groups were just not interested in building in decaying resorts. Their preference was to build or extend in cities and places with an all-the-year-round clientele. St Andrews with its rich golfing heritage was one notable exception. In consequence, places with only small owner-occupied hotels failed to capitalise on the increasingly popular short-stay coach holiday segment of the market. On the other hand, during the 1960s and early 1970s, the North-West Highlands, now boosted by the HIDB, enjoyed a minor tourist boom, with Ullapool, Gairloch and other West Highland destinations increasing in popularity. According to the *Third Statistical Account: Ross and Cromarty*, Lochbroom Parish, which included Ullapool, had by 1982 sixteen hotels, a greatly increased caravan and campsite capacity, new restaurants, cafés, tourist-orientated shops, boat trips and pony trekking facilities. In contrast, the historic town of Cromarty, on an isolated corner on the east side of the county, had experienced a sharp decline in 'the once-important summer hotel trade in family holidays', thus sharing the fate of the larger southern resorts. The opening in 1982 of the Kessock Bridge over the Beauly Firth did provide some compensation by boosting the number of day visitors.

Evidence of Ullapool's mini-boom photographed by the author on a fine August day in 1995.

Although probably far from being the complete picture, it is revealing to find that, according to Scottish Tourist Board bednight statistics for 1973, the Highland village of Ullapool was more popular than Rothesay or Arbroath. Whereas Ayr and Aberdeen of the old seaside resorts did relatively well – marginally ahead of Oban and Inverness – Dunoon and North Berwick had sunk well down the table of popularity, well behind Aviemore and Perth. Again, although just pointers, analysis of the 1976 bednight figures indicates that, when domestic – i.e. British – visitors only were taken into account, Aberdeen, Ayr, Rothesay and Nairn retained a fair measure of popularity but, in contrast, Ullapool was bottom of the league. Dunoon and North Berwick, on the other hand, were still in a relatively low position.

Under the 1969 act, new area boards were also created, with their activities coordinated by the STB. The area boards, thirty-five of them at that time, obviously had a much wider remit than the individual resorts' own agencies. In 1975, the resorts were further weakened when local government was reorganised. The creation of the new Regional and District authorities meant the abolition of the town councils, which up till then had the main responsibility for tourist promotion and had also played a major role in the development of facilities. Elected local community councils had been created but they did not have anything like the same degree of authority and financial clout. The new authorities governed much wider areas, often including large urban areas. Many people in traditional resorts felt, post-1975, that their interests and priorities were being neglected. In traditionally Tory Largs, residents accused the Labour-controlled district and regional councils of neglecting their needs. Inadequate parking in a town that was overrun by day-trippers was one of the main gripes. In the Moray Firth resort of Lossiemouth, there were immediate complaints that the new Moray District was not getting value for money from the regionally appointed area board, the Aberdeen and Grampian Tourist Board. The townsfolk were unhappy, too, with the service they received from their nearest Tourist Information Centre, Elgin TIC. The Lossie folk wanted their own TIC back again. Since then the area board system has been chopped and changed several times, the most recent change coming in 2005.

In the 1970s and 1980s, foreign competition intensified. The large-scale tourist companies offered a product, which, with regard to both price and facilities, was far superior to anything that the domestic market could provide. The Scottish, and indeed many of the English, Welsh and Northern Ireland resorts also, just could not compete and, in consequence, lost what hold they still had on the long-stay domestic market. The effects were widespread. From 1976 to 1980, for instance, the attendance levels at Ayr's Gaiety Theatre had remained fairly constant. In 1981, however, attendances slumped, down by 20 per cent, and that was just one reflection of the decline in the domestic market. The hotels, too, were losing market share. Dunbar alone lost three large hotels, one the fifty-two-room Belle-View which then stood derelict for many years. It was not till 2005 that the decision to demolish it was finally reached. By 1987, the number of Britons going abroad for holidays (of four nights or more) had risen to 20 million. Nearly 12 million of them were on package tours, virtually a six-fold increase since 1970. There are no separate Scottish figures, but in 1991, at the start of the Glasgow Fair, an estimated 30,000 people left Glasgow airport on international flights. In 2005 on one single day, Fair Friday, the same airport handled 41,616 passengers. These outward-bound holidaymakers were the kind of people who, say, forty years earlier would have been heading for Ayr, Stonehaven or some other domestic resort.

The need for overcoats and tweed jackets during the Scottish summer helps to explain why Scots abandoned Troon and similar Scottish resorts and, once cheap package holidays became available, flocked instead to Mediterranean warmth.

CHAPTER 13

Meccas No More

Nature has provided the region with many of the ingredients necessary to a successful tourist industry, but many of the developed areas leave much to be desired. With few exceptions the communities of the area fail to provide a distinctive tourist appeal, lacking both old world charm and the colour and gaiety of a modern resort.

Tourism in the Firth of Clyde Region, Scottish Tourist Board, 1968

The increased popularity of rival domestic resorts and of the foreign package holiday hit the Clyde and other Scottish resorts very badly. For Rothesay, we can trace the process of decline through the harbour passenger figures. In the halcyon year of 1955, the number of passengers going through the turnstiles had been a post-war record. Thereafter the numbers slowly declined for some years and then, between 1968 and 1973, very rapidly. The fact that UK domestic holidaymakers were now using cars for travelling in or to Scotland, 76 per cent by 1973, was one major factor. By the late 1960s, accordingly, Clyde steamer cruising had virtually collapsed. For example, the Three Lochs Tour, a circular by steamer and train embracing Lochgoil, Loch Long and Loch Lomond, had in its heyday been operated every weekday. It was reduced to twice a week in 1971, to once a week in the following year, and abandoned altogether at the end of that summer's season.

Increased car ferry traffic brought some recompense, but it did not make up for the massive decline in the number of day visitors to resorts like Dunoon and Rothesay. For the latter towns, traditionally accessed by steamer, the consequences were catastrophic. Since Rothesay was well away from the main tourist flow, it received relatively few of the bus tours which would have provided some compensation for the loss of steamer-borne traffic. With its long-standing doon-the-watter history, Rothesay also had an image problem. Despite Costa Clyde-style marketing ploys, the number of English visitors continued to fall. They complained that, in comparison with other options, Scottish resorts in general were too expensive, too difficult to get to and sadly increasingly tatty, and the weather could not be relied on. It was very evident too, as a 1975 report acknowledged, that the younger generation, except for the yachting fraternity, was now bypassing Rothesay. To make things worse, as in many other places, the decline in the number of visitors to Rothesay had a cumulative effect on the very attractions that were so necessary for its future. For Rothesay, and indeed other Scottish resorts, fewer visitors meant less cash to spend on repairing the fabric of existing structures let alone building new ones. Hotelkeepers and other providers in their turn had to struggle to maintain a meagre livelihood, and thus had less cash to spend on improvements. Run down and visually blighted as they were, many of the Clyde resorts were, as the above quotation indicates, a complete turn-off.

The decline in the popularity of pleasure sailing on the Clyde, combined with the introduction of roll-on-roll-off ferries, led to the closure of many of the doon-the-watter steamer piers. With the ending of the Three Lochs Tour, Arrochar Pier on Loch Long was closed to steamer traffic in 1972. Going against the grain, however, the pier at Blairmore in Cowal was reopened in 2005, 150 years after it was built. Photograph by the author in 1977.

A demographic collapse compounded the problem for Rothesay. In the second half of the twentieth century, the burgh's population halved, slumping from its 1951 peak of 10,141 to 5,017 in 2001. As the years passed, the local population, an ageing one at that, could no longer sustain essential tourist facilities. One after the other, the cinemas were shut. In 1972 the same fate befell the once highly popular Winter Gardens Pavilion variety-hall. Though the latter facility served for some years as an amusement arcade, its condition deteriorated and it was for long under threat of demolition. Fewer visitors meant that boat hiring ceased to be profitable. At Rothesay it ended about 1970, but at Port Bannatyne boats could be hired at Stewart's slip until the early 1980s. Over the years various attempts had been made to broaden the town's appeal. In 1964 a curious experiment had brought a rollcurling rink to the esplanade. With curling stones fitted with ball-bearings, no ice was required. Despite a publicity stunt involving football players from Glasgow Rangers and Greenock Morton, this odd hybrid of a game did not catch on. In 1968, there was a more practical attempt to draw early season visitors back to the 'Madeira of the Clyde' when the Rothesay Hoteliers' Association started an off-peak package holidays scheme designed to compete with foreign package holidays. The initial venture was abandoned after a few years. The scheme was reintroduced in 1978 and, as before, it targeted the older generation. To launch the 1979 package, hoteliers and their families dressed themselves in Victorian dress. The entertainments on offer included variety shows, ceilidhs, museum admission, sequence dancing and bus tours – all very worthy, but of limited appeal for the younger generation. Although in later years the time scale was extended and a more children-friendly family package launched, the Rothesay package holiday venture did not stem the flow. The conference market was on the decline, too, the loss of the island's large hotels, the Glenburn excepted, having a disastrous effect.

It was not all doom and gloom, however. Rothesay's days as a mass-market destination may have been over, but the hoteliers' attempts to break into the 'second holiday' market were not a complete failure Also, on the plus side there were improvements, albeit rather delayed, to the physical environment. Housing and commercial properties were upgraded. To replace the indoor baths, which had been closed in the 1980s, a new swimming pond was opened in 1989. In the following year, the refurbishment of the long-derelict Winter Gardens was completed, and then in 1992 the new ferry pier buildings were opened (the original building had been lost after a fire). Nevertheless, as has happened in other places, there was a great deal of argument as to the best ways and means of forwarding the interests of the island. For some people, the then Bute and Cowal Tourist Board was to blame. In consequence, in 1994 some of the diminishing number of hoteliers and other proprietors formed a breakaway group and published their own promotional material. For others, it was the degree of Bute estate dominance, which they denounced as being unhealthy and inhibiting development. On the other hand, a change of policy meant that from 1995 the Bute family seat, the quirky Gothic-style Mount Stuart, was opened to the public. Mount Stuart has since proved to be a significant tourist attraction, helping to draw in more coach tours. Rothesay's restored Victorian-period gents' toilets, which contrive to combine public utility and aesthetic appeal, have proved to be another tourist hit. Ladies too, at the attendant's discretion, can view their ceramic charms and polished brass fittings. For Lucinda Lampton, an authority on such conveniences, the Rothesay urinals are 'the most beautiful in the world'.

Dunoon fared very differently. For some years the Cowal resort, as *Take Note* recorded in 1964, had been making a big effort to be pensioner-friendly. Each Monday during the weeks when the concession rate applied, the Town Council provided traditional Scottish entertainment in the Queen's Hall for some 800 to 900 senior citizens. An emergent Folkestone travel company, Saga

Rothesay's
refurbished
Victorian gents' loo,
photographed by the
author in July 2002.

Senior Citizens Holidays, offered over-60s eight or fifteen-day inclusive holidays to Dunoon at prices from £16. These packages 'with all the little details taken care of' were organised in conjunction with British Rail. But, like Rothesay, Dunoon was on a downward slope. Its once vaunted lido, for years regarded as a white elephant, was in 1960 converted into a pottery. In November that year the townsfolk were shocked to learn that Cowal's Holy Loch was going to serve as a base for American submarines equipped with Polaris nuclear missiles. For holidaymakers this might be a major turn-off, but, on the other hand, hoteliers, guest house owners, and other local businesses looked to gain from the American presence, just as they had in the boom wartime years when there had also been a substantial military involvement in the Cowal peninsula. CND (Campaign for Nuclear Disarmament) and other anti-Polaris protestors flocked to Dunoon and demonstrated, vigorously and often rowdily, but to no avail. On the other hand, believing that it would benefit the town, Dunoon folk, by and large, welcomed the American influx.

Then, in 1972, there came another, but less welcome, invasion when hordes of outside workers, many of them Irish, were imported to build and work on an oil rig construction yard at nearby Ardyne Point. To house the many hundreds of workers brought into Cowal, McAlpine, the construction firm involved, purchased a number of local hotels and boarding houses, arousing some disquiet in the process. In some of the remaining guesthouses, holidaymakers were disturbed to find that there were navvies staying there too. Some locals, according to G. G. Giarchi, a sociological investigator, likened the 'Godless' navvies to the Sabbath breakers that had so disturbed their Victorian predecessors. Scarred though the area was by the McAlpine site, to the south of the town, and the American base, to the north, Dunoon was still attracting tourists; and at least it now had an indoor swimming pool. The opening of this pond in 1968 marked the end of a long campaign to provide what was an obvious amenity for a holiday town. But, as with Rothesay, Dunoon's holiday traffic was on a much-reduced scale. Having lost their position as the main destination for the local West of Scotland market, Dunoon and the other Clyde Coast resorts had now ceased to be considered as serious summer options for English holidaymakers. The much warmer and cheaper Spanish Costas had overtaken the Costa Clyde. The growth of the 'retirement industry' provided some compensation. In the 1980s, in towns like Ayr and Largs, a number of hotels and large

It was not all loss for the Clyde. Here we see passengers embarking on the paddle steamer *Waverley* from the restored Tignabruaich Pier in August 2003.

private houses were converted into long-stay accommodation for older people. This evoked some resentment, however, with locals complaining that the Clyde coast was being transformed into the Costa Geriatrica. A high proportion of elderly residents meant, it was feared, an unbalanced community and undue pressure on expensive social and medical services.

Aberdeen too was losing ground. Even its famous golden sands were disappearing and in the 1960s vast sums were expended to retain what was left. Once popular facilities were now regarded as economic liabilities. With its audiences dwindling, the Beach Pavilion was closed in 1961. The stage where highly popular 'Scotch' comedians like Harry Gordon and Dave Willis once served hamely comic fare became a restaurant. At the Beach Ballroom the post-war municipal management tried hard to maintain business by diversifying into other forms of use. But the disco generation had other ideas and ditched the Beach Ballroom in favour of more intimate milieus. The old Beach Baths were closed in 1972 and subsequently demolished, as was the bandstand. In 1986, despite conservationists' protests, another popular links landmark, the Victorian-era Shelter, was razed to the ground. On the plus side, Aberdeen could justifiably boast of its floral displays, with the city winning the Beautiful Britain in Bloom Trophy no fewer than ten times and having, it was claimed, at Duthie Park the largest indoor garden in Europe.

Nevertheless, over the years various grandiose plans for redeveloping the seafront and for new wet weather facilities came to naught. The district council did eventually open a Beach Leisure Centre with 'pleasure pool' and sports hall. Other beach area improvements included, in 1992, an ice rink; then came a hotel and a refurbished amusement park, including a spectacular roller coaster. The funfair, it was asserted, was the largest of its type in Scotland. In 1999 an expensive Leisure Park was ceremoniously opened. It included a multiplex cinema, science discovery centre, nightclub, restaurant and other facilities. The consortium formed to restore the fortunes of the seafront named their new venture the Aberdeen Fun Beach. Sensibly, publicity material stressed the fact that most of the attractions were indoors and 'undercover in climate controlled conditions'. The old 'golden sands' brand was now evidently outdated. Final recognition that the days when sun worshippers packed the beach were a thing of the past had come in 1998. That year the City Council sold its last remaining deckchairs, which had been in store since the mid-1980s. Not that Aberdeen was exceptional in this regard, usage of the no longer fashionable deckchairs having slumped elsewhere also. As for the Art Deco Beach Ballroom, long regarded by some as a liability but now a B-listed building, it underwent some refurbishment and is still serving a useful purpose as an events centre.

As for Portobello, the 1960s and 1970s were ill years too for its holiday trade. British Railways closed the passenger stations at Portobello and its Joppa suburb in 1964; the funfair went in the 1970s. In 1977 the power station was closed. This impinged on the open-air swimming pond since it meant that there would be no more free heated water. Two years later Edinburgh District Council decided, by a small majority, that Porty's once magnificent outdoor swimming pool should be closed, although the Portobello Pool Users' Association had presented a petition signed by more than 2,000 people demanding that it be kept open. The decisive factor, though, was a consultant's report that it would cost more than £200,000 to keep it in use. The pool was then left derelict for some years, a sad blot on the landscape. To add insult to injury, the local seawater was found to be polluted; the beach too was looking very bare and sand had to be pumped from the seabed to restore it to something like its former state. Local business people, with local government backing, did try to improve amenities and add to Portobello's visitor attractions by capitalising on its Victorian seaside heritage. Indeed, when the sun comes out, the day-trippers do arrive. Bed and Breakfast

THE BEACH, ABERDEEN   4053

A busy day at Aberdeen beach in the 1940s, a time when deckchairs were still much in demand. All the visitors are formally and heavily clothed, and it was certainly not through fear of sunstroke. This card was posted to Thornton in Fife in July 1949. It was evidently a Fife holiday week as the sender had 'met many Thornton people here'. The handsome and well-loved Beach Shelter, seen on the left, which had stood on the prom for many years, was demolished in 1986.

establishments also do some trade, but it is Edinburgh not Portobello as a beach resort that is the main attraction. As a popular long-stay destination in its own right, Porty's time has gone.

Portobello was, by no means, the only resort to lose its outdoor swimming pool. By then, these once symbolic structures were deemed by most local authorities to be unnecessary encumbrances. They were certainly expensive to maintain, their seaside location always rendering them liable to storm damage. In the era of cheap foreign travel and of new heated indoor pools, fewer people were willing to pay for the privilege of dooking in cold, wind and rain-swept old-style saltwater ponds. Despite some bitter opposition, pool after pool closed its doors. The once prestigious Prestwick Sea Bathing Lake was shut in 1972, the same year as a new indoor pool was opened in Ayr. Large or small, virtually all shared the same fate. When a ring road was constructed, Invergordon's pool was demolished in 1978, but there was at least a bonus with the Scottish Development Agency paying hefty compensation. Over in the west, the Helensburgh one went in 1977, replaced by an indoor pool; and Troon's pond, which had been expensively but inadequately modernised, fell to the breakers in 1986.

Outmoded they might have been, but all the outdoor pools had their champions. When in 1975 Buckie's Strathlene pool was under threat, locals protested that, if it was closed, the town would lose its sole tourist attraction. For the 1976 season the pond did, nevertheless, receive a face-lift, but in the following year winter storms breached the pool's outer seawalls. When it found that renovation costs were estimated at £18,400, Moray District Council decided that it could no longer afford to maintain the pond. In contrast, in that same year, the neighbouring authority, the then

High tide at the derelict Strathlene swimming pool at Buckie, photographed by the author in September 1999. Compare this view with the photograph in Chapter 6. Winter storms had swept away the changing rooms and seawall and partially filled the pond with beach pebbles. In 2004 the pool was in-filled and the surrounding area landscaped.

Banff and Buchan District Council, did carry out some improvements at Macduff's Tarlair pool, but at the same time it reduced hours and cut the number of staff. Tarlair survived into the 1990s, but eventually it went the same way as its Buckie rival. In the early 1990s major rock concerts were held there, in the natural amphitheatre which housed the pond. They featured top names like, rather appropriately, Wet Wet Wet, also Cliff Richard, Fish and Jethro Tull. Sadly, though, the site is now derelict but it looks as if, with admittedly considerable expenditure, it could be brought back into use again. At the time of writing, Aberdeenshire Council is considering options for the future use of the pool. Storm damage and the rising costs of repairs led also to the closure of the Dunbar pond. Again many locals were bitterly opposed, so the Dunbar Traders Association stepped in and the pool was reopened in 1979 under their auspices. But there were too many problems and in 1982 the Dunbar outdoor pool, once the pride of the community, closed at the end of the summer season. There were protests too at Port Seton when the well-loved pond hall was demolished in 1995 to make way for new houses.

Across the Firth in Fife, St Andrews Town Council had for many years faced criticism over the condition of its Step Rock pool, the Steppie as it was popularly called. Complaints to the press included: 'a relic of a bygone age' and 'exposed to the full fury of the elements and to the vagaries of the various sewers in the proximity'. Its defenders were equally passionate, but were unable to convince the local authority of its value to the community. It was closed in 1981, but it was another seven years before its indoor replacement was built. Elsewhere in Fife, the doors at the Burntisland pool were, despite a bitter rearguard action, shut for good at the end of the 1978 season. In the following year, Kirkcaldy District Council did try to allay local discontent by announcing that a new indoor pool would be erected. It took eighteen years, nevertheless, for that promise to be fulfilled. As for Arbroath's monster-sized pond, in 1973 it was reduced in size in an attempt to make it easier to heat, and thus prolong its life. But, as with most other ponds, these efforts were ultimately unsuccessful and it was closed in 1980.

North Berwick's pond lasted longer than most. As elsewhere, the numbers paying for admission had drastically declined. By the early 1990s, however, each user, the district council complained, cost it almost £10 per head on a pool that was open for only thirteen weeks of the year. However, with a new indoor pool on the way, the old pond, the council decided, had to go. Although the

A Valentine postcard of the Dunbar outdoor pond in its 1931 heyday. There were 2,000 spectators at the gala held in that same year to mark the opening of the new pavilion.

doors were closed on 28 August 1995, a campaign to retain the facility gathered momentum. The Save the Outdoor Pool (STOP) campaigners gathered 6,000 signatures against closure and, at the same time, offered to take over and run the pond but it was to no avail. Now many of the old pools have disappeared altogether, the sites cleared and built over or used for a car park. At Dunbar, the derelict pool was demolished and the beach restored to its natural state. It took twenty-seven years, however, for the Strathlene pool to be cleared, backfilled, and the site transformed into an attractive picnic area. At Leven, the former Letham Glen pond was cleverly transformed into a sunken garden, and the Portobello site is now a games field. Much more survives at some of the East Fife tidal ponds – at St Monans and Cellardyke, for example. The St Andrews Step Rock pool at least fills another role, as a key component in a popular aquarium.

It is not just the outdoor swimming ponds that have gone. Sadly, even children's paddling pools have been falling into disuse, some, as at Portobello, as a result of neglect following local government cost-cutting and others emptied since they do not meet contemporary health and safety regulations. Health and safety factors too led to the closure of Portsoy's tidal open-air swimming pool by Aberdeenshire Council. Although the adjacent beach is still popular, for the pool, however, as at nearby Tarlair, there is a prominent warning notice stating that it is a dangerous area and that, as the water is neither treated nor monitored, it is definitely closed. There are two notable survivals, the Trinkie Pool and the North Baths, and both are at Wick, a town about far north as you can go on the mainland. For some years now the Trinkie, a basic natural seawater pool, has been cleaned and painted by volunteers. But the restoration of the North Baths is a more recent phenomenon. Derelict as recently as 2003, the seawall was rebuilt by dedicated volunteers. In the following year, the North Baths was reopened 100 years after it was built (see photographs on the Wick web site). Of the once numerous local authority outdoor pools, there are only two left in Scotland that are maintained and open to the public, one at Gourock and the other at Stonehaven. It takes the help of volunteers, though, to keep these two viable. In Gourock's case, the pool was reopened in 2012, after a nearly £2 million renovation as a focal point for regenerating the town.

Threatened with closure in 1994, Stonehaven's handsome Art Deco open-air pond was saved from demolition only through a co-operative effort between a group of local volunteers, the Friends of

Children splashing happily in Leven's paddling pond, *c.* 1950. Notice the concrete blocks skirting the beach. They were built during the Second World War to stop the advance of any German tanks that might have landed on the shore.

Stonehaven Open Air Pool, and Aberdeenshire Council. The council was persuaded by the Friends to pay for qualified life-saving staff, maintain the plant and provide an annual capital budget. The Friends agreed to raise funds, help with marketing and provide a team of volunteers to do painting and other basic maintenance work. In 2004, the Scottish Tourist Board awarded this Olympic-sized open-air pool 4 Star status as a Visitor Attraction. Although, as with most ponds, the diving boards have been removed on safety grounds, the water chute has been retained. Unlike most of the prewar ponds, both the Stonehaven and Gourock pools are heated to 84 F (28C), a degree of warmth that would have been incredible to the dookers of their 1930s heyday. As in prewar days, midnight galas are a popular feature. The Friends have carried out quite a number of improvements at Stonehaven. These include pool thermal covers to cut down on heating bills, disabled access, and permanent floodlighting for the evening swims. In 2012 the season lasted from 26 May to 2 September inclusive. Recently, a new children's pond was built within an extended pool perimeter. Elsewhere, while the open-air pools may have gone, many resorts now have an indoor swimming pool, the best of them also serving as multi-activity leisure centres. Ironically, while local government bodies were closing down outdoor pools, new ponds, some of them open air, were being built at some of the large caravan sites or holiday centres, as they are now called.

As for Scotland's beaches today, there are, on holiday occasions, enough stay-at-homes to give an animated enough appearance but only when the weather is really fine. Until recently Scotland's beaches, as with UK beaches in general, compared badly with their Continental counterparts in terms of cleanliness and general safety. Too many of the most popular beaches – on the Forth and on the Ayrshire coast for instance – were badly polluted by sewage. Ayr had a particularly malodorous reputation. Comedians may have poked fun: 'I wasn't really swimming, just going through the motions.' But it was no fun for dookers who suffered ill effects or for people in the resorts whose livelihoods were affected. In 1986 the Director of the River Forth Purification Board was quoted as saying that Edinburgh at one time had the worst set of beaches in Europe because of the city's lack of sewage treatment. Not surprisingly, two years later a survey revealed that no fewer than eleven out of twenty-three of Scotland's most popular beaches failed to meet European standards. Eleven years later the situation was no better with only one Scottish beach, Aberdour Silver Sands, reaching the top grade of Blue Flag standard.

Punch and Judy man at Silver Sands, Aberdour, photographed by the author on 9 August 1999. Fife Council had hired him as part of the entertainment laid on to mark the award of a Blue Flag for the fourth successive year. This performer told the author that, as well as the standard performance, he also did a non-sexist version.

By the twenty-first century, improvements were beginning to take effect. In 2012 sixty-one seaside beaches qualified for a Keep Scotland Beautiful Seaside Award, a record number. Twelve years earlier there had been a mere thirteen. In addition to resort beaches like Portobello, a number of rural beaches qualified for an award. It is noticeable that virtually all the current award-winning beaches are in the north, north-west and east coasts. In Scotland's former doon-the-watter playground, only four qualified for an award. While Ayrshire had just two, Shetland in contrast could boast of five beach awards! For the more demanding Blue Flag criteria, Fife had by far the best record with six Blue Flag beaches in 2012, with Coldingham and Broughty Ferry the only other Scottish ones. Nevertheless, in comparison with Wales, which had forty-three Blue Flag awards for its beaches and five for marinas in 2012, Scotland fared badly with eight for its beaches. The Isle of Anglesey alone had seven blue Flag beaches. Unfortunately, after the Scottish flags had been awarded, three of them – at Aberdour, Leven and Coldingham – were subsequently withdrawn. Exceptionally heavy rain, which can cause sewers to overflow, was a possible source of the pollution. With the degree of pollution seen as marginal, these three beaches, however, retained their other Seaside Award flags. Evidently, though, there is some way to go before Scotland's main beaches can be a source of pride, and be regarded once more as suitable playgrounds for family pleasure and entertainment and, perhaps even more importantly, safe resorts for the health-conscious bather. On the other hand, there are many scenically splendid beaches in the Highlands and Islands where the remoteness and accessibility factors preclude classification.

CHAPTER 14

Postscript:
The Contemporary Scene

Over the last 30 years holidays have become synonymous with sunshine, Duty Free, and going home in a silver bird. We have lost the sexy business, if you like, between 18 and 35-40 and we need to do something to bring that back.

Alistair Risk, Hotelier, giving evidence to the Scottish Affairs Committee of the House of Commons in 1998.

In this final section, I conclude with some purely personal impressions derived from recent visits to some of Scotland's former seaside honey pots. Whereas there is wishful longing for at least a partial return to the good old days, I could find scant sign of them ever regaining 'the sexy business' they once enjoyed. On the other hand, it was also evident that the holiday trade was by no means defunct. It was just of a different type and on a different scale from what it had been when the domestic market was at its peak. In Portobello, where we started, few of the big attractions that made it one of Scotland's holiday hotspots have survived. However, its splendid Victorian indoor pond, now a Swim Centre, is still going strong. Also, on the positive side, Porty's busy High Street has, against all the odds, managed to retain a good selection of wee shops. The sands too are looking great and are regularly raked, but, while children still enjoy making their sandcastles on the beach, there are neither donkeys for hire nor deck chairs for their parents to lounge in. The west end of the prom, as ever, is the busiest section. There are amusement arcades here, including an enclosed 'Fun Park' offering ten-pin bowling, dodgems, and glitzy games machines. On the other hand, the children's paddling pond is gone, replaced by an ornamental garden. A few years ago as I watched this work in progress, other onlookers expressed surprise that it was not for yet another block of private flats. One cynically observed that elsewhere in the area, 'If ye pit yer jaicket [jacket] doon for a game o fitba, by the time ye came back, there wid be a hoose built there.'

With regard to Rothesay, it must be said that the town looks well from the sea, but behind the imposing seafront façades, there is a great deal of shabbiness. Although there has been some very stylish refurbishment, there are quite a few derelict buildings, empty shops and sad-looking gap sites. Fewer visitors means that there is not enough money or sufficient incentive for repairs and restoration. The Pavilion, 1938 'International Style Modernism at its best', is showing its age but there are hopes of restoration. On the profit side, there is a good wee museum and the restored Winter Gardens, now entitled the Isle of Bute Discovery Centre, provides both up-to-date tourist guidance and nostalgic glimpses into the island's doon-the-watter heyday. It also incorporates a theatre-cum-cinema and a bistro. The flowerbeds too are both colourful and carefully tended, and the numerous palm trees testify to the mild winter climate, and to walk along the extensive esplanade presents one with a series of stunning views. Coach tour parties, with the elderly predominant, now visit the island, with the Glenburn Hotel a favourite base. The older generation appreciate the peace and quiet of 'a peaceful island still steeped in tradition', as it is described by a holiday company catering solely for the over-50s. Teenagers and young adults give Bute the go-by. It is too quiet for them except for some specialist festivals. 'There is nothing here but scenery,' today's teenagers lament. Teenagers and young adults, out for their version of a good time, prefer the rather warmer Balearic Islands to the more staid islands of the Clyde. It was very different in the mid-twentieth century when, at the time of the Glasgow September Holiday Weekend, hordes of youngsters invaded Rothesay, and Arran too, and, with their rock music and al fresco drinking, created a great deal of noise and mayhem.

For Rothesay, the heady days of doon-the-watter and fresh air and seaside holidays for the masses are but a memory, leaving just the images that are showcased in the museums and heritage centres. On one of my recent visits to Rothesay, I spent some days there, contriving to travel there and back all the way from Glasgow by the traditional doon-the-watter route on the paddle steamer *Waverley*. It was the first week of the Glasgow Fair, a time when once the town would have been packed to the gunnels, but certainly not any longer. For one thing the number of bed spaces on offer was but a fraction of its heyday capacity. Even so, in that Fair Holiday week there were Vacancies Available signs in a lot of windows, and quite a few For Sale notices too. Perhaps even more significant were the notices in a travel agency window: adverts for foreign holiday packages. On asking my B & B landlord what was his busy time nowadays, I was told that there was no busy season now, though the weekends did bring in visitors for special events like the Bute Highland Games. Other highlights are the weekend-long festivals: cycling in September, jazz in April and folk music in July. As at other Clyde resorts, the *Waverley*'s summer excursions help bring in day-trippers and, as the last sea-going paddle steamer in the world, she is a major tourist attraction in her own right. For car-borne tourists, Caledonian MacBrayne's 'island-hopping' fare schemes go a little way to break down the notion that the Firth of Clyde islands are just cul-de-sacs. If we can judge by recent local tourist board brochures, Bute is in process of reinventing itself. In, for example, *Bute the Unexplored Island* the emphasis is on history and heritage, green tourism, and activities such as golf, angling, walking, cycling and watersports. With regard to heritage, Mount Stuart, the Bute family's Gothic Revival mansion, and its gardens, as already noted, are a major attraction. Likewise, the Winter Gardens and the Pavilion, each in its time a symbol

Rothesay's restored Winter Gardens, now entitled the Isle of Bute Discovery Centre, photographed by the author in August 1990. The author's late wife looks on appreciatively.

of modernity, are now seen as just as much part of the resort's history and heritage as the medieval Rothesay Castle. The island's contemporary image is a world away from its brash doon-the-watter heyday, when Rothesay at Glasgow Fair time, it was said, was not a place for sensitive souls.

As for Dunoon, now with the Americans and their submarines and their nuclear weapons gone and the Ardyne rig construction site also but a memory, the town is trying to remake itself. Sandbank and the other Holy Loch settlements, also Blairmore facing Loch Long, look to be picking up. The old Blairmore Pier has been restored, thanks to the Friends of Blairmore Pier Trust, and in 2005 the paddle steamer *Waverley* was once again making scheduled calls after a gap of years. At the least, Dunoon with its wider and beautiful hinterland and its old claim to be a 'gateway to the Highlands' is, in this respect, better placed than its old rival Rothesay. A new linkspan pier was ready for the 2005 tourist season, with a large sign above the ramp boldly proclaiming, in English and Gaelic, 'Dunoon Gateway to the National Park' (Loch Lomond and the Trossachs). Unfortunately this multi-million pound facility is seldom used, as no suitable vessels have been constructed for it. Not surprisingly, though, the population is dropping – down by over 6 per cent in the ten years between 1991 and 2001. Yet, with a population of 9,628, it has fared better than Rothesay and, compared with its 1891 figure, it is actually up by nearly 1,000. An international film festival is a new venture for the summer of 2013, to be held in the restored Victorian Burgh Hall – a good instance of how heritage and up-to-date events can be combined to create a new visitor attraction.

Some resorts have survived the difficult years better than others – St Andrews and Oban most notably. St Andrews is in a unique position, because of its status as 'the home of golf' and also because of the appeal of its own remarkable history and heritage and that of the East Neuk generally. Old tourist attractions have been replaced by new – the British Golf Museum for one, and the once popular Step Rock open-air swimming pool now houses an aquarium. Broadly speaking, there are two tourist worlds at St Andrews. Golfers and their spouses coming from elsewhere in Britain and overseas head for the West End, towards the Old Course and its satellite courses and up-market shops. There too they find short-stay accommodation in B&Bs and hotels. A more recent facility, and one which, as we have seen was not universally welcomed, is the giant St Andrews Bay hotel and golf complex. Intrusive though this hotel may be, it at least greatly expands

Gourock outdoor swimming pool, photographed by the author in August 1998. Of Scotland's significant open-air pools, this is one of the only two survivors. The other is at Stonehaven.

the area's potential for the conference market. Holidaymakers of the more traditional long-stay type are accommodated at the other end of the town, at the Kinkell Braes caravan site or at other fringe-area holiday parks. Oban, on the other hand, was not, despite the appeal of its Ganavan Sands, really a traditional seaside resort in the mould of, say, Saltcoats or Rothesay. Although there are fewer visitors than formerly, the town maintains its traditional role as 'the Charing Cross' of the Highlands – as port of access for Mull and other islands, as a touring and yachting centre in an area of great natural beauty and now as the 'Seafood Capital of Scotland'.

Right across Scotland, the resorts have had to adapt to new needs and demands. Angus Council, for example, has upgraded its Arbroath West Links leisure area, transforming it into 'a miniature fun world with a variety of exciting activities for all ages and abilities.' These include mini formula-one cars, evidently designed to appeal to the young. But an older attraction that appeals to young and old, Kerr's Miniature Railway, still has its devotees. In Scotland as a whole, there is more emphasis on short break holidays and attracting the niche markets, customer-tailoring holidays towards special interest groups – golfers and yachties being two of the main target groups. Resorts, the island resorts in particular, are now offering much more for outdoor enthusiasts with, for example, trails for walkers and mountain bikers. Companies in the adventure holiday market offer high-speed power boat journeys and helicopter tours. For east coast divers, though, St Abbs is the place to go. Theme weekends and festivals are another option. We find, for instance, that Largs has a festival that makes the most of its fleeting Viking connection. In early September Millport has its Country and Western Festival, when pubs become Wild West saloons and shops are transformed into Nashville emporia. Walking festivals have been gaining favour. The Dunoon area's October Cowalfest cleverly combines the arts with outdoor activities. Nautical themes are also popular, Portsoy having its Traditional Boat Festival in early summer and Ullapool for some years celebrating its enticingly entitled Fish Week in May. A celebrated fish and chip shop is one of the attractions that draw tourists to Anstruther in the East Neuk of Fife. Anstruther and the other East Neuk towns and villages benefit from their distinctive architectural heritage and more recent cultural festivals. Even seemingly unlikely interests can draw in extra tourists, like the National Cartoon Festival which was put on in Ayr from 1998 to 2002. With Scotland's uncertain weather, indoor attractions, as at Eyemouth with its two museums and maritime centre, are a necessity.

Kerr's Miniature Railway was snapped by the author in July 1998 just as a mainline train was passing. Like its big brother systems, the wee Arbroath line has been modernised over the years. The contemporary publicity material tells us that the railway is family run, non-profit making and staffed by volunteers. 'Our great wee trains have delighted nearly two million passengers since opening in 1935.'

There are, too, some well-planned information-cum-visitor centres such as Arbroath Abbey Visitor Centre and the afore-mentioned Isle of Bute Discovery Centre at Rothesay, which entertain as well as inform. At North Berwick a new popular attraction is the Scottish Seabird Centre, situated, ironically enough, on the site of the former pavilion – the domain of the pierrots of yesteryear. With video cameras on the gannet-breeding colonies on the Bass Rock and on other Firth of Forth islands, the centre has become a major asset helping to 'tranform the economic fortunes of North Berwick'. Once tourists came to shoot the gannets; now they just shoot with cameras.

As we have seen, many resorts have been popular with retirees, which has both advantages and disadvantages. Nevertheless, the flow of active and inactive retirees continues. Currently, the resorts with the highest proportion of older residents are, according to the 2001 census, Crail, Elie, Millport and Port Bannatyne in Bute. In some coastal towns, a number of landlords now prefer to accommodate homeless persons and thus enjoy the luxury of a steady and regular income. Necessary this service may be, but from the point of view of potential visitors it is a case of a resort going downmarket. Resorts that are readily accessible to major centres of populations fill an alternative role as dormitory towns, with towns like Stonehaven and North Berwick in the east and Largs, Troon and Helensburgh in the west more upmarket than others. Even Rothesay and, more especially, Dunoon have their quota of commuters, using reasonably regular ferry and train services. For more remote towns like Campbeltown and Girvan this is hardly an option. While visits by touring yachties and golfing enthusiasts bring some compensation to Campeltown, its position on the tourist periphery remains a handicap. Judging, though, by the number of caravans at nearby Southend and elsewhere in the peninsula, Kintyre (promoted as Scotland's only 'Mainland Island'), nevertheless, has many devotees.

However, for many people nowadays there are destinations within Scotland itself which have more allure than the traditional seaside resort. Most obviously, there are the big cities, Edinburgh and Glasgow, with their bright lights and all kinds of attractions including shopping malls, with shopping now regarded as a recreational activity. While Edinburgh has always been a tourist destination, Glasgow now rivals it as a cultural centre. Beyond the cities, there are some remote areas, too, which, though far from being mass destinations, have raised their tourist profile. Orkney is a case in point where, though hardly a Tenerife, tourist providers have had unprecedented success in developing niche markets in archaeological heritage, wreck diving and wildlife. Cruise liners, too, bring in large

In its Doon-the-Watter heyday, Campbeltown was well served by steamers. In this Valentine 1950 image, day excursionists have been photographed returning to their excursion steamer.

On a trip doon the watter on the *Waverley* there are no mythical monsters to look out for, but a folk music band provides an agreeable substitute. Photographed by the author in August 1992.

numbers of day visitors. Some country towns and country places have also been developed into tourist magnets. People looking for a day out can now choose from a wide variety of inland country parks, heritage centres, shopping malls, Scottish National Trust properties and other historic attractions including industrial heritage sites like Summerlee in Coatbridge and New Lanark. The latter has been recognized as a World Heritage Site. Even places that people were once glad to leave have, in some instances, been transformed into attractive visitor centres. In Fife, for instance, a once blighted mining area was transformed in the 1970s into a 1,200-acre park: the Lochore Meadows Country Park. The estimated number of visitors to the park comes to nearly 400,000. Thirty or forty years ago the chances are that many of these day-trippers would have gone instead to nearby Aberdour or one of the other Fife beach resorts. Coach companies offering short break holidays gravitate towards the cities and the few resorts which still possess large hotels. As for business tourism, a fast developing and valuable sector, it is the big cities, particularly Edinburgh and Glasgow, that gain the most. Aberdeen, however, with its impressive exhibition and conference centre, gets a fair share of this market. The city still has a role as a touring centre with easy access to Royal Deeside and Aberdeenshire's well advertised 'Castle Country'. Outwith Scotland, there are in this age of global tourism a huge number of choices, many of them far more exotic than anything that our ageing resorts can offer.

As for those overseas visitors who manage to escape the clutches of London's multifarious tourist attractions, they have other priorities. Rightly or wrongly, for many overseas visitors, the traditional seaside towns do not fit their preconceptions of Scotland as a land of myth, legend and romance. Tourists leaving the cities head instead to the so-called Golden Triangle from Edinburgh to Inverness via Perth, then down the Great Glen where, to quote Alastair Borthwick, the Loch Ness Monster lives during the tourist season, and then on to the Fort William/Oban area. This 'milk run' route is widely promoted and is too often seen by visitors and operators alike as the be-all and virtually end-all of Scottish tourism. How different it might have been had that tourist's favourite, the mythical Nessie, surfaced not in Loch Ness but in Loch Fyne or another of the sea lochs of the Firth of Clyde. Through its publicity literature and promotion pictures, the Scottish Tourist Board has presented a romantic and semi-mythic image of Scotland as a place whose prime attractions are, to quote a recent Visit Scotland brochure, 'the awesome scenery, the proud history, the rare wildlife, the vibrant people.' Except for the Arran villages, which were always exceptions to the rule, the traditional seaside resorts cannot readily be assimilated into this kind of stereotyped promotion. In the face of an overall decline in tourist arrivals from the mid-1980s onward, the Scottish Tourist Board and area tourist boards have striven to improve overall standards of accommodation, marketing and service with some, but not universal, success. For the STB, now restyled as Visit Scotland, its main recent achievement, the creation of a website for information, was welcomed but its online booking service was not successful and was eventually discontinued. In 2005 also, the tourist area board system was brought to an end. The area boards were merged with Visit Scotland and replaced with so-called hub areas which serve as subsidiaries of the national agency.

What the seaside resorts lack, though, are the big-scale visitor attractions which are found in competitor destinations like Blackpool and nearer home in Edinburgh (Our Dynamic Earth) and Glasgow (Science Centre). Such attractions require large-scale investment, and as far as the great majority of resort towns are concerned, raising the large amount of capital required would be a very difficult task. This was the case with an ambitious Girvan project to build a £10 million seabird centre at the town's harbour. Despite having the support of the RSPB, the Ailsa Craig Centre, as it was to be called, failed to receive lottery support. Future development is now the responsibility of South Ayrshire Council. The coastal towns have to compete also with huge, well-financed English theme parks, like Alton Towers, situated for the most part in attractive, inland locations. In contrast, most seaside resorts, in England and Wales no less than in Scotland, are regarded by a large part of the population as fuddy-duddy, out-of-date, and just unfashionable. In comparison with their warm and often brand-new foreign equivalents, British seaside resorts have lost their novelty value. On the other hand, in some areas the loss of tourists may be less than it appears, since many visitors are now accommodated in out-of-town holiday parks. The Seton Sands Holiday Village in East Lothian, for instance, is said to attract around 30,000 visitors a year. In the days when in popular resorts 'everybody let', the impact was fairly obvious and the financial benefits were spread throughout the town. When, however, holidaymakers are concentrated in self-contained caravan sites, the local benefits are diminished. Car-owning park residents often bring their own foodstuffs with them and spread their other spending over a wider area than their less mobile predecessors would have done.

Yet, the most unexpected trends can lead to strange reversals of fortunes. For instance, Coulport on Loch Long, once a dead-end holiday development, is now part of the Clyde Naval Base and hosts an armament depot for Polaris and Trident nuclear missiles. Coulport today is a very different place from the hamlet where on 2 July 1886 five excursion steamers docked at the pier for a very special event – an open-air performance of Handel's *Messiah*. In recent years, Leith too has been

Kathleen Simpson views a busy Aberdeen beach scene in August 1982. When the sun shines, the crowds can still come out, but certainly not as in former days, when cool, cloudy conditions were no deterrent.

The tiny fishing settlement of Crovie is one of the scenic villages that draw tourists to the south Moray Firth coast. Most of the dwellings are now holiday homes.

Stonehaven by the sea in Edwardian days.

The paddle steamer *Waverley* departing from the recently restored Millport pier, photographed by the author in August 2003.

transformed in a more visitor-friendly fashion. Leith was the very first place in Scotland to be developed as a sea bathing resort. Its extensive sandy beach, bathing machines and indoor seawater baths attracted valetudinarians and other tourists. With port extension and industrialisation, all this came to an end. But who two decades ago would have forecast Leith's present part-gentrified status as a haven for foodies and with its Ocean Terminal shopping mall a port of call for shoppers and, with the Royal Yacht *Britannia* as a prime attraction, for tourists and sightseers also? Reflecting new leisure patterns, a number of new marinas have been built in recent years. Stranraer has been one of the gainers from this. Likewise, the Clyde Marina, a new leisure development, is bringing some new life to an otherwise forlorn-looking Ardrossan. In addition, the Ayrshire tourist economy has benefited from Ryanair's low-cost flights from and to Prestwick airport. Even before Ryanair came on the scene, the county still had something to offer tourists. South Ayrshire, according to a submission to a House of Commons Committee in February 1999, had an excellent and wide range of 'indoor and outdoor sports facilities, water sports, parks, museums, galleries and theatres, together with the highest concentration of quality golf courses in Britain, including two Open Championship courses at Turnberry and Royal Troon'. It was an area, the submission continued, where tourism was a major element of the local economy and was a tourist destination that could be considered to be 'a microcosm of the wider Scottish tourism scene'. South Ayrshire had seen substantial investment in the tourism infrastructure by both private and public bodies resulting in a considerable increase in the number of day visits and short break holidays. South Ayrshire is not alone in this regard.

While the Scottish seaside resorts' long-stay holiday market has largely gone, there are signs of a limited degree of revival, with their tourist providers now successfully setting their sights on capturing the short-break trade and by exploiting niche markets. Coastal towns and villages with heritage appeal and natural attractions will always attract tourists. One such area is the Moray Firth coast from Inverness to Peterhead. In 2013, the influential *National Geographic* magazine reckoned it to be one of the world's top rated coastal destinations. With outstanding cliff scenery, excellent beaches, opportunities for whale and dolphin watching, and pretty coastal villages, this 'undiscovered gem … is attractive to walkers, cyclists, wild life watchers and surfers'. In contrast, such tourist hot spots such as Portugal's Algarve, Spain's Costa Blanca and Dubai were poorly rated for environmental quality.

Nevertheless, for Scottish seaside resorts, therefore, I venture to suggest that, unless global warming changes the climate in some unexpected way, the traditional long-stay market will never return. But who knows? Perhaps, sometime in the future Spaniards and Greeks, in their desperation to escape the intolerable heat of their own furnace-like lands, will flock to bathe in the clean and pleasantly warm beaches of Auld Scotia's shores. In that event, resorts like Stonehaven would doubtless be once more ready to greet long-stay visitors frae a the airts:

We've the Prom wi' seats a' ready
Where the weary can sit doon,
An' we've some fine walks an' woodlands
Where the loving ones can spoon.
An' the beautiful surroundings
Are a pleasure tae the e'e
For there's naught can touch the beauty
Of Stonehaven by the sea.

'The Glesca Fair' by Walter Donald

Select Bibliography

A. B. Adamson, *In the Wind's Eye North Berwick Golf Club* (1980)

T. Alexander, *Remember When We Lived on Arran* (1986)

D. Anderson, *Old Dunbar* (2000)

Anon., *One Hundred Years of Kinghorn Golf Club 1887–1987* (ND)

S. Baker (ed.), *East Lothian 1945–2000 Fourth Statistical Account*, Vol. I

N. E. M. Bailey, *A Scottish Childhood* Vol. II (1998)

J. Bald, *Aberdour Golf Club – the First Hundred Years* (1997)

M. Bellamy, *Millport & the Cumbraes* (2003)

E. Bishop, *For You I Remember* (1980)

G. Blake, *The Firth of Clyde* (1952)

A. G. Bradley, *The Gateway of Scotland* (1912)

British Tourist Authority, *The British on Holiday 1951–1970* (1971)

I. Brodie, *Steamers of the Forth* (1976)

A. W. Brotchie & J. J. Herd, *Old Broughty Ferry & Monifieth* (1980)

F. Bruce, *Scottish Showbusiness: Music Hall, Variety and Pantomime* (2000)

J. Burnett, 'Small Showmen and Large Firms: The development of Glasgow Fair in the nineteenth century' in *Review of Scottish Culture* 17, 2004–2005 eds. K. Veitch and A. Fenton.

E. Caldwell, *Around Leven* (2000)

J. R. D. Campbell, *Millport and the Cumbraes* (1975)

E. Casciani, *Oh, How We Danced* (1994)

E. Christie, *The Haven under the Hill: The Story of Stonehaven* (1977)

I. L. Cormack, *The Rothesay Tramway Company 1879–1949* (1986)

E. Cowan, *Spring Remembered* (1974)

D. Daiches: See below C Macafee and I. Macleod (eds.)

N. Davey & J. Perkins, *Broughty Ferry – Village to Suburb* (1976)

T. M. Devine & R. J. Finlay (eds.), *Scotland in the 20th Century* (1996)

C. L. D Duckworth & G. E. Langmuir, *Clyde River and Other Steamers* (1972 edition)

A. J. Durie, *George Washington Wilson, Sport and Leisure in Victorian Scotland* (1988)

A. J. Durie, *Scotland for the Holidays – Tourism in Scotland c. 1780–1939* (2003)

K. Durland, *Among the Fife Miners* 1904

East Lothian Museum Council, *Brrr! Stories of Dunbar's Outdoor Pool* video & booklet (1997)

E. Eunson & J. Band, *Largo An Illustrated History* (2000)

G. Eyre Todd, *Doon the Watter – Caledonian Excursions Official Guide* (1906)

H. B. Farnie, *Handy-Book of the Fife Coast* (c. 1860)

R. Finlay, *Modern Scotland* (2004)

A. S. Fraser, *The Hills of Home* (1973)

A. S. Fraser, *In Memory Long* (1977)

W. H. Fraser & C. H. Lee (eds.), *Aberdeen 1800–2000 A New History* (2000)

A. Gemmell, *Discovering Arran* (1998)

G. G. Giarchi, *Between McAlpine and Polaris* (1984)

K. Grimman, *Seaside All Year* (1987)

J. C. Hill, *Innellan* (1943)

J. House, *Dunoon 1868–1968* (N.D.)

D. L. G. Hunter, *From SMT to Eastern Scottish* (1987)

G. Irving, *The Good Auld Days* (1977)

B. A. Jamieson, *North Berwick Biarritz of the North* (1992)

B. A. Jamieson, *North Berwick Between the Wars* (1996)

T. Johnston, *Memories* (1952)

S. G. Jones, *Workers at Play: A Social and Economic History of Leisure 1918–1939* (1986)

E. King, *The Hidden History of Glasgow's Women – The New Factor* (1993)

Kintyre Civic Society, *The Campbeltown Book* (2003)

M. Knox (ed.), *Cockenzie and Port Seton in Days Gone By* (N.D.)

M. Lindsay, *Clyde Waters* 1958

I. McCrorie & J. Monteith, *Clyde Piers* (1982)

C. Macafee & I. Macleod (eds.), *The Nuttis Schell: Essays on the Scots Language* [see essay by David Daiches on pierrots' songs, etc.]

I. Maclagan, *Rothesay Harbour* (N.D.)

R. MacLellan & R. Smith, *Tourism in Scotland* (1998)

J. Macleay, *Old Dunoon and Cowal* (2002)

A. Millar, *Kilfinnan Parish History and Memories* [re. Tignabruaich area] (ND)

M. Mitchell & D. Macdonald, *70 Years at Stonehaven Open Air Pool* (2004)

J. Moore, *The Gaiety* (2001)

D. Morrison & I. Reynolds, *Changed Days in Montrose* (1999)

H. V. Morton, *In Scotland Again* (1933)

I. S. Munro, *The Island of Bute* (1973)

N. Munro, *The Clyde* (1907)

Murray's *Handbook for Travellers in Scotland* (1875)

Murray's *Handbook for Travellers in Scotland* (1894)

S. Noble (ed.), *200 Hundred Years of Helensburgh 1802–2002* (2002)

C. A. Oakley, *Scottish Industry Today* (1937)

B. D. Osborne, *Helensburgh & Garelochside in Old Pictures* (1984)

Oxford Dictionary of National Biography (for John Henry Iles)

D. A. Pattison, *Tourism in the Firth of Clyde* (1967, Glasgow University Ph. D. Thesis)

R. Forsyth, *Memories of Dunoon and Cowal* (1983)

D. Phillips-Birt, *The History of Yachting* (1974)

Portobello History Society, *It always seemed to be sunny: Memories of Portobello*; a video (2004)

R. J. M. Pugh, *Swords, Loaves and Fishes: A History of Dunbar* (2003)

W. Robbie, *Aberdeen – its Traditions and History* (1893)

I. Robertson, 'Population Trends of Great Cumbrae Island' in *Scottish Geographical Magazine* (April 1973)

G. Rountree, *A Govan Childhood The Nineteen Thirties* (1993)

Saltire Review Vol. 6 Spring 1959 No. 18

J. Sandeman, *Bute's War* (2005)

Scottish Tourist Board, *Tourism in the Firth of Clyde* (1968)

Scottish Women's Rural Institute, *Arran: History of the Villages of the Isle of Arran* (c. 1985)

A. Shaw (ed.), *Rothesay's Yesterdays* (1991)

G. Shaw & A. Williams (eds.), *The Rise and Fall of British Coastal Resorts* (1997)

J. Smith, *Liquid Assets – the lidos and open air swimming pools of Britain* (2005)

M. Smith, *Britain's Light Railways* (1994)

R. Smith, *The Making of Scotland* (2001)

E. Simpson, *Aberdour & Burntisland in Old Picture Postcards* (1993)

E. Simpson, 'Aberdour: the Evolution of a Seaside Resort' in G. Cruickshank (ed.), *A Sense of Place* (1988)

E. Simpson, *Discovering Moray, Banff and Nairn* (1998)

E. Simpson, *Going on Holiday* (1997)

E. Simpson, *St Andrews in Old Picture Postcards* (2001)

I. Sommerville, *Burntisland Voices* (2005)

J. Strawhorn, *The History of Prestwick* (1994)

SWRI Arran Federation, *History of the Villages of the Isle of Arran* (1983)

Transactions of the Aberdeen Philosophical Society, Vol. II, 1892

Transactions of the Royal Sanitary Association of Scotland, 1950.

'Mirren Tate', *The Trials of a Seaside Landlady* (N.D.)

J. Thomas, *A Regional History of the Railways of Great Britain Vol. 6 Scotland: the Lowlands & the Borders* (1971)

J. Thomas & D. Turnock, *A Regional History of the Railways of Great Britain Vol. 15 North of Scotland* (1989)

G. Twaddle, *Old Bute* (2000)

C. Thorburn (ed.), *Recollections – a trip down memory lane in and around Tignabruaich* (*c.* 2000)

J. K. Walton, *Blackpool* (1998)

F. Waters (ed), *Thurso Then & Now* (1972)

H. Watson, *Kilrenny and Cellardyke* (1951)

I. Watson, *Harry Gordon – the Laird of Inversnecky* (1993)

R. Wilkinson, *Memories of Maryhill* (1993)

B. Willsher, *St Andrews Citizens – Their Societies Past and Present* (2003)

N. Wood, *Health Resorts of the British Isles* (1912)

Sources and Acknowledgements

I have delved into many old newspaper files, some local and some national, most notably the *Glasgow Herald*, the Aberdeen *Press and Journal* and the *Scotsman*, and also into very many resort guidebooks, frequently anonymous, usually undated and far too many to list here. Old postcards, as can be seen from some of the examples printed in this book, are another useful source of mainly visual information, although the written messages can also illuminate. I owe, therefore, a great debt of gratitude to firms like the Dundee businesses of J. Valentine & Sons Ltd. and J. B. White & Co., whose postcards I have collected for many years. The minutes of the old burgh councils, and their various sub-committees, have been another fertile source. I have quarried the Scottish Tourist Board's magazine *Take Note* (1946–66), also its annual reports and other publications, and, as the text indicates, the *Third Statistical Account of Scotland* (1951–88) various volumes passim. Illustrations and the holiday guidebooks referred to in the text are drawn mainly from my own personal archive. I am obliged, though, for the loan of photographs from the personal collections of Alan Brotchie, Archie Foley and Carol McNeill.

I am grateful to the following authors and publishers: Ian Brodie and publisher David & Charles for permission to use the quotation from the *Steamers of the Forth*; also Maurice Lindsay and his publisher, Robert Hale Ltd., for permitting me to quote extensively (in chapter 7) from his book *Clyde Waters*. I have quoted from a number of other authors, but unfortunately I have not been able to trace them. My sincere gratitude is therefore due to all the other writers quoted in this book and to the commercial artists whose images adorn these pages. I am also indebted to various institutions and the staff, some of them volunteers, who serve them – museums such as at Burntisland, Dunoon, Millport, North Berwick, Rothesay, and St Andrews; and archive depositories such as Aberdeen City Archives (covering both the city and Aberdeenshire records), Aberdeenshire Local Studies Centre, Angus Council Archive Centre, Burntisland Heritage Trust, Fife Council Archive Centre, Buteshire Natural History Society, the University of St Andrews Library, the National Archives of Scotland, and the National Library of Scotland. I must too express my appreciation for the services of public library staff in Aberdeen, Arbroath, Cupar, Dalgety Bay, Dunfermline, Edinburgh (Central and Leith), Elgin, Inverness, Kirkcaldy, Montrose, Rothesay, and St Andrews.

Over many years, I have had assistance from, and tapped into the memories of, many individuals, some now sadly deceased. I give grateful thanks to the following: David M. Anderson, William Bissett, Alan Brotchie, Flora Calder, Shirley Cunningham, Stewart Dowie, Archie Foley, Wilma Forret, Allan A. Fraser, Helen Fraser, Jane Handley, Margaret R. Hunter, Walter Hutchison, Matthew Kerr, William and Ian Landles, John Macfarlane, Fiona McGregor, James H. McIvor, Kenneth McKellar (Rothesay), Carol McNeill, Ron Malcolm, Angus Martin, Michael Minty, Mary Mitchell, Anne Paterson, Mary Patullo, Jess Sandeman, Barbara Scott, Iain Sommerville, Bill Stratton, Carole Thomson, Anita Walker, Betty Willsher, and that grand old trouper from Kinghorn – Nellie Phillips. A special debt of gratitude is due to my daughter Rhona Mackenzie and my old friends Jennifer Heath and George Robertson who scrutinised the text on my behalf, also to Fraser Simpson and Anne Paterson for technical assistance and my very efficient Amberley editors Louis Archard and Campbell McCutcheon. Any errors, however, are purely my responsibility. My apologies to anyone whose name I have inadvertently omitted.

Index